Dear Friends,

Want to eat healthier, lose weight and live a better life? This cookbook is for you! Our simple 1500 calorie eating plan will help you achieve these goals. Eating better and losing weight is easier when the food is *flavorful, satisfying*—and *never boring*. (Always check with your healthcare provider before making any diet changes.)

We've organized taste-tempting recipes by meal occasion. Choose a recipe from each meal chapter—Breakfast, Lunch, Dinner—and <u>two</u> recipes from the Snacks and Desserts chapter. Then round out your meals with fruits, veggies and healthy side dishes and snacks. No matter what combination of recipes you choose, you'll end up eating 1500 calories or less each day (the average number of calories a woman needs to lose weight). All these mouthwatering recipes have been approved by our dieticians and include a complete nutritional analysis.

As an added bonus, you can trim *more* calories from many recipes by following our *A Little Bit Less* tips. Have higher-calorie needs or are extra-hungry? *A Little Bit More* tips show you healthy ways to add bulk to a dish. More or less—the change in calories is included.

A healthy lifestyle is more than just good eating—so inside you'll also find helpful information on how to embrace a healthy lifestyle, make physical activity part of your busy day and know if you're at a healthy weight. We've taken the guesswork out of sticking to your 1500-calorie goal by including a list of 100-calories-or-less foods you can enjoy. Check out our 7 days of sample menus—a week's-worth of enticing recipes to keep you full and satisfied. With all these fantastic recipes and information, you'll be so inspired; success can begin with your very next meal!

Sincerely,

Betty Crocker

Contents

Embracing a Healthy Lifestyle

Having a healthy lifestyle is what it's all about. It's making lifelong habits to promote long-term health while reducing risk of health problems, increasing your energy level and improving your mood. If you want to achieve a healthy weight or maintain one, don't worry, we don't mean dieting. Diets are a temporary solution. Often as soon as you go off the diet, the weight begins to return. Achieving lifestyle changes means eating nutritiously, exercising, limiting alcohol and avoiding smoking and drugs.

To control your weight, shed pounds by eating nutritious, lower-calorie foods from all food groups and set a goal of getting at least 60 minutes of physical activity per day. When you're active and eating well, your body can settle into a weight that's healthy for you.

Choose MyPlate for Healthful Eating

MyPlate is the USDA guide to building a healthy plate at mealtime. The MyPlate symbol shows the five food groups (fruit, vegetable, grain, protein and dairy) within a place setting—and includes awareness of portion sizes. The symbol visually shows that half the plate should be made up of fruits and veggies— and that we need less protein than grains.

Dairy is important to the diet too. MyPlate helps reinforce the message about making healthier food choices from the 2010 Dietary Guidelines for Americans, which suggest:

- Enjoy your food, but eat less. Eat slowly and avoid eating while engaging in other activities such as reading or watching TV so that you don't overeat.

- Avoid oversized portions. Use a smaller plate (such as a salad plate), bowl and glass to avoid serving yourself portions that are too big. When eating out, opt for the smaller size of a dish (when two sizes are offered), share with someone else or immediately have your server box up half of your meal to take home for eating at another time.

- Make half your plate fruits and vegetables. Fruits and vegetables contain sources of fiber, vitamins and minerals. They are generally low in calories, so it's easy to fill up without eating too many calories.

- Switch to fat-free or low-fat (1%) milk. It's a simple way to reduce the calories and fat you consume. These products have the same amount of calcium and other essential nutrients as full-fat products but contain fewer calories and less fat.

- Make at least half your grains whole grains. Read labels carefully, looking for the word "whole" in front of the word "grain" to assure you're choosing whole-grain options for bread, tortillas, cereals, rice and pasta.

- Compare sodium in foods—and choose foods with the lower number. Look for products that are labeled "low sodium," "reduced sodium" or "no salt added." When these versions aren't available, read the nutrition facts labels to compare foods.

- Drink water to keep calories down. By drinking water before and during eating, you can fool your body into thinking it's full, so you may end up eating less.

Check out www.chooseMyPlate.gov to learn more. Look for the online tools to personalize and manage your diet quality and physical activity choice. Start small by making changes to your diet one day at a time.

How Many Calories Do I Need Per Day?

To maintain your weight, calories in must equal calories out. This means that you will maintain your weight as long as you are eating as many calories as you are expending through exercise and bodily functions.

To lose weight, you need to eat fewer calories than you burn. You can do this in two ways: cut calories and/or increase physical activity. The recommended way to achieve weight loss is to combine both. In essence, move more and eat less.

A reduction of 3500 calories in your diet will result in a loss of 1 pound of body fat. Experts recommend losing 1 to 2 pounds per week to lose weight and keep it off. Achieve this by reducing some of the calories you consume (500–1000 calories per day) and/or increasing your activity level. (The more you burn through exercise, the fewer calories you may need to reduce to lose up to 2 pounds per week.)

How to Use This Book

The average woman needs about 1,500 calories a day to lose weight, and this book makes it simple using four chapters: Breakfast, Lunch, Dinner and Snacks & Desserts. Each day, you get to choose a delicious, satisfying recipe from each of the meal chapters—and two recipes from the Snacks & Desserts chapter! Round out your meals with fruits, veggies and healthy side dishes or snacks (See Snacks with 100 Calories or Less, page 9, to help you.) No matter what recipe you choose from each chapter, you'll end up eating about 1,500 calories or less. When you want to consume fewer calories, look for our **A Little Bit Less** tips with many of the recipes. They will show you ways to trim calories from the recipes. If you find yourself extra-hungry, look for recipes with **A Little Bit More** tips for ways to bulk up the dishes.

This is no diet. It's healthy food that you and your family can enjoy.

How Do I Know If I'm at a Healthy Weight?

BMI—also known as body mass index—is a measure used to estimate appropriate weight for height. Knowing your BMI gives you an awareness of where your body weight is—and where it needs to be. The goal is to have a BMI that is less than 25. Overweight (BMI = 25 to 29.9 kg/m^2) and obese (BMI = 30 kg/m2 or greater) describe ranges for adult weights that are higher than what is considered healthy for a certain height.

To calculate a BMI:

$$BMI = \left\{ \frac{\text{Weight (lb)}}{(\text{Height (in)} \times \text{Height (in)})} \right\} \times 703$$

Don't want to get out a calculator? Look for many free BMI calculators online, which will help you figure out your BMI when you enter your height and weight. You can search the Internet for tools to help you calculate and interpret the BMI for a child or teen.

Be Active Every Day

There are lots of little things you can do that can add up to big results. You don't have to do one long exercise activity to burn calories. Break it up into little segments throughout the day and still get the calorie-burning effects.

Use waiting time as calorie-burning time: jog in place while you wait. Lift small weights as you watch TV. Use your laundry basket as a large weight and lift and lower it as you walk.

Why Is Physical Activity Important?

Besides a healthy body weight, take a peek at other benefits you may get from exercising:

Increase your chance of living longer

Decrease your chance of becoming depressed

May reduce the risk of dementia or slow the condition's progression once it starts

Strengthens muscles and bones and improves flexibility

Helps you feel better about yourself

Lets you sleep better

Walking is an easy way to burn calories without the need for special equipment. Experts suggest starting with 2,000 steps per day (or about 1 mile). Work up to 10,000 steps per day (about 5 miles) most days of the week.

MODERATE PHYSICAL ACTIVITIES

Walking briskly (3 miles per hour)

Bicycling (less than 10 miles per hour)

Raking leaves for 30 minutes

Dancing

Stair climbing for 15 minutes

Water aerobics

VIGOROUS PHYSICAL ACTIVITIES

Running/jogging (5-6 miles per hour)

Walking very fast (4½ miles per hour)

Hiking uphill

Aerobic dancing

Swimming laps

Jumping rope

Snacks with 100 Calories or Less

Whether you are craving something sweet, savory, crunchy or smooth, before you let anything go past your lips, stop and think about what kind of food will really satisfy you. If you take the time to do this, you may prevent yourself from eating more than you want to in the quest to feel satiated. Use this list to round out your meals and to select snacks that will keep you from getting too hungry while sticking to your calorie limit for the day. To stay satisfied, choose snacks that contain a little protein, fiber and fat, along with some carbohydrate. To keep sodium in check, choose low-sodium versions whenever possible. Be sure to look for healthy choices from the list of common snacks (below) that are all 100 calories or less.

GRAINS

3 oz cooked whole-grain noodles with 1 fresh tomato and ½ oz grated hard cheese

Scant ½ cup cooked brown rice

½ cup cooked oatmeal

1 slice whole wheat bread with 1 teaspoon fruit spread

1 bag 100-calorie microwave popcorn

4 whole-grain baked tortilla chips and 1½ tablespoons spicy black bean dip

4 whole-grain baked tortilla chips and 1 tablespoon guacamole

1 (6-inch) corn tortilla with 1 oz low-fat Cheddar cheese, melted

6 saltines or thin wheat crackers with 2 teaspoons peanut butter (or any nut butter)

7 whole wheat pita chips and 1 tablespoon hummus

NUTS AND SEEDS

24 pistachios

16 peanuts

9 walnut halves

14 almonds

2 tablespoons sunflower seeds

VEGETABLES

1⅓ cups tomato soup (made with water)

1¾ cups tomato and vegetable juice

½ of a 3-oz baked potato with ¼ cup salsa and 1 tablespoon light sour cream

Up to 2 cups raw vegetables (carrots, broccoli, celery, cucumber, tomatoes, sugar snap peas) with 2 tablespoons light ranch dressing

½ cup cooked green peas

1½ cups cooked green beans

1½ cups cooked broccoli

1½ cups cooked carrots

¾ cup cooked corn

MEATS/FISH/EGGS

3 thin slices lunch meat

⅓ cup cut-up roasted chicken breast (without skin)

3 oz tuna (packed in water)

3 oz shrimp

Hard-boiled egg with 1 Melba toast

DAIRY

½ cup low-fat cottage cheese with 5 strawberries

¾-oz cheese stick (most varieties)

One wedge (from a 6-oz container) spreadable light cheese with 8 reduced-fat wheat crackers

½ mini bagel with 1 tablespoon light cream cheese

1 cup fat-free (skim) milk

5 oz low-fat chocolate milk

3 oz Greek strawberry yogurt

FRUIT

½ apple with 2 teaspoons peanut butter

29 frozen grapes

1¼ cups cantaloupe, watermelon or honeydew melon

3 clementines

1½ cups mixed berries

1 cup mango chunks

1 frozen fruit and juice bar

SWEET TREATS

1 (2-inch) slice angel food cake

2 apple cinnamon– or caramel-flavored rice cakes

10 animal crackers

3 gingersnaps

½ cup fat-free chocolate pudding

4 milk chocolate candy drops

2 silky smooth dark chocolate pieces

2 pieces strawberry twist candy

10 large jelly beans

5 pieces hard candy

A Week's-Worth of Delicious Menus

We've put together several special, satisfying menus for you to follow, if you wish—each irresistible and around 1,500 calories per day. Use these ideas for inspiration to get you started—then feel free to come up with your own menus to meet your family's needs.

Busy Weekday

Short on time? Each recipe takes 20 minutes or less to prepare.

BREAKFAST

Pineapple-Mango Smoothies (180 calories)   p. 65

100% whole wheat bagel with 1 tablespoon peanut butter (340 calories)

LUNCH

Turkey-Apple Salad Wraps (260 calories)   p. 111

½ cup baby carrots (30 calories)

DINNER

Citrus-Glazed Salmon (320 calories)   p. 222

½ cup cooked orzo (100 calories)

½ cup steamed broccoli (30 calories)

SNACK AND DESSERT

Smoky Spinach Hummus with Popcorn Chips (120 calories)   p. 278

Banana Brownie Skillet (200 calories)   p. 302

Total: 1,490 calories

Company for the Weekend

Family or friends staying over? Try these simple yet special meals for entertaining weekend guests.

BREAKFAST

Easy Cranberry-Orange Scones (260 calories)   p. 47

Hard-boiled egg (70 calories)

½ cup grapes (50 calories)

LUNCH

Grilled Chicken Sandwiches with Lime dressing (290 calories)

Cantaloupe wedge (40 calories)

½ cup cut-up bell pepper slices with 1 tablespoon light dill dip (40 calories)

DINNER

Pork Mole-Fajita Quesadillas (360 calories)   p. 206

½ cup cooked brown rice with chopped cilantro (110 calories)

SNACK AND DESSERT

BLT Tomato Cups (3 appetizers) (75 calories)   p. 269

Triple Chocolate Pie (190 calories)   p. 301

Total: 1,485 calories

Viva Italia

Savor the flavors of Italy without the cost of a trip!

BREAKFAST

Savory Italian Frittata (140 calories)   p. 27

1 large orange (80 calories)

Purchased caramel macchiato made with skim milk (190 calories)

LUNCH

Italian Bean Soup with Greens (220 calories)   p. 134

1 slice multi-grain (whole-grain) bread (70 calories)

DINNER

Tomato-Basil Pasta Primavera (280 calories)   p. 244

1 cup salad greens with 1 tablespoon reduced-calorie Italian dressing (30 calories)

½ cup sliced strawberries (30 calories)

1 glass (5 oz) Pinot Grigio (120 calories)

SNACK AND DESSERT

Bruschetta—3 pieces (150 calories)

Bittersweet Chocolate Cake with Berries (170 calories)   p. 294

Total: 1,520 calories

Mexican Fiesta

Recreate the flavors from a favorite vacation destination.

BREAKFAST
Mexican Breakfast Pizzas (200 calories)

LUNCH
Zesty Mexican Soup (160 calories) p. 139

5 whole-grain wheat saltine crackers (60 calories)

DINNER
Easy Green Enchiladas (410 calories) p. 183

½ cup fat-free refried beans (90 calories)

SNACK AND DESSERT
Seven-Layer Taco Dip with 1 oz baked tortilla chips (290 calories) p. 274

Dark Chocolate Cupcakes (170 calories) p. 295

Total: 1,510 calories

Summer's Bounty

Celebrate the fresh produce of the season.

BREAKFAST
Whole-Grain Mixed-Berry Coffeecake (160 calories) p. 52

1 container (6 oz) peach Yoplait® Greek fat free yogurt (160 calories)

1 glass (8 oz) orange juice (120 calories)

LUNCH
Grilled Fajita Pitas (230 calories) p. 106

1 cup diced watermelon (50 calories)

1 oz whole-grain multi-grain chips (140 calories)

DINNER
Marinated Pork with Summer Corn Salad (250 calories) p. 205

1½ cups 3-color coleslaw tossed with 1 tablespoon reduced-fat coleslaw dressing (80 calories)

1 fresh peach (60 calories)

SNACK AND DESSERT
Sweet Pea–Wasabi Hummus with Wonton Chips (90 calories) p. 276

Cherry-Raspberry Ice Cream (120 calories) p. 328

Total: 1,430 calories

Warming Winter Day

Hearty foods will keep you warm and toasty all day long.

BREAKFAST
Potato, Bacon and Egg Scramble (180 calories) p. 17

1 slice 100% whole wheat bread, toasted with 2 teaspoons reduced-sugar red raspberry preserves (90 calories)

6 oz cocoa mix prepared with water (110 calories)

LUNCH
Calico Bean Chili (310 calories) p. 151

1 medium apple (95 calories)

8 oz fat-free (skim) milk (90 calories)

DINNER
Mexican Ground Beef and Noodles (330 calories) p. 194

Caesar salad (1 cup shredded romaine, 1 tablespoon light Caesar dressing) (60 calories)

SNACK AND DESSERT
Sweet Almond Snack Mix (130 calories) p. 283

Creamy Custards (240 calories) p. 324

Total: 1,495 calories

Celebrate-All-Day Birthday

Honor the birthday person for the entire day.

BREAKFAST
Honey-Lemon Fruit Parfaits (120 calories) p. 64

Whole wheat English muffin with 1 tablespoon low-fat cream cheese (150 calories)

1 glass (8 oz) fat-free (skim) milk (90 calories)

LUNCH
Vegetable-Cashew Noodle Bowl (330 calories) p. 122

½ cup mandarin orange segments (50 calories)

DINNER
Three-Cheese Manicotti (410 calories) p. 238

1 cup salad greens with 1 tablespoon balsamic vinaigrette dressing (50 calories)

1 slice garlic bread (frozen, prepared) (150 calories)

SNACK AND DESSERT
Lemon-Dill Dip with ½ cup vegetable dippers (50 calories) p. 270

Incredible Apple Tart (130 calories) p. 298

Total: 1,520 calories

Chapter 1
Breakfast

arepas with perico-style eggs

Prep Time: 45 Minutes   **Start to Finish:** 55 Minutes   **Makes:** 4 servings

260 Calories

AREPAS

1	cup whole-grain corn flour
½	cup frozen whole kernel corn, thawed
⅓	cup finely shredded sharp Cheddar cheese
¼	teaspoon salt
1	cup fat-free (skim) milk
1	teaspoon canola oil

PERICO-STYLE EGGS

3	eggs
1	tablespoon fat-free (skim) milk
¼	teaspoon salt
¼	teaspoon pepper
¼	cup chopped green bell pepper
¼	cup chopped tomato
2	medium green onions, chopped (2 tablespoons)
	Fresh parsley sprigs, if desired

1. In medium bowl, mix flour, corn, cheese and ¼ teaspoon salt. In microwavable measuring cup, heat 1 cup milk on High 1 minute 30 seconds or until hot but not boiling. Stir milk into corn mixture; let stand 10 minutes.

2. In 8-inch nonstick skillet, heat ½ teaspoon of the oil over medium-high heat. Stir batter. Pour ¼ cup batter into skillet; spread to 4-inch round. Cook about 30 seconds or until light golden brown on bottom and edges are dry. Turn and cook about 30 seconds longer. Transfer to heatproof plate; cover to keep warm. Repeat with remaining batter and ½ teaspoon oil.

3. In medium bowl, beat eggs, 1 tablespoon milk, ¼ teaspoon salt and the pepper; set aside. Heat same skillet over medium heat with any remaining oil. Add bell pepper; cook and stir 1 minute. Pour egg mixture over bell pepper. Cook until eggs are set but slightly moist, stirring occasionally from outside edge to center of pan. Stir in tomato and onions.

4. To serve, place 2 arepas on each of 4 plates. Serve with egg mixture. Garnish with parsley.

1 Serving: Calories 260 (Calories from Fat 90); Total Fat 10g (Saturated Fat 3.5g; Trans Fat 0g); Cholesterol 150mg; Sodium 430mg; Total Carbohydrate 32g (Dietary Fiber 3g); Protein 12g **% Daily Value:** Vitamin A 15%; Vitamin C 10%; Calcium 15%; Iron 8% **Exchanges:** 1½ Starch, ½ Other Carbohydrate, ½ Vegetable, ½ Very Lean Meat, ½ Lean Meat, 1½ Fat **Carbohydrate Choices:** 2

a little bit more

Sprinkle 1 tablespoon finely shredded sharp
Cheddar cheese over each serving of hot eggs
to add 30 calories.

bmt scrambled eggs

Prep Time: 25 Minutes   **Start to Finish:** 25 Minutes   **Makes:** 4 servings

100 Calories

½ cup sliced fresh mushrooms	⅛ teaspoon pepper
4 medium green onions, thinly sliced (¼ cup)	½ cup shredded reduced-fat Cheddar cheese (2 oz)
1 teaspoon canola oil	1 slice turkey bacon, crisply cooked, crumbled
1 cup fat-free egg product	8 grape or cherry tomatoes, cut in half
¼ cup fat-free (skim) milk	
⅛ teaspoon salt	

1. Spray 12-inch skillet with cooking spray; heat over medium heat. Add mushrooms and onions; cook 5 to 7 minutes, stirring occasionally, until tender. Stir in oil.

2. In medium bowl, beat egg product, milk, salt and pepper with whisk. Pour into skillet. Cook, without stirring, until mixture begins to set on bottom and around edge. Gently lift cooked portions with spatula so that thin, uncooked portion can flow to bottom.

3. Sprinkle with cheese and bacon. Cook 2 to 3 minutes longer or until egg mixture is cooked through but still glossy and moist (do not overcook). Remove from heat immediately. Top with tomatoes.

1 Serving: Calories 100 (Calories from Fat 50); Total Fat 5g (Saturated Fat 2.5g; Trans Fat 0g); Cholesterol 15mg; Sodium 390mg; Total Carbohydrate 3g (Dietary Fiber 1g); Protein 11g **% Daily Value:** Vitamin A 20%; Vitamin C 2%; Calcium 15%; Iron 8% **Exchanges:** ½ Vegetable, 1 Very Lean Meat, ½ Lean Meat, ½ Fat **Carbohydrate Choices:** 0

a little bit more

Serve half of a toasted whole wheat English muffin with 1 teaspoon fruit preserves for about 90 extra calories per serving.

potato, bacon and egg scramble

Prep Time: 20 Minutes   **Start to Finish:** 20 Minutes   **Makes:** 5 servings

180 Calories

1¼ lb small red potatoes (8 or 9), cubed	⅛ teaspoon pepper
1½ cups fat-free egg product or 6 eggs, beaten	1 tablespoon olive or canola oil
⅓ cup fat-free (skim) milk	4 medium green onions, sliced (¼ cup)
¼ teaspoon salt	3 slices bacon, crisply cooked, crumbled

1. In 2-quart saucepan, heat 1 inch water to boiling. Add potatoes. Cover; return to boiling. Reduce heat to medium-low. Cover; cook 6 to 8 minutes or until potatoes are tender. Drain. In medium bowl, beat egg product, milk, salt and pepper with whisk until well mixed; set aside.

2. In 10-inch skillet, heat oil over medium-high heat. Cook potatoes in oil 3 to 5 minutes, turning occasionally, until light brown. Stir in onions. Cook and stir 1 minute.

3. Pour egg mixture into skillet. As mixture begins to set at bottom and side, gently lift cooked portions with spatula so that thin, uncooked portion can flow to bottom. Avoid constant stirring. Cook 3 to 4 minutes or until eggs are thickened throughout but still moist. Sprinkle with bacon.

1 Serving: Calories 180 (Calories from Fat 45); Total Fat 5g (Saturated Fat 1g; Trans Fat 0g); Cholesterol 5mg; Sodium 380mg; Total Carbohydrate 23g (Dietary Fiber 3g); Protein 11g **% Daily Value:** Vitamin A 20%; Vitamin C 10%; Calcium 8%; Iron 20% **Exchanges:** 1 Starch, 1 Vegetable, ½ Very Lean Meat, ½ High-Fat Meat **Carbohydrate Choices:** 1½

asiago-vegetable strata

Prep Time: 30 Minutes   **Start to Finish:** 5 Hours 25 Minutes   **Makes:** 12 servings

160 Calories

1 large onion, chopped (1 cup)	6 eggs
2 cups sliced fresh mushrooms (from 8-oz package)	1½ cups fat-free (skim) milk
2 cups small fresh broccoli florets	¾ teaspoon dried oregano leaves
4 plum (Roma) tomatoes, chopped (2 cups)	¼ teaspoon salt
6 cups cubes (1 inch) 12-grain bread (7 slices)	¼ teaspoon black pepper
	¼ teaspoon ground red pepper (cayenne)
	1 cup shredded Asiago cheese (4 oz)

1. Spray 12-inch skillet with cooking spray; heat over medium-high heat. Add onion, mushrooms and broccoli; cook 5 to 6 minutes, stirring frequently, until crisp-tender. Stir in tomatoes. Remove from heat.

2. Spray 13×9-inch (3-quart) glass baking dish with cooking spray. Arrange bread cubes in baking dish. Spoon vegetable mixture over bread cubes. In medium bowl, beat eggs, milk, oregano, salt, black pepper and red pepper with whisk. Pour egg mixture over vegetables. Sprinkle with cheese. Cover; refrigerate 4 hours or overnight.

3. Heat oven to 350°F. Uncover baking dish. Bake 45 to 50 minutes or until set in center (some moisture will appear in center and will dry upon standing). Let stand 5 minutes before cutting.

1 Serving: Calories 160 (Calories from Fat 60); Total Fat 7g (Saturated Fat 3.5g; Trans Fat 0g); Cholesterol 105mg; Sodium 300mg; Total Carbohydrate 14g (Dietary Fiber 2g); Protein 10g **% Daily Value:** Vitamin A 10%; Vitamin C 15%; Calcium 15%; Iron 6% **Exchanges:** ½ Starch, 1 Vegetable, 1 Medium-Fat Meat, ½ Fat **Carbohydrate Choices:** 1

a little bit more

Add 1 cup chopped turkey pepperoni (about 3 ounces) with the cooked veggies for an additional 210 calories per serving.

chicken fajita strata

Prep Time: 30 Minutes   **Start to Finish:** 4 Hours 30 Minutes   **Makes:** 12 servings

210 Calories

2 tablespoons canola oil
2 teaspoons chili powder
1 teaspoon ground cumin
½ teaspoon salt
1 clove garlic, finely chopped
1 lb boneless skinless chicken breasts, cut into thin strips
1 medium onion, cut into thin wedges
1 medium green bell pepper, cut into strips
1 to 2 medium jalapeño chiles, seeded, finely chopped
12 soft yellow corn tortillas (6 inch; 10 oz), cut into 1-inch strips

½ cup shredded reduced-fat Cheddar cheese (2 oz)
1 cup reduced-fat sour cream
3 tablespoons chopped fresh cilantro
¼ teaspoon ground red pepper (cayenne)
1 carton (8 oz) fat-free egg product (1 cup)
¾ cup fat-free (skim) milk
1 can (10¾ oz) condensed 98% fat-free cream of chicken soup with 45% less sodium
1 medium tomato, chopped

1. In small bowl, stir together oil, chili powder, cumin, salt and garlic. Place chicken in resealable food-storage plastic bag; add chili powder mixture. Seal bag and shake to coat chicken with spices. Refrigerate 30 minutes.

2. Heat 10-inch nonstick skillet over medium-high heat. Add chicken mixture; cook 5 to 7 minutes, stirring frequently, until chicken is no longer pink in center. Transfer from skillet to plate. In same skillet, cook onion, bell pepper and chiles over medium-high heat 5 to 7 minutes, stirring frequently, until crisp-tender.

3. Spray 13×9-inch (3-quart) glass baking dish with cooking spray. Arrange half of the tortilla strips in baking dish. Top with chicken, half of the vegetable mixture and ¼ cup of the cheese. Repeat layers with remaining tortilla strips, vegetables and ¼ cup cheese. In medium bowl, stir sour cream, 2 tablespoons of the cilantro, the red pepper, egg product, milk and soup with whisk. Pour over chicken mixture. Cover; refrigerate 2 hours or overnight.

4. Heat oven to 350°F. Uncover baking dish. Bake 48 to 52 minutes or until egg mixture is set. Sprinkle with tomato and remaining 1 tablespoon cilantro. Let stand 5 minutes before serving.

1 Serving: Calories 210 (Calories from Fat 80); Total Fat 9g (Saturated Fat 3g; Trans Fat 0g); Cholesterol 35mg; Sodium 380mg; Total Carbohydrate 17g (Dietary Fiber 2g); Protein 15g **% Daily Value:** Vitamin A 20%; Vitamin C 10%; Calcium 10%; Iron 8% **Exchanges:** 1 Starch, ½ Vegetable, 1½ Very Lean Meat, 1½ Fat **Carbohydrate Choices:** 1

a little bit more

Top each serving with 2 tablespoons refrigerated salsa for an additional 10 calories.

canadian bacon bagel sandwiches

Prep Time: 10 Minutes   **Start to Finish:** 10 Minutes   **Makes:** 2 sandwiches

230 Calories

4   teaspoons spicy brown or country-style Dijon mustard

2   everything-flavored thin bagels

2   slices (1 oz each) Canadian bacon (from 6-oz package)

2   large slices tomato

½   cup loosely packed fresh spinach leaves

2   thin slices (⅔ oz each) reduced-fat Swiss cheese

1. Heat contact grill or panini maker for 5 minutes. Spread 1 teaspoon mustard on cut sides of each bagel. On bagel bottoms, place 1 slice Canadian bacon, 1 slice tomato, ¼ cup spinach and 1 slice cheese. Cover with bagel tops.

2. Place sandwiches on grill. Close grill, pressing down lightly; cook 2 to 3 minutes or until sandwiches are hot and cheese is melted. Serve immediately.

1 Sandwich: Calories 230 (Calories from Fat 60); Total Fat 7g (Saturated Fat 3.5g; Trans Fat 0g); Cholesterol 25mg; Sodium 920mg; Total Carbohydrate 26g (Dietary Fiber 6g); Protein 16g **% Daily Value:** Vitamin A 25%; Vitamin C 6%; Calcium 20%; Iron 10% **Exchanges:** 1½ Starch, ½ Vegetable, 1½ Lean Meat, ½ Fat **Carbohydrate Choices:** 2

a little bit more

Extra-hungry? Use 2 slices of Canadian bacon per sandwich for an additional 140 calories.

breakfast panini

Prep Time: 10 Minutes   **Start to Finish:** 10 Minutes   **Makes:** 2 panini

300 Calories

2 eggs	2 thin slices onion
½ teaspoon salt-free seasoning blend	4 very thin slices reduced-sodium cooked ham (from deli)
2 tablespoons chopped fresh chives	2 thin slices reduced-fat Cheddar cheese
2 whole wheat thin bagels	
2 slices tomato	

1. Spray 8-inch skillet with cooking spray; heat over medium heat. In medium bowl, beat eggs, seasoning blend and chives with whisk until well mixed. Pour into skillet. As eggs begin to set at bottom and side, gently lift cooked portions with spatula so that thin, uncooked portion can flow to bottom. Avoid constant stirring. Cook 3 to 4 minutes or until eggs are thickened throughout but still moist and creamy; remove from heat.

2. Heat contact grill or panini maker for 5 minutes. For each panini, divide cooked eggs evenly between bagel bottoms. Top each with 1 tomato slice, 1 onion slice, 2 ham slices and 1 cheese slice. Cover with bagel tops.

3. Place sandwiches on grill. Close grill, pressing down lightly; cook 2 to 3 minutes or until hot and cheese is melted. Serve immediately.

1 Panini: Calories 300 (Calories from Fat 100); Total Fat 11g (Saturated Fat 4.5g; Trans Fat 0g); Cholesterol 205mg; Sodium 490mg; Total Carbohydrate 32g (Dietary Fiber 3g); Protein 18g **% Daily Value:** Vitamin A 15%; Vitamin C 4%; Calcium 15%; Iron 15% **Exchanges:** 1½ Starch, ½ Other Carbohydrate, 1 Very Lean Meat, 1 Lean Meat, 1½ Fat **Carbohydrate Choices:** 2

a little bit more
Spread each cut side of bagels with 1½ teaspoons reduced-fat mayonnaise and 1 teaspoon Dijon mustard for an additional 25 calories panini.

veggie-stuffed omelet

Prep Time: **15 Minutes**   Start to Finish: **15 Minutes**   Makes: **1 serving**

150 Calories

1 teaspoon olive or canola oil	½ cup fat-free egg product or 2 eggs, beaten
2 tablespoons chopped red bell pepper	1 tablespoon water
1 tablespoon chopped onion	Dash salt
¼ cup sliced fresh mushrooms	Dash pepper
1 cup loosely packed fresh baby spinach leaves	1 tablespoon shredded reduced-fat Cheddar cheese

1. In nonstick omelet pan or 8-inch skillet, heat oil over medium-high heat. Cook bell pepper, onion and mushrooms in oil 2 minutes, stirring frequently, until onion is tender. Stir in spinach; cook and stir just until spinach wilts. Transfer vegetables from skillet to small bowl; cover to keep warm.

2. In medium bowl, beat egg product, water, salt and pepper with whisk until well mixed. Reheat same skillet over medium-high heat. Quickly pour egg mixture into pan. While sliding pan back and forth rapidly over heat, quickly stir with spatula to spread eggs continuously over bottom of pan as they thicken. Let stand over heat a few seconds to lightly brown bottom of omelet. Do not overcook; omelet will continue to cook after folding.

3. Spoon vegetable mixture over half of omelet; sprinkle with cheese. With spatula, loosen edge of omelet and fold other half over vegetables. Gently slide out of pan onto plate. Serve immediately.

1 Serving: Calories 150 (Calories from Fat 60); Total Fat 6g (Saturated Fat 1.5g; Trans Fat 0g); Cholesterol 0mg; Sodium 460mg; Total Carbohydrate 6g (Dietary Fiber 2g); Protein 16g **% Daily Value:** Vitamin A 100%; Vitamin C 30%; Calcium 10%; Iron 20% **Exchanges:** 1½ Vegetable, 2 Very Lean Meat, 1 Fat **Carbohydrate Choices:** ½

a little bit more

A slice of toasted whole wheat bread spread with 2 teaspoons almond butter makes a great partner for this omelet, adding 140 calories.

savory italian frittata

Prep Time: 25 Minutes **Start to Finish:** 25 Minutes **Makes:** 6 servings

140 Calories

8	eggs	½	teaspoon salt
1	tablespoon chopped fresh or 1 teaspoon dried basil leaves	⅛	teaspoon pepper
1	tablespoon chopped fresh or 1 teaspoon dried sage leaves	¼	cup diced lean turkey ham, prosciutto or cooked ham (2 oz)
1	tablespoon chopped fresh mint leaves or 1 teaspoon mint flakes	1	tablespoon butter or margarine
1	tablespoon freshly grated Parmesan cheese	1	small onion, finely chopped (¼ cup)

1. In medium bowl, beat eggs, herbs, cheese, salt and pepper with whisk until well mixed. Stir in turkey ham.

2. In 10-inch nonstick skillet, melt butter over medium-high heat. Cook onion in butter 4 to 5 minutes, stirring frequently, until crisp-tender; reduce heat to medium-low.

3. Pour egg mixture into skillet. Cover; cook 9 to 11 minutes or until eggs are set around edge and light brown on bottom. Cut into wedges.

1 Serving: Calories 140 (Calories from Fat 90); Total Fat 10g (Saturated Fat 3.5g; Trans Fat 0g); Cholesterol 260mg; Sodium 420mg; Total Carbohydrate 2g (Dietary Fiber 0g); Protein 10g **% Daily Value:** Vitamin A 10%; Vitamin C 0%; Calcium 6%; Iron 6% **Exchanges:** 1½ Very Lean Meat, 2 Fat **Carbohydrate Choices:** 0

a little bit less

Save 55 calories per serving by substituting 2 cups fat-free egg product for the eggs.

skillet eggs with summer squash hash

Prep Time: 35 Minutes   **Start to Finish:** 1 Hour 15 Minutes   **Makes:** 4 servings

260 Calories

2 medium zucchini (1 lb)
2 medium yellow summer squash (1 lb)
1 teaspoon salt
1 tablespoon olive oil
¼ cup chopped red onion
1 small tomato, chopped (½ cup)

½ cup diced cooked 95% fat-free ham
1 tablespoon chopped fresh dill weed
1 teaspoon grated lemon peel
4 eggs
⅛ teaspoon pepper

1. Shred the zucchini and yellow squash and place in large colander. Stir in salt; let stand in sink 30 minutes to drain. Rinse gently to remove excess salt; squeeze squash mixture to remove as much liquid as possible. Set aside.

2. In 12-inch nonstick skillet, heat oil over medium-high heat. Cook onion in oil 2 minutes, stirring frequently. Stir in squash mixture. Cook 8 minutes, stirring occasionally, until vegetables are crisp-tender. Add tomato, ham, dill and lemon peel. Cook and stir 1 minute longer. Reduce heat to medium.

3. Spread squash mixture evenly in skillet. Make 4 (2½-inch-wide) indentations in mixture with back of spoon. Break eggs, one at a time, into custard cup or saucer; pour into indentations. Sprinkle eggs with pepper. Cover; cook 8 to 10 minutes or until whites and yolks are firm, not runny.

1 Serving: Calories 260 (Calories from Fat 120); Total Fat 13g (Saturated Fat 3.5g; Trans Fat 0g); Cholesterol 225mg; Sodium 1550mg; Total Carbohydrate 10g (Dietary Fiber 2g); Protein 24g **% Daily Value:** Vitamin A 15%; Vitamin C 30%; Calcium 6%; Iron 15% **Exchanges:** 2 Vegetable, 2 Very Lean Meat, 1 Medium-Fat Meat, 1½ Fat **Carbohydrate Choices:** ½

a little bit more

Add 1 cup finely chopped red bell pepper with the zucchini and squash—for a dish that's rich in vitamin C, beta-carotene and another 10 calories per serving.

mexican breakfast pizzas

Prep Time: 15 Minutes   Start to Finish: 25 Minutes   Makes: 4 servings

200 Calories

¼   lb bulk turkey breakfast sausage

2   whole-grain lower-carb lavash flatbreads or tortillas (10 inch)

¼   cup chunky-style salsa

½   cup black beans with cumin and chili spices (from 15-oz can)

1   small tomato, chopped (½ cup)

½   cup frozen whole kernel corn, thawed

¼   cup shredded reduced-fat Cheddar cheese (1 oz)

1   tablespoon chopped fresh cilantro

2   teaspoons crumbed cotija (white Mexican) cheese

1. Heat oven to 425°F. In 8-inch skillet, cook sausage over medium heat 4 to 5 minutes, stirring occasionally, until thoroughly cooked; drain.

2. On 1 large cookie sheet, place flatbreads. Spread each with 2 tablespoons salsa. Top each with half of the sausage, beans, tomatoes, corn and Cheddar cheese.

3. Bake about 8 minutes or until cheese is melted. Sprinkle with cilantro and cotija cheese; cut into wedges. Serve immediately.

1 Serving: Calories 200 (Calories from Fat 70); Total Fat 8g (Saturated Fat 2g; Trans Fat 0g); Cholesterol 25mg; Sodium 710mg; Total Carbohydrate 19g (Dietary Fiber 6g); Protein 14g **% Daily Value:** Vitamin A 15%; Vitamin C 4%; Calcium 8%; Iron 10% **Exchanges:** 1 Starch, ½ Other Carbohydrate, 1 Very Lean Meat, ½ Lean Meat, 1 Fat **Carbohydrate Choices:** 1

a little bit more

A dollop of reduced-fat sour cream (about 2 teaspoons) per slice of pizza might seem decadent but only adds 15 calories.

whole-grain strawberry pancakes

Prep Time: 30 Minutes   Start to Finish: 30 Minutes   Makes: 7 servings

270 Calories

1½ cups whole wheat flour
3 tablespoons sugar
1 teaspoon baking powder
½ teaspoon baking soda
½ teaspoon salt
3 eggs or ¾ cup fat-free egg product

1 container (6 oz) vanilla thick and creamy low-fat yogurt
¾ cup water
3 tablespoons canola oil
1¾ cups sliced fresh strawberries
1 container (6 oz) strawberry thick and creamy low-fat yogurt

1. In large bowl, mix flour, sugar, baking powder, baking soda and salt; set aside. In medium bowl, beat eggs, vanilla yogurt, water and oil with whisk until well blended. Pour egg mixture all at once into flour mixture; stir until moistened.

2. Heat griddle or skillet over medium-high heat (375°F). Grease with canola oil if necessary (or spray with cooking spray before heating). For each pancake, pour slightly less than ¼ cup batter onto hot griddle. Cook until puffed and dry around edges and bubbles form on top. Turn and cook other sides until golden brown.

3. Top each serving (2 pancakes) with ¼ cup strawberries and about 1 heaping tablespoon strawberry yogurt.

1 Serving: Calories 270 (Calories from Fat 90); Total Fat 10g (Saturated Fat 2g; Trans Fat 0g); Cholesterol 85mg; Sodium 380mg; Total Carbohydrate 37g (Dietary Fiber 4g); Protein 7g **% Daily Value:** Vitamin A 6%; Vitamin C 20%; Calcium 15%; Iron 8% **Exchanges:** 1½ Starch, 1 Other Carbohydrate, ½ Medium-Fat Meat, 1½ Fat **Carbohydrate Choices:** 2½

a little bit more

Have a craving for chocolate? Drizzle pancakes with 2 tablespoons fat-free chocolate syrup before topping with strawberries and yogurt for an extra 100 calories per serving.

apple griddle cakes

Prep Time: 40 Minutes   Start to Finish: 40 Minutes   Makes: 4 servings

220 Calories

1	cooking apple (such as Jonathan or Granny Smith), finely chopped (about ¾ cup)
1	teaspoon fresh lemon juice
¾	cup whole wheat flour
1	tablespoon sugar
1	teaspoon baking powder
¼	teaspoon apple pie spice or ground cinnamon
⅛	teaspoon salt

¾	cup fat-free (skim) milk
1	egg white
2	tablespoons canola oil
1	cup unsweetened applesauce
⅛	teaspoon apple pie spice or ground cinnamon
	Additional apple pie spice or ground cinnamon, if desired
	Fresh fruit, if desired

1. In small bowl, toss apple and lemon juice; set aside. In medium bowl, mix whole wheat flour, sugar, baking powder, ¼ teaspoon apple pie spice and the salt.

2. In another small bowl, beat milk, egg white and oil with whisk. Add milk mixture all at once to flour mixture; stir just until moistened (batter should be lumpy). Gently fold in apple mixture.

3. Spray griddle or skillet with cooking spray; heat over medium-high heat (375°F). For each pancake, pour slightly less than ¼ cup batter onto hot griddle; spread batter into 3- to 4-inch round. Cook until edges are slightly dry and bubbles form on top. Turn and cook other sides until golden brown.

4. Meanwhile, in small bowl, mix applesauce and ⅛ teaspoon apple pie spice. Top each serving (2 pancakes) with ¼ cup applesauce. Sprinkle with additional apple pie spice and serve with fruit.

1 Serving: Calories 220 (Calories from Fat 70); Total Fat 8g (Saturated Fat 0.5g; Trans Fat 0g); Cholesterol 0mg; Sodium 230mg; Total Carbohydrate 32g (Dietary Fiber 4g); Protein 5g **% Daily Value:** Vitamin A 2%; Vitamin C 0%; Calcium 15%; Iron 6% **Exchanges:** 1 Starch, 1 Other Carbohydrate, ½ Very Lean Meat, 1½ Fat **Carbohydrate Choices:** 2

a little bit more

Stir in 4 slices crumbled crisply cooked turkey bacon with the apple mixture and add only 35 calories per serving.

buckwheat pancakes with butter-pecan syrup

Prep Time: 25 Minutes **Start to Finish:** 25 Minutes **Makes:** 5 servings

320
Calories

SYRUP

1	tablespoon butter or margarine
3	tablespoons chopped pecans
½	cup maple-flavored syrup

PANCAKES

1	egg
½	cup buckwheat flour
½	cup whole wheat flour
1	cup fat-free (skim) milk
1	tablespoon sugar
2	tablespoons canola oil
3	teaspoons baking powder
¼	teaspoon salt
	Whole bran or wheat germ, if desired

1. In 1-quart saucepan, melt butter over medium heat. Cook pecans in butter, stirring frequently, until browned. Stir in syrup; heat until hot. Remove from heat; keep warm.

2. In medium bowl, beat egg with whisk until fluffy. Beat in remaining pancake ingredients except bran just until smooth.

3. Heat griddle or skillet over medium-high heat (375°F). Grease with canola oil if necessary (or spray with cooking spray before heating). For each pancake, pour about 3 tablespoons batter onto hot griddle. Cook until puffed and dry around edges and bubbles form on top. Sprinkle each pancake with 1 teaspoon bran. Turn and cook other sides until golden brown.

4. Top each serving (2 pancakes) with about 2 tablespoons syrup.

1 Serving: Calories 320 (Calories from Fat 110); Total Fat 12g (Saturated Fat 2.5g; Trans Fat 0g); Cholesterol 45mg; Sodium 480mg; Total Carbohydrate 45g (Dietary Fiber 3g); Protein 6g **% Daily Value:** Vitamin A 4%; Vitamin C 0%; Calcium 25%; Iron 8% **Exchanges:** 2½ Starch, ½ Other Carbohydrate, 2 Fat **Carbohydrate Choices:** 3

a little bit more

Kick-start your day with some fruit by slicing ½ medium banana over each serving of pancakes before topping with syrup for 55 additional calories.

chocolate crepes with banana-pecan topping

Prep Time: 35 Minutes   **Start to Finish:** 35 Minutes   **Makes:** 8 servings

170 Calories

⅓ cup whole wheat flour	1 teaspoon canola oil
2 tablespoons packed brown sugar	½ teaspoon vanilla
2 tablespoons unsweetened baking cocoa	4 medium bananas
⅛ teaspoon salt	¼ cup fat-free caramel topping
⅔ cup fat-free (skim) milk	¼ teaspoon rum extract
¼ cup fat-free egg product	¼ cup coarsely chopped pecans, toasted*

1. In medium bowl, mix flour, brown sugar, cocoa and salt. Add milk, egg product, oil and vanilla; stir with whisk until combined.

2. Lightly oil 7- to 8-inch crepe pan or nonstick skillet; heat over medium heat. For each crepe, pour about 2 tablespoons batter into pan. Immediately rotate pan until thin film covers bottom. Cook 30 to 45 seconds or until top is set and dry. Invert pan to remove crepe. Stack crepes between waxed paper; cover to keep warm. Repeat with remaining batter, oiling pan occasionally.

3. Cut bananas in half lengthwise, then crosswise. Lightly oil nonstick grill pan or large nonstick skillet; heat over medium heat. Add bananas; cook 3 to 4 minutes, turning once, until browned and softened.

4. Meanwhile, in 1-quart saucepan, heat caramel topping over low heat until hot. Remove from heat; stir in rum extract.

5. On each of 8 plates, place 1 crepe (folding as desired). Top evenly with banana pieces, caramel sauce and pecans.

*To toast nuts, cook in an ungreased skillet over medium heat for 5 to 7 minutes, stirring frequently, until nuts begin to brown, then stirring constantly until nuts are light brown.

1 Serving: Calories 170 (Calories from Fat 30); Total Fat 3.5g (Saturated Fat 0g; Trans Fat 0g); Cholesterol 0mg; Sodium 95mg; Total Carbohydrate 30g (Dietary Fiber 3g); Protein 3g **% Daily Value:** Vitamin A 4%; Vitamin C 4%; Calcium 4%; Iron 4% **Exchanges:** 1 Starch, ½ Fruit, ½ Other Carbohydrate, ½ Fat **Carbohydrate Choices:** 2

a little bit more

Top each serving with a tablespoon of miniature semisweet chocolate chips for an added 50 calories.

fruit-topped whole-grain waffles

Prep Time: 20 Minutes   **Start to Finish:** 20 Minutes   **Makes:** 4 servings

340 Calories

TOPPING
- 1 cup fresh or frozen (thawed) blueberries
- 1 cup sliced fresh strawberries
- ¼ cup real maple syrup

WAFFLES
- ½ cup all-purpose flour
- ½ cup whole wheat flour
- ¼ cup quick-cooking oats
- 2 teaspoons sugar
- 1 teaspoon baking powder
- ½ teaspoon baking soda
- 1¼ cups buttermilk
- ¼ cup fat-free egg product
- 2 tablespoons canola or soybean oil

1. In medium bowl, stir together topping ingredients; set aside.

2. Heat waffle maker. (Waffle makers without a nonstick coating may need to be brushed with vegetable oil or sprayed with cooking spray before batter for each waffle is added.) In large bowl, mix flours, oats, sugar, baking powder and baking soda. Add buttermilk, egg product and oil; beat with whisk until well blended.

3. Pour about ½ cup batter onto hot waffle maker. (Check manufacturer's directions for recommended amount of batter.) Close lid of waffle maker. Bake about 3 minutes or until steaming stops and waffle is golden brown. Repeat with remaining batter.

4. Top each serving (2 waffles) with ½ cup fruit topping.

1 Serving: Calories 340 (Calories from Fat 90); Total Fat 9g (Saturated Fat 1.5g; Trans Fat 0g); Cholesterol 5mg; Sodium 540mg; Total Carbohydrate 55g (Dietary Fiber 4g); Protein 9g **% Daily Value:** Vitamin A 6%; Vitamin C 25%; Calcium 20%; Iron 10% **Exchanges:** 3 Starch, ½ Fruit, 1½ Fat **Carbohydrate Choices:** 3½

a little bit more
Can't go without syrup? Drizzling the waffles with 2 tablespoons reduced-calorie maple-flavored syrup adds 60 calories per serving.

whole-grain raspberry french toast

Prep Time: 20 Minutes   **Start to Finish:** 20 Minutes   **Makes:** 2 servings

310 Calories

TOPPING

- 3 tablespoons raspberry fruit spread
- 1 cup frozen raspberries
- 1 tablespoon finely chopped crystallized ginger or ¼ teaspoon ground ginger

FRENCH TOAST

- ½ cup fat-free egg product or 2 eggs, beaten
- ¼ cup fat-free (skim) milk
- 2 teaspoons sugar
- 1 teaspoon vanilla
- ¼ teaspoon ground cinnamon
- 3 slices white whole-grain bread, cut diagonally in half

1. In 1-quart saucepan, heat fruit spread and raspberries over low heat, stirring occasionally, until warm. Remove from heat. Stir in ginger; set aside.

2. In shallow bowl, beat egg product, milk, sugar, vanilla and cinnamon with whisk until blended.

3. Spray griddle or skillet with cooking spray; heat over medium-high heat (375°F). Dip each slice of bread into egg mixture, turning to coat both sides; let stand in egg mixture to soak 30 to 60 seconds. Place bread on hot griddle; cook 4 to 6 minutes, turning once, until golden brown on both sides.

4. Serve French toast with topping.

1 Serving: Calories 310 (Calories from Fat 20); Total Fat 2.5g (Saturated Fat 0g; Trans Fat 0g); Cholesterol 0mg; Sodium 330mg; Total Carbohydrate 57g (Dietary Fiber 11g); Protein 14g **% Daily Value:** Vitamin A 15%; Vitamin C 30%; Calcium 15%; Iron 15% **Exchanges:** 1½ Starch, ½ Fruit, 2 Other Carbohydrate, 1½ Very Lean Meat **Carbohydrate Choices:** 4

berry french toast stratas

Prep Time: 20 Minutes   **Start to Finish:** 50 Minutes   **Makes:** 6 servings

190 Calories

3 cups mixed fresh berries (such as blueberries, raspberries or cut-up strawberries)	½ cup fat-free (skim) milk
	½ cup fat-free half-and-half
	2 tablespoons honey
1 tablespoon granulated sugar	1½ teaspoons vanilla
4 cups cubes (¾ inch) whole wheat bread (about 5 slices)	1 teaspoon ground cinnamon
	¼ teaspoon ground nutmeg
1½ cups fat-free egg product or 6 eggs, beaten	½ teaspoon powdered sugar, if desired

1. Heat oven to 350°F. Generously spray 12 regular-size muffin cups with cooking spray. In medium bowl, mix fruit and granulated sugar; set aside.

2. Divide bread cubes evenly among muffin cups. In large bowl, beat remaining ingredients except powdered sugar with whisk until well mixed. Pour egg mixture over bread cubes, pushing down lightly with spoon to soak bread cubes. (If all egg mixture doesn't fit into cups, let cups stand up to 10 minutes, gradually adding remaining egg mixture as bread cubes soak it up.)

3. Bake 20 to 25 minutes or until centers are set. Cool 5 minutes; remove from muffin cups. Place 2 stratas on each of 6 plates. Top each serving with ½ cup fruit mixture; sprinkle evenly with powdered sugar.

1 Serving: Calories 190 (Calories from Fat 15); Total Fat 1.5g (Saturated Fat 0g; Trans Fat 0g); Cholesterol 0mg; Sodium 280mg; Total Carbohydrate 31g (Dietary Fiber 5g); Protein 11g **% Daily Value:** Vitamin A 15%; Vitamin C 20%; Calcium 10%; Iron 10% **Exchanges:** 1 Starch, ½ Fruit, ½ Other Carbohydrate, 1 Very Lean Meat **Carbohydrate Choices:** 2

cinnamon french toast sticks with spicy cider syrup

Prep Time: 20 Minutes   **Start to Finish:** 20 Minutes   **Makes:** 10 servings

280 Calories

SYRUP
1	cup sugar
3	tablespoons all-purpose flour
¼	teaspoon ground cinnamon
¼	teaspoon ground nutmeg
2	cups apple cider
2	tablespoons fresh lemon juice
¼	cup butter or margarine, cut into 8 pieces

FRENCH TOAST
½	cup all-purpose flour
1¼	cups milk
2	teaspoons ground cinnamon
1	teaspoon vanilla
2	eggs
10	slices firm-textured whole-grain sandwich bread, cut into thirds

1. In 2-quart saucepan, mix sugar, 3 tablespoons flour, ¼ teaspoon cinnamon and the nutmeg. Stir in cider and lemon juice. Cook over medium heat, stirring constantly, until mixture thickens and boils. Boil and stir 1 minute; remove from heat. Stir in butter; cover to keep warm.

2. In small bowl, beat ½ cup flour, the milk, 2 teaspoons cinnamon, the vanilla and eggs with whisk until smooth.

3. Heat griddle or skillet over medium-high heat (375°F). Grease griddle with oil if necessary (or spray with cooking spray before heating). Dip sticks of bread into batter; drain excess batter back into bowl. Place bread on hot griddle; cook about 4 minutes on each side or until golden brown.

4. Serve French toast sticks with warm syrup.

1 Serving: Calories 280 (Calories from Fat 70); Total Fat 7g (Saturated Fat 4g; Trans Fat 0g); Cholesterol 50mg; Sodium 200mg; Total Carbohydrate 46g (Dietary Fiber 2g); Protein 7g **% Daily Value:** Vitamin A 6%; Vitamin C 0%; Calcium 8%; Iron 8% **Exchanges:** 2½ Starch, ½ Other Carbohydrate, 1 Fat **Carbohydrate Choices:** 3

a little bit more
Serve with ½ cup of fresh orange segments for only 40 extra calories and a boost of vitamin C.

bran muffins

Prep Time: 15 Minutes   **Start to Finish:** 50 Minutes   **Makes:** 12 muffins

160 Calories

1¼ cups Fiber One® cereal or
2 cups bran cereal flakes

1⅓ cups milk

½ cup raisins, dried cherries or dried
cranberries, if desired

½ teaspoon vanilla

¼ cup canola oil

1 egg

1¼ cups all-purpose or whole
wheat flour

½ cup packed brown sugar

3 teaspoons baking powder

¼ teaspoon salt

¼ teaspoon ground cinnamon,
if desired

1. Heat oven to 400°F. Grease bottoms only of 12 regular-size muffin cups with shortening or cooking spray, or place paper baking cup in each muffin cup.

2. Place cereal in resealable plastic food-storage bag; seal bag and crush with rolling pin or meat mallet (or crush in food processor). In medium bowl, stir crushed cereal, milk, raisins and vanilla until well blended. Let stand about 5 minutes or until cereal has softened. Beat in oil and egg with fork.

3. In another medium bowl, stir remaining ingredients until well blended; stir into cereal mixture just until moistened. Divide batter evenly among muffin cups.

4. Bake 18 to 25 minutes or until toothpick inserted in center comes out clean. If baked in greased pan, cool 5 minutes in pan, then remove from pan to cooling rack; if baked in paper baking cups, immediately remove from pan to cooling rack. Serve warm, if desired.

1 Muffin: Calories 160 (Calories from Fat 50); Total Fat 5g (Saturated Fat 0.5g; Trans Fat 0g); Cholesterol 15mg; Sodium 210mg; Total Carbohydrate 26g (Dietary Fiber 3g); Protein 3g **% Daily Value:** Vitamin A 0%; Vitamin C 0%; Calcium 15%; Iron 10% **Exchanges:** 1 Starch, ½ Other Carbohydrate, 1 Fat **Carbohydrate Choices:** 2

a little bit more

Serve these muffins warm with an orange and honey butter: Mix ½ cup softened butter, 6 tablespoons orange marmalade and 2 tablespoons honey. A 1-tablespoon serving is 100 calories.

upside-down date-bran muffins

Prep Time: 20 Minutes   **Start to Finish:** 40 Minutes   **Makes:** 12 muffins

230 Calories

MUFFINS
1	cup Fiber One cereal
1	cup buttermilk
¼	cup canola oil
1	teaspoon vanilla
1	egg
1¼	cups whole wheat flour
¾	cup chopped dates
½	cup packed brown sugar
1	teaspoon baking soda
¼	teaspoon salt

TOPPING
3	tablespoons packed brown sugar
2	tablespoons butter or margarine, melted
1	tablespoon light corn syrup

1. Heat oven to 400°F. Grease bottoms and sides of 12 regular-size muffin cups with shortening or cooking spray. Do not use paper baking cups.

2. In blender or food processor, place cereal, buttermilk, oil, vanilla and egg. Cover; let stand 10 minutes. Meanwhile, in small bowl, stir topping ingredients until well mixed. Place 1 teaspoon topping in bottom of each muffin cup.

3. Blend cereal mixture in blender on medium speed until smooth; set aside. In medium bowl, stir flour, dates, ½ cup brown sugar, the baking soda and salt until well mixed. Pour cereal mixture over flour mixture; stir just until moistened (batter will be thick). Divide batter evenly among muffin cups.

4. Bake 14 to 18 minutes or until toothpick inserted in center comes out clean. Immediately place cookie sheet upside down on muffin pan; turn cookie sheet and pan over to remove muffins. Serve warm, if desired.

1 Muffin: Calories 230 (Calories from Fat 70); Total Fat 8g (Saturated Fat 2g; Trans Fat 0g); Cholesterol 20mg; Sodium 220mg; Total Carbohydrate 35g (Dietary Fiber 4g); Protein 3g **% Daily Value:** Vitamin A 0%; Vitamin C 0%; Calcium 6%; Iron 8% **Exchanges:** 1 Starch, 1½ Other Carbohydrate, 1½ Fat **Carbohydrate Choices:** 2

blueberry-orange muffins

Prep Time: 20 Minutes   **Start to Finish:** 45 Minutes   **Makes:** 12 muffins

150 Calories

¾ cup buckwheat flour
⅔ cup whole wheat flour
⅔ cup all-purpose flour
¼ cup sugar
1½ teaspoons baking powder
1 teaspoon ground cinnamon
½ teaspoon baking soda
½ teaspoon salt
2 eggs

1 cup mashed cooked butternut squash
½ cup fat-free (skim) milk
½ teaspoon grated orange peel
¼ cup orange juice
2 tablespoons canola oil
¾ cup fresh or frozen (do not thaw) blueberries
1 to 2 tablespoons old-fashioned oats

1. Heat oven to 400°F. Place paper baking cup in each of 12 regular-size muffin cups; spray paper cups with cooking spray.

2. In large bowl, mix flours, sugar, baking powder, cinnamon, baking soda and salt. In medium bowl, beat eggs, squash, milk, orange peel, orange juice and oil with whisk. Make well in center of flour mixture; add egg mixture all at once. Stir just until moistened (batter should be lumpy). Fold in blueberries.

3. Divide batter evenly among muffin cups, filling each almost full. Sprinkle with oats.

4. Bake 17 to 20 minutes or until toothpick inserted in center comes out clean. Cool in pan on cooling rack 5 minutes. Remove from pan; serve warm.

1 Muffin: Calories 150 (Calories from Fat 35); Total Fat 3.5g (Saturated Fat 0.5g; Trans Fat 0g); Cholesterol 30mg; Sodium 230mg; Total Carbohydrate 25g (Dietary Fiber 2g); Protein 4g **% Daily Value:** Vitamin A 45%; Vitamin C 4%; Calcium 6%; Iron 6% **Exchanges:** 1½ Starch, ½ Fat **Carbohydrate Choices:** 1½

a little bit more

Add an orange drizzle for an extra punch of citrus flavor. Mix ½ cup powdered sugar, ¼ teaspoon grated orange peel and 2 to 3 teaspoons orange juice until thin enough to drizzle. Drizzle over warm muffins for an added 20 calories per serving.

easy cranberry-orange scones

Prep Time: 20 Minutes   **Start to Finish:** 1 Hour   **Makes:** 8 scones

260 Calories

1 cup whole wheat flour	⅓ cup cold butter
1 cup all-purpose flour	⅓ cup fat-free (skim) milk
¼ cup granulated sugar	¼ cup orange juice
2 teaspoons grated orange peel	½ cup sweetened dried cranberries
1½ teaspoons cream of tartar	⅓ cup powdered sugar
¾ teaspoon baking soda	2 to 3 teaspoons fat-free (skim) milk
¼ teaspoon salt	

1. Heat oven to 350°F. In large bowl, mix flours, granulated sugar, orange peel, cream of tartar, baking soda and salt. Cut in butter, using pastry blender or fork, until mixture looks like fine crumbs. Stir in ⅓ cup milk, the orange juice and cranberries just until dry ingredients are moistened.

2. On ungreased cookie sheet, pat dough into 8-inch round. Cut into 8 wedges with sharp knife dipped in flour, but do not separate wedges.

3. Bake 20 to 25 minutes or until golden brown. Cool 5 minutes; transfer from cookie sheet to cooling rack. Cool 10 minutes.

4. In small bowl, mix powdered sugar and 2 to 3 teaspoons milk until smooth and thin enough to drizzle. Drizzle over scones. Serve warm, if desired.

1 Scone: Calories 260 (Calories from Fat 70); Total Fat 8g (Saturated Fat 5g; Trans Fat 0g); Cholesterol 20mg; Sodium 260mg; Total Carbohydrate 42g (Dietary Fiber 2g); Protein 4g **% Daily Value:** Vitamin A 6%; Vitamin C 2%; Calcium 2%; Iron 8% **Exchanges:** 1½ Starch, 1½ Other Carbohydrate, 1½ Fat **Carbohydrate Choices:** 3

glazed whole wheat cinnamon rolls

Prep Time: 30 Minutes   **Start to Finish:** 3 Hours 10 Minutes   **Makes:** 10 rolls

240 Calories

DOUGH
- 1½ to 2 cups all-purpose flour
- ¼ cup granulated sugar
- 1 teaspoon salt
- 1 package regular active or fast-acting dry yeast
- 1 cup warm water (105°F to 115°F)
- 1 tablespoon canola oil
- 2 teaspoons vanilla
- 1½ cups white whole wheat or whole wheat flour

FILLING
- 2 teaspoons butter, softened
- 2 tablespoons granulated sugar
- 1 teaspoon ground cinnamon
- 3 tablespoons miniature semisweet chocolate chips

GLAZES
- 1 oz bittersweet baking chocolate, chopped
- ½ teaspoon butter
- ⅓ cup powdered sugar
- 1 to 2 teaspoons water or milk

1. In large bowl, mix 1½ cups of the all-purpose flour, ¼ cup granulated sugar, the salt and yeast. Beat in warm water, oil and vanilla with electric mixer on low speed 30 seconds, scraping bowl frequently. Beat on medium speed 1 minute, scraping bowl occasionally. Stir in whole wheat flour and enough remaining ½ cup all-purpose flour to make dough easy to handle.

2. On lightly floured surface, knead dough about 5 minutes or until smooth and springy. Cover dough with bowl; let rest 10 minutes. On lightly floured surface, flatten dough with hands or rolling pin into 12½×9-inch rectangle. Spread with 2 teaspoons butter. In small bowl, mix 2 tablespoons granulated sugar and the cinnamon; sprinkle over butter. Sprinkle with chocolate chips.

3. Roll up rectangle tightly, beginning at 1 long side; pinch edge of dough into roll to seal. Stretch and shape until even. Cut roll into 10 (1¼-inch) slices. Spray 13×9-inch pan with cooking spray; place rolls slightly apart in pan. Cover loosely with plastic wrap and cloth towel. Let rise in warm place (80°F to 85°F) 1 hour 30 minutes to 2 hours or until doubled in size.

4. Heat oven to 375°F. Uncover rolls. Bake 20 to 25 minutes or until golden brown. Transfer from pan to cooling rack. Cool 5 minutes.

5. Meanwhile, in small microwavable bowl, microwave bittersweet chocolate and ½ teaspoon butter on High 30 seconds; stir until melted and smooth. Drizzle over tops of rolls. In small bowl, stir powdered sugar and enough water until glaze is thin enough to drizzle. Drizzle over chocolate glaze. Serve warm.

1 Roll: Calories 240 (Calories from Fat 50); Total Fat 5g (Saturated Fat 2g; Trans Fat 0g); Cholesterol 0mg; Sodium 250mg; Total Carbohydrate 42g (Dietary Fiber 3g); Protein 5g **% Daily Value:** Vitamin A 0%; Vitamin C 0%; Calcium 0%; Iron 10% **Exchanges:** 1½ Starch, 1½ Other Carbohydrate, 1 Fat **Carbohydrate Choices:** 3

blueberry-peach coffee cake

Prep Time: 25 Minutes   **Start to Finish:** 1 Hour 35 Minutes   **Makes:** 9 servings

210 Calories

1 cup all-purpose flour	¼ cup sugar
⅓ cup yellow cornmeal	¼ cup honey
1½ teaspoons grated lemon peel	¼ cup canola oil
1 teaspoon baking powder	1 cup fresh or frozen blueberries
½ teaspoon baking soda	½ cup chopped fresh peach or frozen sliced peaches, thawed, drained and chopped
¼ teaspoon salt	
¾ cup plain fat-free yogurt	1 tablespoon all-purpose flour
2 egg whites	

1. Heat oven to 350°F. Lightly spray 8-inch square pan with cooking spray. In large bowl, mix 1 cup flour, cornmeal, lemon peel, baking powder, baking soda and salt; set aside.

2. In medium bowl, mix yogurt, egg whites, sugar, honey and oil. Make well in center of flour mixture; add yogurt mixture all at once and stir just until combined. In small bowl, gently toss blueberries, peach and 1 tablespoon flour until coated.

3. Spread about half of the batter in pan. Sprinkle with fruit mixture. Spoon mounds of remaining batter over fruit, then spread evenly over fruit (batter may not completely cover fruit).

4. Bake 40 minutes or until golden brown and toothpick inserted near center comes out clean. Cool on cooling rack 30 minutes. Cut into squares; serve warm.

1 Serving: Calories 210 (Calories from Fat 60); Total Fat 6g (Saturated Fat 0.5g; Trans Fat 0g); Cholesterol 0mg; Sodium 220mg; Total Carbohydrate 34g (Dietary Fiber 1g); Protein 4g **% Daily Value:** Vitamin A 0%; Vitamin C 2%; Calcium 8%; Iron 6% **Exchanges:** 1½ Starch, 1 Other Carbohydrate, 1 Fat **Carbohydrate Choices:** 2

a little bit more

Add ½ cup chopped walnuts with the fruit for another 45 calories per serving.

berry-cheesecake coffee cake

Prep Time: 20 Minutes   **Start to Finish:** 1 Hour 5 Minutes   **Makes:** 10 servings

210 Calories

1¼ cups all-purpose flour	¼ cup fat-free egg product
1¼ teaspoons baking powder	1 teaspoon vanilla
1 teaspoon grated lemon or orange peel	½ cup buttermilk
¼ teaspoon baking soda	2 oz ⅓-less-fat cream cheese (Neufchâtel)
¼ teaspoon salt	2 tablespoons fat-free egg product
1 cup granulated sugar	1 cup fresh or frozen raspberries
3 tablespoons butter, softened	Sifted powdered sugar

1. Heat oven to 375°F. Lightly spray 9-inch round pan with cooking spray. In medium bowl, mix flour, baking powder, lemon peel, baking soda and salt; set aside.

2. In medium bowl, beat ¾ cup of the granulated sugar and the butter with electric mixer on medium speed until combined. Add ¼ cup egg product and the vanilla. Beat 1 minute. On low speed, alternately add flour mixture and buttermilk, beating just until combined after each addition. Pour into pan.

3. In small bowl, beat cream cheese and remaining ¼ cup granulated sugar on medium speed until combined. Add 2 tablespoons egg product; beat until combined. Sprinkle raspberries over batter in pan. Spoon cream cheese mixture over raspberries, allowing some of the berries to show.

4. Bake 35 minutes or until toothpick inserted near center comes out clean. Cool on cooling rack 10 minutes. Sprinkle with powdered sugar. Cut into wedges; serve warm. If desired, garnish each serving with additional raspberries.

1 Serving: Calories 210 (Calories from Fat 45); Total Fat 5g (Saturated Fat 3g; Trans Fat 0g); Cholesterol 15mg; Sodium 230mg; Total Carbohydrate 36g (Dietary Fiber 1g); Protein 3g **% Daily Value:** Vitamin A 6%; Vitamin C 4%; Calcium 6%; Iron 6% **Exchanges:** 1 Starch, 1½ Other Carbohydrate, 1 Fat **Carbohydrate Choices:** 2½

a little bit more

A tasty drink to serve with this yummy coffee cake would be hot cocoa. One serving of instant cocoa mix (no sugar added) prepared with water adds 60 calories.

whole-grain mixed berry coffee cake

Prep Time: 15 Minutes   **Start to Finish:** 1 Hour   **Makes:** 8 servings

160
Calories

¼ cup low-fat granola
½ cup buttermilk
⅓ cup packed brown sugar
2 tablespoons canola oil
1 teaspoon vanilla
1 egg
1 cup whole wheat flour

½ teaspoon baking soda
½ teaspoon ground cinnamon
⅛ teaspoon salt
1 cup mixed fresh berries (such as blueberries, raspberries and blackberries)

1. Heat oven to 350°F. Spray 8- or 9-inch round pan with cooking spray. Place granola in resealable food-storage plastic bag or between sheets of waxed paper; slightly crush with rolling pin. Set aside.

2. In large bowl, stir buttermilk, brown sugar, oil, vanilla and egg until smooth. Stir in flour, baking soda, cinnamon and salt just until moistened. Gently fold in half of the berries. Spoon into pan. Sprinkle with remaining berries and the granola.

3. Bake 28 to 33 minutes or until golden brown and top springs back when touched in center. Cool in pan on cooling rack 10 minutes. Serve warm.

1 Serving: Calories 160 (Calories from Fat 45); Total Fat 5g (Saturated Fat 1g; Trans Fat 0g); Cholesterol 25mg; Sodium 150mg; Total Carbohydrate 26g (Dietary Fiber 2g); Protein 3g **% Daily Value:** Vitamin A 0%; Vitamin C 2%; Calcium 4%; Iron 4% **Exchanges:** 1 Starch, ½ Other Carbohydrate, 1 Fat **Carbohydrate Choices:** 2

a little bit more

Spread 1 tablespoon orange marmalade on each serving of coffee cake for only 50 additional calories.

cranberry-sweet potato bread

Prep Time: 20 Minutes **Start to Finish:** 2 Hours 45 Minutes **Makes:** 2 loaves (12 slices each)

240 Calories

2⅓ cups sugar
⅔ cup water
⅔ cup canola oil
1 teaspoon vanilla
2 cups mashed cooked dark-orange sweet potatoes (about 1¼ lb)
4 eggs
3⅓ cups all-purpose flour

2 teaspoons baking soda
1½ teaspoons salt
1 teaspoon ground cinnamon
½ teaspoon ground nutmeg
½ teaspoon baking powder
1 cup sweetened dried cranberries
1 cup chopped pecans, if desired

1. Heat oven to 350°F. Grease 2 (8×4- or 9×5-inch) loaf pans and lightly flour. In large bowl, mix sugar, water, oil, vanilla, sweet potatoes and eggs until well blended.

2. In medium bowl, mix flour, baking soda, salt, cinnamon, nutmeg and baking powder. Add dry ingredients to sweet potato mixture, stirring just until moistened. Stir in cranberries and pecans. Spoon into pans.

3. Bake 60 to 70 minutes or until toothpick inserted in center comes out clean. Cool 15 minutes; transfer from pans to cooling rack. Cool completely, about 1 hour. Store tightly wrapped in refrigerator.

1 Slice: Calories 240 (Calories from Fat 60); Total Fat 7g (Saturated Fat 1g; Trans Fat 0g); Cholesterol 30mg; Sodium 290mg; Total Carbohydrate 42g (Dietary Fiber 1g); Protein 3g **% Daily Value:** Vitamin A 60%; Vitamin C 0%; Calcium 2%; Iron 6% **Exchanges:** ½ Starch, 2½ Other Carbohydrate, 1½ Fat **Carbohydrate Choices:** 3

a little bit less

Cut the loaves just a bit thinner to make 18 slices per loaf to save on calories. A ½-inch-thick slice will be 160 calories.

blueberry-almond brown bread

Prep Time: 15 Minutes   **Start to Finish:** 3 Hours 10 Minutes   **Makes:** 1 loaf (16 slices)

180 Calories

2½ cups white whole wheat flour
½ cup old-fashioned oats
⅓ cup ground flaxseed or flaxseed meal
½ cup packed dark brown sugar
¼ cup chopped blanched slivered almonds

1 teaspoon baking soda
1 teaspoon salt
½ cup dried blueberries or currants
1⅔ cups buttermilk
2 teaspoons vanilla
1 tablespoon old-fashioned oats

1. Heat oven to 375°F. Spray 9×5-inch loaf pan with cooking spray.

2. In large bowl, stir flour, ½ cup oats, flaxseed, brown sugar, almonds, baking soda and salt. Add blueberries; stir to coat in flour mixture. Stir in buttermilk and vanilla just until mixed. Spread in pan; sprinkle with 1 tablespoon oats.

3. Bake 45 to 50 minutes or until toothpick inserted in center comes out clean and top is golden brown. Cool 5 minutes. Loosen sides of loaf from pan; remove from pan to cooling rack. Cool completely, about 2 hours.

1 Slice: Calories 180 (Calories from Fat 30); Total Fat 3g (Saturated Fat 0.5g; Trans Fat 0g); Cholesterol 0mg; Sodium 250mg; Total Carbohydrate 33g (Dietary Fiber 4g); Protein 5g **% Daily Value:** Vitamin A 0%; Vitamin C 0%; Calcium 6%; Iron 4% **Exchanges:** 1½ Starch, ½ Other Carbohydrate, ½ Fat **Carbohydrate Choices:** 2

a little bit more

Serve a slice of this hearty bread with a tablespoon of cherry preserves for a pop of color and flavor and only 50 extra calories.

chunky gingered applesauce

Prep Time: 30 Minutes   **Start to Finish:** 30 Minutes   **Makes:** 7 servings (½ cup each)

80 Calories

4 medium tart cooking apples (such as Granny Smith, Greening or Rome), coarsely chopped (4 cups)	¼ cup finely chopped crystallized ginger
½ cup water	1 tablespoon packed brown sugar
	¼ teaspoon ground cinnamon

1. In 3-quart saucepan, mix apples, water, ginger and brown sugar. Heat to boiling; reduce heat. Cover; simmer 10 to 15 minutes, stirring occasionally, until apples are tender. Drain off excess liquid.

2. Stir cinnamon into applesauce. Serve warm or chilled.

1 Serving: Calories 80 (Calories from Fat 0); Total Fat 0g (Saturated Fat 0g; Trans Fat 0g); Cholesterol 0mg; Sodium 0mg; Total Carbohydrate 19g (Dietary Fiber 2g); Protein 0g **% Daily Value:** Vitamin A 0%; Vitamin C 2%; Calcium 0%; Iron 0% **Exchanges:** ½ Fruit, 1 Other Carbohydrate **Carbohydrate Choices:** 1

a little bit more

Applesauce and cottage cheese are a terrific combination! Serve ½ cup 2% reduced-fat cottage cheese under or alongside the applesauce for a healthy breakfast or snack. The cottage cheese adds protein and 100 calories per serving.

oatmeal-peanut butter breakfast cookies

Prep Time: 35 Minutes   **Start to Finish:** 50 Minutes   **Makes:** 1 dozen cookies

210 Calories

½ cup mashed banana (about 1 large)
½ cup chunky natural peanut butter (unsalted and unsweetened)
½ cup honey
1 teaspoon vanilla

1 cup old-fashioned oats
½ cup whole wheat flour
¼ cup instant nonfat dry milk
2 teaspoons ground cinnamon
¼ teaspoon baking soda
1 cup dried cranberries or raisins

1. Heat oven to 350°F. Lightly spray 2 cookie sheets with cooking spray. In large bowl, stir banana, peanut butter, honey and vanilla. In small bowl, mix oats, flour, dry milk, cinnamon and baking soda. Stir oat mixture into banana mixture until combined. Stir in cranberries.

2. Onto cookie sheets, drop ¼ cupfuls of dough 3 inches apart. With small spatula dipped in water, flatten and spread each mound of dough to 2¾-inch round, about ½ inch thick.

3. Bake 14 to 16 minutes or until browned. Transfer from cookie sheets to cooling racks.

4. Store cooled cookies in tightly covered container or resealable plastic food-storage bag up to 3 days or freeze up to 2 months.

1 Cookie: Calories 210 (Calories from Fat 60); Total Fat 6g (Saturated Fat 1g; Trans Fat 0g); Cholesterol 0mg; Sodium 30mg; Total Carbohydrate 33g (Dietary Fiber 3g); Protein 4g **% Daily Value:** Vitamin A 0%; Vitamin C 0%; Calcium 2%; Iron 4% **Exchanges:** 1½ Starch, ½ Other Carbohydrate, 1 Fat **Carbohydrate Choices:** 2

a little bit more
Dip these breakfast treats into an 8-oz glass of light vanilla soymilk for added calcium and an extra 80 calories per serving.

tropical fruit 'n ginger oatmeal

Prep Time: 15 Minutes   **Start to Finish:** 45 Minutes   **Makes:** 4 servings

220 Calories

2¼	cups water	
¾	cup steel-cut oats	
2	teaspoons finely chopped gingerroot	
⅛	teaspoon salt	
½	medium banana, mashed	
1	container (6 oz) vanilla thick and creamy low-fat yogurt	

1	medium mango, seed removed, peeled and chopped (1 cup)
½	cup sliced fresh strawberries
2	tablespoons shredded coconut, toasted*
2	tablespoons chopped walnuts

1. In 1½-quart saucepan, heat water to boiling. Stir in oats, gingerroot and salt. Reduce heat; simmer gently uncovered 25 to 30 minutes, without stirring, until oats are tender yet slightly chewy.

2. Stir banana into oatmeal. Divide among 4 bowls. Top each serving with yogurt, mango, strawberries, coconut and walnuts. Serve immediately.

   *To toast coconut, sprinkle in an ungreased skillet and cook over medium-low heat 6 to 14 minutes, stirring frequently until browning begins, then stirring constantly until golden brown.

1 Serving: Calories 220 (Calories from Fat 50); Total Fat 6g (Saturated Fat 2g; Trans Fat 0g); Cholesterol 0mg; Sodium 105mg; Total Carbohydrate 38g (Dietary Fiber 4g); Protein 5g **% Daily Value:** Vitamin A 20%; Vitamin C 35%; Calcium 10%; Iron 6% **Exchanges:** 1½ Starch, 1 Fruit, 1 Fat **Carbohydrate Choices:** 2½

a little bit less

Trim the calories for this breakfast meal by skipping the banana, using fat-free yogurt and omitting the coconut for a savings of 50 calories per serving.

caribbean steel-cut oats with fruit and yogurt

Prep Time: 40 Minutes   **Start to Finish:** 40 Minutes   **Makes:** 4 servings

330 Calories

1¾ cups water
1 can (14 oz) reduced-fat (lite) coconut milk
¾ teaspoon ground cinnamon
⅛ teaspoon salt, if desired
1 cup steel-cut oats (from 24-oz container)

1 tablespoon honey
1 container (6 oz) French vanilla fat-free yogurt
1 large mango, seed removed, peeled and chopped (about 1½ cups)
1 cup fresh raspberries

1. In 2-quart saucepan, mix water, coconut milk, ½ teaspoon of the cinnamon and the salt. Heat to boiling over medium-high heat. Stir in oats; reduce heat to low. Simmer uncovered 30 to 35 minutes, stirring occasionally, until oats are tender yet slightly chewy. Remove from heat. Stir in honey.

2. Divide oats among 4 bowls; top each with generous 2 tablespoons yogurt, about ⅓ cup mango and ¼ cup raspberries. Sprinkle evenly with remaining ¼ teaspoon cinnamon.

1 Serving: Calories 330 (Calories from Fat 80); Total Fat 8g (Saturated Fat 6g; Trans Fat 0g); Cholesterol 0mg; Sodium 230mg; Total Carbohydrate 57g (Dietary Fiber 7g); Protein 7g **% Daily Value:** Vitamin A 20%; Vitamin C 35%; Calcium 10%; Iron 10% **Exchanges:** 1 Starch, 1 Fruit, 1½ Other Carbohydrate, ½ Skim Milk, 1½ Fat **Carbohydrate Choices:** 4

a little bit less
Serve yourself a smaller portion by turning this recipe into 6 servings instead of 4; each smaller serving will provide 220 calories.

triple-berry oatmeal-flax muesli

Prep Time: 5 Minutes   **Start to Finish:** 40 Minutes   **Makes:** 6 servings

290 Calories

2¾ cups old-fashioned oats or rolled barley	1½ cups fat-free (skim) milk
½ cup sliced almonds	¼ cup ground flaxseed or flaxseed meal
2 containers (6 oz each) banana crème or French vanilla fat-free yogurt	½ cup fresh blueberries
	½ cup fresh raspberries
	½ cup sliced fresh strawberries

1. Heat oven to 350°F. On ungreased cookie sheet with sides, spread oats and almonds. Bake 18 to 20 minutes, stirring occasionally, until light golden brown. Cool 15 minutes.

2. In large bowl, mix yogurt and milk until well blended. Stir in flaxseed and toasted oats and almonds. Top each serving with berries.

1 Serving: Calories 290 (Calories from Fat 80); Total Fat 8g (Saturated Fat 1g; Trans Fat 0g); Cholesterol 0mg; Sodium 55mg; Total Carbohydrate 42g (Dietary Fiber 7g); Protein 11g **% Daily Value:** Vitamin A 8%; Vitamin C 10%; Calcium 20%; Iron 15% **Exchanges:** 2½ Starch, ½ Skim Milk, 1 Fat **Carbohydrate Choices:** 3

honey-lemon fruit parfaits

Prep Time: 15 Minutes   **Start to Finish:** 20 Minutes   **Makes:** 6 parfaits

120 Calories

¾ cup fat-free (skim) milk
Dash salt
⅓ cup uncooked whole wheat couscous
½ cup lemon cream pie fat-free yogurt (from 6-oz container)
½ cup fat-free sour cream
1 tablespoon honey

¼ teaspoon grated lemon peel
3 cups mixed fresh fruit (such as blueberries, raspberries and/or sliced strawberries, kiwifruit, nectarines or star fruit)
Chopped crystallized ginger, if desired
Fresh mint leaves or sprigs, if desired

1. In 2-quart saucepan, heat milk and salt to boiling; stir in couscous. Cover; simmer 1 minute. Remove from heat; let stand 5 minutes. Fluff with fork; cool.

2. In small bowl, mix yogurt, sour cream, honey and lemon peel. In medium bowl, toss with desired fruit.

3. To serve, divide half of the fruit mixture among 6 parfait glasses or dessert dishes. Spoon couscous and half of the yogurt mixture evenly over fruit. Top with remaining fruit mixture and yogurt mixture. Garnish with crystallized ginger and mint.

1 Parfait: Calories 120 (Calories from Fat 0); Total Fat 0g (Saturated Fat 0g; Trans Fat 0g); Cholesterol 0mg; Sodium 75mg; Total Carbohydrate 25g (Dietary Fiber 3g); Protein 4g **% Daily Value:** Vitamin A 4%; Vitamin C 20%; Calcium 10%; Iron 2% **Exchanges:** 1 Starch, ½ Fruit **Carbohydrate Choices:** 1½

a little bit more
Add ¼ cup low-fat granola over each yogurt layer (3 cups total for 6 servings) for extra crunch and 160 calories per serving.

pineapple-mango smoothies

Prep Time: 5 Minutes   **Start to Finish:** 5 Minutes   **Makes:** 2 servings (1 cup each)

180 Calories

1	container (6 oz) fat-free Greek plain yogurt	¼	cup mango syrup (from jar of sliced mango)
⅓	cup fresh or canned drained pineapple chunks	3	or 4 ice cubes
⅓	cup chopped refrigerated sliced mango (from 24-oz jar)		

In blender, place all ingredients. Cover; blend on high speed about 30 seconds or until smooth. Pour into 2 glasses. Serve immediately.

1 Serving: Calories 180 (Calories from Fat 0); Total Fat 0g (Saturated Fat 0g; Trans Fat 0g); Cholesterol 5mg; Sodium 50mg; Total Carbohydrate 38g (Dietary Fiber 0g); Protein 7g **% Daily Value:** Vitamin A 15%; Vitamin C 40%; Calcium 20%; Iron 0% **Exchanges:** ½ Starch, ½ Fruit, 1 Other Carbohydrate, ½ Skim Milk **Carbohydrate Choices:** 2½

a little bit more

Blend 2 tablespoons Fiber One cereal and 1 tablespoon flaxseed in blender before adding remaining ingredients for an added 3 grams of fiber and 35 calories per serving.

green goodness
smoothies

Prep Time: 5 Minutes   **Start to Finish:** 5 Minutes   **Makes:** 4 servings (1 cup each)

1	cup pear nectar
2	cups loosely packed chopped fresh spinach
½	cup chopped seeded peeled cucumber

½	cup plain fat-free yogurt
2	tablespoons honey
2	cups ice cubes

In blender, place all ingredients. Cover; blend on high speed about 1 minute or until smooth. Pour into 4 glasses. Serve immediately.

1 Serving: Calories 100 (Calories from Fat 5); Total Fat 0.5g (Saturated Fat 0g; Trans Fat 0g); Cholesterol 0mg; Sodium 40mg; Total Carbohydrate 22g (Dietary Fiber 1g); Protein 2g **% Daily Value:** Vitamin A 30%; Vitamin C 25%; Calcium 8%; Iron 4% **Exchanges:** ½ Starch, 1 Other Carbohydrate, ½ Vegetable **Carbohydrate Choices:** 1½

a little bit more

Get a nutritional boost of omega-3's and additional fiber by adding a tablespoon of flaxseed with the other ingredients. Be sure to blend long enough to grind up the flaxseed to reap the nutritional benefits of adding it.

tropical papaya smoothies

Prep Time: 10 Minutes   **Start to Finish:** 10 Minutes   **Makes:** 2 servings (1½ cups each)

150 Calories

½   medium papaya, peeled, seeded and chopped (¾ cup)
½   cup frozen unsweetened whole strawberries
½   cup fat-free (skim) milk
½   cup plain fat-free yogurt

1   tablespoon honey
3   large ice cubes
    Sliced papaya or sliced fresh strawberries, if desired
    Fresh mint leaves or sprigs, if desired

1. In blender, place chopped papaya, frozen strawberries, milk, yogurt and honey. Cover; blend on high speed until smooth. With blender running, add ice cubes, one at a time, blending until ice is crushed and mixture is smooth.

2. Pour into 2 tall glasses. Garnish with sliced papaya or fresh strawberries and mint. Serve immediately.

1 Serving: Calories 150 (Calories from Fat 0); Total Fat 0g (Saturated Fat 0g; Trans Fat 0g); Cholesterol 0mg; Sodium 80mg; Total Carbohydrate 30g (Dietary Fiber 2g); Protein 6g **% Daily Value:** Vitamin A 20%; Vitamin C 120%; Calcium 20%; Iron 4% **Exchanges:** ½ Starch, 1 Fruit, ½ Skim Milk **Carbohydrate Choices:** 2

Chapter 2
Lunch

caprese turkey salad with guacamole

Prep Time: 40 Minutes   **Start to Finish:** 40 Minutes   **Makes:** 4 servings

350 Calories

DRESSING
- ¼ cup balsamic vinegar
- ¼ cup water
- 2 tablespoons olive oil
- 2 tablespoons chopped fresh basil leaves
- ¼ teaspoon salt
- ½ teaspoon salt-free garlic-pepper blend

GUACAMOLE SAUCE
- ½ medium avocado
- 2 tablespoons fat-free (skim) milk
- 2 tablespoons fat-free sour cream

- 2 teaspoons fresh lemon juice
- ¼ teaspoon salt-free garlic-pepper blend

SALAD
- 1 package (20 oz) turkey breast tenderloins
- 6 cups mixed salad greens
- 1 pint grape tomatoes, cut in half (about 1½ cups)
- ¼ cup thinly sliced red onion
- ½ cup cherry-size fresh mozzarella cheese balls, cut in half

1. Spray grill rack with cooking spray. Heat gas or charcoal grill. In small bowl, mix all dressing ingredients with whisk until well blended. Reserve ¼ cup for brushing turkey. Set remaining dressing aside until serving time.

2. In blender, place all sauce ingredients. Cover; blend on medium speed until smooth. Transfer to small bowl; refrigerate until serving time.

3. Brush turkey with reserved ¼ cup dressing. Place turkey on grill over medium heat. Cover grill; cook 8 to 10 minutes, turning once, until juice of turkey is clear when center of thickest part is cut (at least 165°F). Transfer tenderloins from grill to cutting board; cut crosswise into ½-inch strips.

4. In medium bowl, toss salad greens with 1 cup of the tomatoes, the onion and remaining dressing. Divide among 4 plates. Arrange turkey strips over salads. Top evenly with guacamole sauce, cheese and remaining ½ cup tomatoes. Serve guacamole with salad.

1 Serving: Calories 350 (Calories from Fat 140); Total Fat 15g (Saturated Fat 4.5g; Trans Fat 0g); Cholesterol 110mg; Sodium 330mg; Total Carbohydrate 12g (Dietary Fiber 4g); Protein 40g **% Daily Value:** Vitamin A 110%; Vitamin C 15%; Calcium 20%; Iron 20% **Exchanges:** 2 Vegetable, 5 Very Lean Meat, 2½ Fat **Carbohydrate Choices:** 1

a little bit less
Omit the guacamole to save 40 calories per serving.

curried chicken salad with jicama

Prep Time: 30 Minutes **Start to Finish:** 1 Hour 30 Minutes **Makes:** 6 servings

210 Calories

1 orange, peeled, sectioned	2 teaspoons reduced-sodium soy sauce
3 cups cubed cooked chicken breast	1 teaspoon curry powder
1½ cups seedless red grapes, halved	3 small papayas, peeled, halved lengthwise and seeded
½ cup chopped peeled jicama	Fresh chives, if desired
1 cup thinly sliced celery	
¼ cup fat-free mayonnaise or salad dressing	
¼ cup lemon cream pie or lemon burst fat-free yogurt (from 6-oz container)	

1. Cut orange sections into halves or quarters; place in large bowl. Add chicken, grapes, jicama and celery.

2. In small bowl, stir mayonnaise, yogurt, soy sauce and curry powder until well blended. Pour over chicken mixture; toss gently to coat. Cover; refrigerate at least 1 hour or up to 24 hours.

3. To serve, spoon 1 cup salad into each papaya half. Garnish with chives.

1 Serving: Calories 210 (Calories from Fat 35); Total Fat 3.5g (Saturated Fat 1g; Trans Fat 0g); Cholesterol 60mg; Sodium 210mg; Total Carbohydrate 21g (Dietary Fiber 3g); Protein 22g **% Daily Value:** Vitamin A 20%; Vitamin C 110%; Calcium 6%; Iron 6% **Exchanges:** ½ Starch, 1 Fruit, 3 Very Lean Meat, ½ Fat **Carbohydrate Choices:** 1½

a little bit less

Reduce the chicken in this recipe to 2 cups for a savings of 40 calories per serving.

nut and berry salad toss

Prep Time: 25 Minutes **Start to Finish:** 25 Minutes **Makes:** 4 servings (2 cups each)

290 Calories

VINAIGRETTE
- ⅓ cup raspberry vinegar
- 2 tablespoons finely chopped fresh mint
- 2 tablespoons honey
- 1 tablespoon canola oil
- ¼ teaspoon salt

SALAD
- 4 cups fresh baby spinach leaves
- 2 cups chopped cooked chicken breast
- 2 cups sliced fresh strawberries
- ½ cup fresh or frozen (thawed) blueberries
- 2 tablespoons coarsely chopped walnuts, toasted*
- ¼ cup crumbled chèvre (goat) cheese (1 oz)
- ½ teaspoon freshly ground pepper

1. In jar with tight-fitting lid, place vinegar, mint, honey, oil and salt; shake well.

2. In large bowl, toss spinach, chicken, strawberries, blueberries, walnuts and cheese. Divide among salad plates. Drizzle with vinaigrette and sprinkle with pepper.

*To toast nuts, cook in an ungreased skillet over medium heat for 5 to 7 minutes, stirring frequently, until nuts begin to brown, then stirring constantly until nuts are light brown.

1 Serving: Calories 290 (Calories from Fat 100); Total Fat 11g (Saturated Fat 3g; Trans Fat 0g); Cholesterol 65mg; Sodium 500mg; Total Carbohydrate 22g (Dietary Fiber 3g); Protein 24g **% Daily Value:** Vitamin A 60%; Vitamin C 100%; Calcium 8%; Iron 15% **Exchanges:** ½ Starch, ½ Fruit, ½ Other Carbohydrate, ½ Vegetable, 3 Very Lean Meat, 2 Fat **Carbohydrate Choices:** 1½

a little bit less

Saving up calories so you can have a snack later? Skip the walnuts and cheese for a savings of 50 calories per serving. With all the flavorful ingredients in this salad, you won't even miss them.

tangy spinach and apple salad

Prep Time: 15 Minutes   **Start to Finish:** 15 Minutes   **Makes:** 4 servings

160 Calories

VINAIGRETTE

- ¼ cup white balsamic or regular balsamic vinegar
- 2 tablespoons olive oil
- 2 teaspoons chopped fresh thyme leaves or ½ teaspoon dried thyme, crushed
- 1 teaspoon Dijon mustard
- ¼ teaspoon salt

SALAD

- 6 cups fresh baby spinach leaves
- 1 medium Granny Smith apple, sliced
- ¼ cup thin wedges red onion
- 2 tablespoons chopped dried tart red cherries
- ⅓ cup crumbled reduced-fat feta cheese

1. In jar with tight-fitting lid, place all vinaigrette ingredients; shake well.

2. In large bowl, toss spinach, apple, onion and cherries. Drizzle with vinaigrette; toss gently to coat. Top with cheese.

1 Serving: Calories 160 (Calories from Fat 70); Total Fat 8g (Saturated Fat 1.5g; Trans Fat 0g); Cholesterol 0mg; Sodium 360mg; Total Carbohydrate 17g (Dietary Fiber 2g); Protein 3g **% Daily Value:** Vitamin A 90%; Vitamin C 25%; Calcium 10%; Iron 10% **Exchanges:** ½ Starch, ½ Other Carbohydrate, 1 Vegetable, 1½ Fat **Carbohydrate Choices:** 1

a little bit more

Want to feel full longer? Add 2 cups cut-up cooked chicken breast to this salad to give it staying power. It will add 120 calories per serving.

chipotle shrimp ceviche salad

Prep Time: 20 Minutes   **Start to Finish:** 20 Minutes   **Makes:** 4 servings

220 Calories

DRESSING

- ¾ cup low-sodium vegetable juice
- 2 tablespoons fresh lime juice
- 1 chipotle chile in adobo sauce (from 7-oz can), chopped
- ½ teaspoon salt
- ¼ teaspoon coarsely ground black pepper

SALAD

- 1 cup cherry tomatoes, cut in half
- 1 cup coarsely chopped English (seedless) cucumber
- ¼ cup finely chopped red onion
- 2 tablespoons chopped fresh cilantro
- 4 cups torn romaine lettuce
- 1 package (12 oz) frozen cooked deveined peeled small shrimp, thawed
- ½ large avocado, thinly sliced
- 16 baked tortilla chips

1. In medium bowl, mix all dressing ingredients until well blended. Stir in tomatoes, cucumber, onion and cilantro.

2. On each of 4 salad plates, place 1 cup lettuce and about 1 cup vegetable mixture. Arrange shrimp, avocado and tortilla chips on top. Serve immediately.

1 Serving: Calories 220 (Calories from Fat 50); Total Fat 6g (Saturated Fat 0.5g; Trans Fat 0g); Cholesterol 180mg; Sodium 1230mg; Total Carbohydrate 19g (Dietary Fiber 4g); Protein 22g **% Daily Value:** Vitamin A 110%; Vitamin C 20%; Calcium 10%; Iron 10% **Exchanges:** 1 Starch, 1 Vegetable, 2½ Very Lean Meat, 1 Fat **Carbohydrate Choices:** 1

a little bit less

Save 30 calories from this recipe to use later in the day by omitting the avocado.

italian wheat berry salad

Prep Time: 20 Minutes   **Start to Finish:** 2 Hours 30 Minutes   **Makes:** 4 servings

240 Calories

SALAD

- 3½ cups water
- 1 cup uncooked wheat berries
- 2 large tomatoes, chopped (2 cups)
- ¼ cup chopped dry-pack sun-dried tomatoes
- 2 tablespoons coarsely chopped fresh basil leaves
- ¼ cup crumbled reduced-fat feta cheese (1 oz)
  Fresh basil sprigs, if desired

DRESSING

- 2 tablespoons low-sodium vegetable juice
- 2 tablespoons red wine vinegar
- 1 tablespoon olive oil
- 1 clove garlic, finely chopped
- 1 teaspoon finely chopped shallot
- ¼ teaspoon Italian seasoning
- ¼ teaspoon salt
- ¼ teaspoon pepper

1. In 2-quart saucepan, heat water and wheat berries to boiling; reduce heat to low. Cover; simmer 60 to 70 minutes or until wheat berries are tender but still chewy. Drain.

2. In small bowl, stir all dressing ingredients with whisk until blended. In medium bowl, toss wheat berries, tomatoes, sun-dried tomatoes and chopped basil. Pour dressing over mixture and mix well. Cover; refrigerate 1 to 3 hours to blend flavors.

3. Divide salad evenly among 4 plates or bowls. Top each serving with 1 tablespoon cheese. Garnish with basil sprigs.

1 Serving: Calories 240 (Calories from Fat 45); Total Fat 5g (Saturated Fat 1g; Trans Fat 0g); Cholesterol 0mg; Sodium 320mg; Total Carbohydrate 39g (Dietary Fiber 7g); Protein 9g **% Daily Value:** Vitamin A 20%; Vitamin C 15%; Calcium 6%; Iron 10% **Exchanges:** 2½ Starch, ½ Vegetable, 1 Fat **Carbohydrate Choices:** 2½

a little bit more

Like a little meat in your salad? Add 1 cup chopped cooked chicken breast to the recipe for 60 additional calories per serving.

hearty grain and veggie salad

Prep Time: 20 Minutes   **Start to Finish:** 40 Minutes   **Makes:** 6 servings

200 Calories

1¼ cups water	¼ teaspoon pepper
½ cup uncooked quinoa, rinsed, well drained	1 can (15 oz) red kidney beans, drained, rinsed
½ teaspoon salt	1 cup chopped yellow bell pepper
1 cup fresh basil leaves	½ cup chopped seeded tomato (1 small)
2 tablespoons grated Parmesan cheese	½ cup sliced green onions (8 medium)
2 tablespoons fresh lemon juice	4 cups torn Bibb lettuce
2 tablespoons olive oil	
4 cloves garlic, finely chopped	

1. In 1-quart saucepan, heat water, quinoa and ¼ teaspoon of the salt to boiling; reduce heat. Cover; simmer 15 minutes. Remove from heat; let stand to cool slightly.

2. Meanwhile, in food processor, place basil, cheese, lemon juice, oil, garlic, pepper and remaining ¼ teaspoon salt. Cover; process until nearly smooth, stopping to scrape down side as needed.

3. Drain any remaining liquid from quinoa. In medium bowl, toss quinoa, beans, bell pepper, tomato and onions. Add basil mixture; stir to coat.

4. To serve, place ⅔ cup lettuce on each of 6 plates; top with ¾ cup quinoa mixture.

1 Serving: Calories 200 (Calories from Fat 60); Total Fat 6g (Saturated Fat 1g; Trans Fat 0g); Cholesterol 0mg; Sodium 370mg; Total Carbohydrate 26g (Dietary Fiber 5g); Protein 8g **% Daily Value:** Vitamin A 35%; Vitamin C 90%; Calcium 10%; Iron 15% **Exchanges:** 1 Starch, ½ Other Carbohydrate, 1 Vegetable, ½ Very Lean Meat, 1 Fat **Carbohydrate Choices:** 2

a little bit more

Round out your meal with cubed cantaloupe. A 1¼ cup serving adds only 100 calories and is an excellent source of vitamins A and C.

fruited tabbouleh with walnuts and feta

Prep Time: 20 Minutes   **Start to Finish:** 3 Hours 20 Minutes   **Makes:** 10 servings (½ cup each)

160 Calories

1 cup uncooked bulgur	⅓ cup loosely packed fresh mint leaves, chopped
1 cup boiling water	
¼ cup fresh orange juice	1 tablespoon grated orange peel
2 tablespoons olive oil	½ teaspoon salt
½ medium unpeeled cucumber, seeded, chopped (about 1 cup)	1 orange, peeled, sectioned and chopped
½ cup chopped red onion	⅓ cup chopped walnuts, toasted
½ cup sweetened dried cranberries	½ cup crumbled feta cheese (2 oz)
⅓ cup loosely packed fresh Italian (flat-leaf) parsley, chopped	

1. Place bulgur in large heatproof bowl. Pour boiling water over bulgur; stir. Let stand about 1 hour or until water is absorbed.

2. Stir in orange juice, oil, cucumber, onion, cranberries, parsley, mint, orange peel and salt; toss well. Cover; refrigerate 2 to 3 hours or until well chilled.

3. Just before serving, stir in chopped orange. Sprinkle with walnuts and cheese.

   *To toast them, sprinkle nuts in ungreased heavy skillet. Cook over medium heat 5 to 7 minutes, stirring occasionally until nuts begin to brown, then stirring constantly until golden brown.

1 Serving: Calories 160 (Calories from Fat 60); Total Fat 7g (Saturated Fat 1.5g; Trans Fat 0g); Cholesterol 5mg; Sodium 190mg; Total Carbohydrate 20g (Dietary Fiber 4g); Protein 3g **% Daily Value:** Vitamin A 6%; Vitamin C 25%; Calcium 6%; Iron 4% **Exchanges:** 1 Starch, ½ Other Carbohydrate, 1½ Fat **Carbohydrate Choices:** 1

southwestern quinoa salad

Prep Time: 15 Minutes   **Start to Finish:** 1 Hour   **Makes:** 6 servings

320 Calories

SALAD

- 1 large onion, chopped (1 cup)
- 1 cup uncooked quinoa, rinsed, well drained
- 1½ cups reduced-sodium chicken broth
- 1 cup packed fresh cilantro leaves
- ¼ cup raw unsalted hulled pumpkin seeds (pepitas)
- 2 cloves garlic, sliced
- ⅛ teaspoon ground cumin
- 2 tablespoons chopped green chiles (from 4.5-oz can)
- 1 tablespoon olive oil
- 1 can (15 oz) no-salt-added black beans, drained, rinsed
- 6 medium plum (Roma) tomatoes, chopped (2 cups)
- 2 tablespoons fresh lime juice

GARNISH

- 1 avocado, pitted, peeled and thinly sliced
- 6 small sprigs fresh cilantro, leaves torn

1. Spray 3-quart saucepan with cooking spray; heat over medium heat. Add onion; cook 6 to 8 minutes, stirring occasionally, until golden brown. Stir in quinoa and broth. Heat to boiling; reduce heat. Cover; simmer 10 to 15 minutes or until all liquid is absorbed. Remove from heat.

2. Meanwhile, in small food processor, place cilantro, pumpkin seeds, garlic and cumin. Cover; process, using quick on-and-off motions, 5 to 10 seconds. Scrape side. Add chiles and oil. Cover; process, using quick on-and-off motions, until paste forms.

3. Add cilantro mixture to cooked quinoa. Stir in beans, tomatoes and lime juice. Refrigerate at least 30 minutes to blend flavors.

4. To serve, divide salad evenly among 6 plates; top each serving with 2 to 3 slices avocado and 1 sprig cilantro.

1 Serving: Calories 320 (Calories from Fat 110); Total Fat 12g (Saturated Fat 2g; Trans Fat 0g); Cholesterol 0mg; Sodium 180mg; Total Carbohydrate 38g (Dietary Fiber 8g); Protein 13g **% Daily Value:** Vitamin A 15%; Vitamin C 15%; Calcium 8%; Iron 20% **Exchanges:** 2½ Starch, ½ Vegetable, ½ Very Lean Meat, 2 Fat **Carbohydrate Choices:** 2½

veggie thai noodle salad

Prep Time: 30 Minutes   **Start to Finish:** 30 Minutes   **Makes:** 8 servings (¾ cup each)

170 Calories

1 package (7 oz) vermicelli, broken in half
1 medium carrot, shredded
1 cup sliced quartered cucumber
1 cup coarsely chopped red bell pepper
⅓ cup sliced green onions (about 5 medium)
¼ cup chopped fresh cilantro
½ cup Thai peanut sauce

1. Cook and drain vermicelli as directed on package. Rinse with cold water to cool; drain well.

2. In large bowl, toss vermicelli and remaining ingredients until evenly coated with sauce.

1 Serving: Calories 170 (Calories from Fat 40); Total Fat 4.5g (Saturated Fat 1g; Trans Fat 0g); Cholesterol 0mg; Sodium 140mg; Total Carbohydrate 26g (Dietary Fiber 2g); Protein 6g **% Daily Value:** Vitamin A 40%; Vitamin C 20%; Calcium 0%; Iron 6% **Exchanges:** 1 Starch, ½ Other Carbohydrate, 1 Vegetable, 1 Fat **Carbohydrate Choices:** 2

a little bit more

You can easily make this salad more hearty by tossing in ½ pound frozen (thawed) cooked medium shrimp, peeled (tail shells removed) and deveined, and 1 medium mango, seed removed, peeled and cut into bite-size pieces, with the vermicelli for an additional 45 calories per serving.

tailgate pasta salad

Prep Time: 25 Minutes   **Start to Finish:** 2 Hours 25 Minutes   **Makes:** 6 servings (1⅓ cups each)

250 Calories

SALAD
4	cups uncooked gemelli pasta (8 oz)
1	medium zucchini, cut in half lengthwise, thinly sliced (2 cups)
1	can (14 oz) artichoke hearts, drained, chopped
1	cup cherry tomatoes, cut in half
4	oz fresh baby spinach leaves
½	cup chopped fresh basil leaves

DRESSING
2	tablespoons olive oil
3	tablespoons red wine vinegar
1	teaspoon coarse-grained mustard
½	teaspoon salt
½	teaspoon pepper
1	clove garlic, crushed

1. Cook and drain pasta as directed on package. Rinse with cold water to cool; drain well.

2. In large bowl, toss pasta, zucchini, artichoke hearts, tomatoes, spinach and ¼ cup of the basil. In small bowl, stir dressing ingredients with whisk until blended. Pour dressing over salad; toss to coat.

3. Cover; refrigerate 2 to 3 hours to blend flavors. Just before serving, sprinkle remaining ¼ cup basil over salad.

1 Serving: Calories 250 (Calories from Fat 50); Total Fat 6g (Saturated Fat 1g; Trans Fat 0g); Cholesterol 0mg; Sodium 360mg; Total Carbohydrate 41g (Dietary Fiber 7g); Protein 9g **% Daily Value:** Vitamin A 45%; Vitamin C 15%; Calcium 6%; Iron 15% **Exchanges:** 2 Starch, 1½ Vegetable, 1 Fat **Carbohydrate Choices:** 3

a little bit more
Toss 1 can (9 ounces) chunk light tuna in water, drained and flaked, with the other salad ingredients for an additional 50 calories per serving.

moroccan carrot salad

Prep Time: 15 Minutes   **Start to Finish:** 2 Hours 15 Minutes   **Makes:** 5 servings

250 Calories

DRESSING
¼	cup fresh orange juice
2	tablespoons olive oil
1	teaspoon grated orange peel
1	teaspoon ground cumin
1	teaspoon paprika
¼	teaspoon salt
⅛	to ¼ teaspoon ground red pepper (cayenne)
⅛	teaspoon ground cinnamon

SALAD
1	can (15 oz) chickpeas (garbanzo beans), drained, rinsed
1	bag (10 oz) julienne carrots
¼	cup golden raisins
3	tablespoons salted roasted whole almonds, coarsely chopped
¼	cup coarsely chopped fresh cilantro or Italian (flat-leaf) parsley

1. In small bowl, stir all dressing ingredients with whisk until blended.

2. In large bowl, toss beans, carrots and raisins. Add dressing; toss until well coated. Cover; refrigerate at least 2 hours or overnight, stirring occasionally. Just before serving, sprinkle with almonds and cilantro.

1 Serving: Calories 250 (Calories from Fat 90); Total Fat 10g (Saturated Fat 1g; Trans Fat 0g); Cholesterol 0mg; Sodium 270mg; Total Carbohydrate 32g (Dietary Fiber 6g); Protein 7g **% Daily Value:** Vitamin A 200%; Vitamin C 20%; Calcium 8%; Iron 15% **Exchanges:** 1½ Starch, ½ Other Carbohydrate, 1 Vegetable, 2 Fat **Carbohydrate Choices:** 2

chicken jalapeño panini

Prep Time: 25 Minutes   **Start to Finish:** 25 Minutes   **Makes:** 4 panini

390 Calories

4   wedges light spreadable Swiss cheese, unwrapped

3   tablespoons reduced-fat cream cheese (from 8-oz container)

1½ teaspoons chili powder

2   teaspoons salt-free garlic-pepper blend

1   teaspoon ground cumin

4   boneless skinless chicken breasts (1¼ lb), trimmed of any visible fat

4   seven-grain thin sandwich rounds, toasted

20 pickled jalapeño slices (from 12-oz jar), drained

4   large slices tomato

1. Heat contact grill or panini maker for 5 minutes. In small bowl, mix Swiss cheese, cream cheese and chili powder until smooth; set aside. In another small bowl, mix garlic-pepper blend and cumin; set aside.

2. Between pieces of plastic wrap or waxed paper, place each chicken breast smooth side down; gently pound with flat side of meat mallet or rolling pin until about 4½ inches across. Sprinkle about 1½ teaspoons of the cumin mixture over chicken; rub into chicken. Place chicken, seasoning side down, on grill. Sprinkle remaining cumin mixture evenly over chicken. Close grill; cook 3 to 4 minutes or until chicken is no longer pink in center. Transfer to plate; cover to keep warm. Wipe grill with damp paper towel if necessary.

3. For each panini, spread 1 tablespoon cheese mixture on cut sides of each sandwich round. Place 5 jalapeño slices on bottom round; top with grilled chicken and 1 slice tomato. Cover with top round. Place panini on grill (in batches if necessary). Close grill, pressing down lightly; cook until bread is toasted and panini are hot.

1 Panini: Calories 390 (Calories from Fat 140); Total Fat 16g (Saturated Fat 8g; Trans Fat 0.5g); Cholesterol 125mg; Sodium 880mg; Total Carbohydrate 19g (Dietary Fiber 2g); Protein 43g **% Daily Value:** Vitamin A 25%; Vitamin C 4%; Calcium 20%; Iron 15% **Exchanges:** 1½ Other Carbohydrate, 1 Very Lean Meat, 5 Lean Meat **Carbohydrate Choices:** 1

a little bit more

Add a slice of crisply cooked turkey bacon, cut in half, to each sandwich (on top of the cooked chicken) for an additional 35 calories.

greek chicken burgers with tzatziki sauce

Prep Time: 30 Minutes   **Start to Finish:** 30 Minutes   **Makes:** 4 burgers

270 Calories

SAUCE

1	medium cucumber
½	cup fat-free Greek plain yogurt (from 6-oz container)
2	tablespoons chopped onion
2	teaspoons chopped fresh mint

BURGERS

1	lb ground chicken breast
1	cup chopped fresh spinach
¼	cup chopped pitted kalamata olives
1	tablespoon cornstarch
1	tablespoon chopped fresh oregano leaves
2	cloves garlic, chopped
¼	teaspoon salt
¼	teaspoon pepper
2	whole wheat pita (pocket) breads (6 inch), cut in half to form pockets
½	cup chopped tomato (1 small)

1. Set oven control to broil. Cut 8 slices from cucumber; set aside. Chop enough remaining cucumber to equal ½ cup; place in small bowl. Stir in yogurt, onion and mint. Refrigerate until serving time.

2. In large bowl, mix chicken, spinach, olives, cornstarch, oregano, garlic, salt and pepper. Shape into 4 oval patties, ½ inch thick. Place on broiler pan. Broil with tops about 5 inches from heat 10 to 12 minutes, turning once, until thermometer inserted in center of patties reads at least 165°F.

3. Place 1 burger in each pita half. Add tomato, reserved cucumber slices and about 3 tablespoons sauce.

1 Burger: Calories 270 (Calories from Fat 50); Total Fat 6g (Saturated Fat 1.5g; Trans Fat 0g); Cholesterol 70mg; Sodium 460mg; Total Carbohydrate 24g (Dietary Fiber 3g); Protein 32g **% Daily Value:** Vitamin A 25%; Vitamin C 6%; Calcium 10%; Iron 15% **Exchanges:** 1½ Starch, 1 Vegetable, 2½ Very Lean Meat, 1 Lean Meat **Carbohydrate Choices:** 1½

a little bit more

Sprinkle 1 tablespoon crumbled feta cheese in each pita half for an additional 75 calories per serving.

cheese-stuffed turkey sliders

Prep Time: 35 Minutes **Start to Finish:** 35 Minutes **Makes:** 5 servings (2 sliders each)

380 Calories

1 medium yellow onion, cut into ¼-inch slices (about 1¼ cups)	¼ teaspoon coarse ground black pepper
1 package (20 oz) lean (at least 93%) ground turkey	5 slices (1½ oz each) reduced-fat sharp Cheddar cheese
3 tablespoons dry whole wheat bread crumbs	10 mini sandwich buns
3 tablespoons fat-free (skim) milk	2 medium plum (Roma) tomatoes, each cut into 5 slices
2 teaspoons Worcestershire sauce	10 dill pickle chips (from 16-oz jar)
1 teaspoon Dijon mustard	

1. Spray 12-inch skillet with cooking spray; heat over medium-high heat. Add onion; cook 6 to 8 minutes, stirring occasionally, until softened and lightly browned. Transfer from skillet to bowl; cover to keep warm.

2. In large bowl, gently mix turkey, bread crumbs, milk, Worcestershire sauce, mustard and pepper with fork until well combined. Shape mixture by heaping tablespoonfuls into 20 balls. Flatten each ball into 3-inch patty. Cut each cheese slice in half crosswise; place 1 piece of cheese in the center of each of 10 patties. Top each with another patty; press edges together to seal.

3. Heat same skillet over medium-high heat. Add patties. Cover; cook 4 to 6 minutes, turning once, until turkey is no longer pink. Let stand 2 minutes.

4. On each bun bottom, place about 1 tablespoon onion, 1 burger, 1 tomato slice and 1 pickle chip. Cover with bun tops.

1 Serving: Calories 380 (Calories from Fat 130); Total Fat 14g (Saturated Fat 4.5g; Trans Fat 0.5g); Cholesterol 70mg; Sodium 700mg; Total Carbohydrate 32g (Dietary Fiber 2g); Protein 30g **% Daily Value:** Vitamin A 8%; Vitamin C 4%; Calcium 20%; Iron 20% **Exchanges:** 2 Starch, 3½ Lean Meat, ½ Fat **Carbohydrate Choices:** 2

a little bit more

For about 15 extra calories per serving, add 1 tablespoon ketchup.

cheesy pizza burgers

Prep Time: 40 Minutes   **Start to Finish:** 40 Minutes   **Makes:** 4 burgers

310 Calories

¼ cup fat-free egg product
¼ cup quick-cooking oats
4 teaspoons chopped fresh oregano
⅛ teaspoon salt
⅛ teaspoon pepper
1 lb ground turkey breast

4 whole wheat burger buns, split
4 thin slices (½ oz each) provolone cheese
½ cup tomato pasta sauce (any variety), heated

1. Heat gas or charcoal grill. In medium bowl, mix egg product, oats, 2 teaspoons of the oregano, the salt and pepper. Add turkey; mix well. Shape mixture into 4 patties, ¾ inch thick.

2. Place patties on grill over medium heat. Cover grill; cook 14 to 18 minutes, turning once, until meat thermometer inserted in center of patties reads at least 165°F. Place buns, cut sides down, on grill and place 1 cheese slice on each burger for last 2 minutes of cooking time; cook until buns are toasted and cheese is melted.

3. On each bun bottom, place 1 burger, 2 tablespoons warmed pasta sauce and ½ teaspoon oregano. Cover with bun tops.

1 Burger: Calories 310 (Calories from Fat 60); Total Fat 7g (Saturated Fat 3g; Trans Fat 0g); Cholesterol 85mg; Sodium 590mg; Total Carbohydrate 25g (Dietary Fiber 4g); Protein 38g **% Daily Value:** Vitamin A 10%; Vitamin C 0%; Calcium 20%; Iron 20% **Exchanges:** 1 Starch, ½ Other Carbohydrate, 4½ Very Lean Meat, ½ High-Fat Meat **Carbohydrate Choices:** 1½

a little bit less

Omit the cheese and save 50 calories per serving to enjoy later in the day!

rice and bean burgers

Prep Time: 30 Minutes   **Start to Finish:** 30 Minutes   **Makes:** 4 burgers

300 Calories

1   can (15 oz) red kidney beans, drained, rinsed
1   medium onion, finely chopped (½ cup)
¼   cup finely chopped celery
¼   cup soft whole wheat bread crumbs
2   tablespoons chopped fresh cilantro
1   clove garlic, finely chopped
½   teaspoon dried oregano leaves
½   teaspoon ground cumin
⅛   teaspoon salt
¼   teaspoon pepper
¾   cup cooked brown rice
4   whole wheat burger buns, split, toasted
2   tablespoons fat-free mayonnaise
    Fresh spinach leaves, sliced tomato and red onion, if desired

1. In medium bowl, coarsely mash beans with potato masher or fork. Stir in chopped onion, celery, bread crumbs, cilantro, garlic, oregano, cumin, salt and pepper. Stir in rice. Shape mixture into 4 patties, ½ inch thick.

2. Heat grill pan or large skillet over medium heat. Add patties; cook 10 to 12 minutes, turning once, until thoroughly heated.

3. Spread cut sides of bun bottoms with mayonnaise; top with burgers, tomato, spinach and red onion. Cover with bun tops.

1 Burger: Calories 300 (Calories from Fat 25); Total Fat 3g (Saturated Fat 0.5g; Trans Fat 0g); Cholesterol 0mg; Sodium 580mg; Total Carbohydrate 53g (Dietary Fiber 10g); Protein 14g **% Daily Value:** Vitamin A 0%; Vitamin C 4%; Calcium 10%; Iron 20% **Exchanges:** 3½ Starch, ½ Vegetable, ½ Very Lean Meat **Carbohydrate Choices:** 3½

burgers with dill sauce

Prep Time: 30 Minutes   **Start to Finish:** 30 Minutes   **Makes:** 4 burgers

200 Calories

1   small onion, finely chopped
    (¼ cup)
¼   cup chopped fresh Italian
    (flat-leaf) parsley
2   cloves garlic, finely chopped
¼   teaspoon salt
1   lb extra-lean (at least 90%)
    ground beef
⅓   cup plain fat-free yogurt
1   tablespoon stone-ground or
    Dijon mustard

1   tablespoon chopped fresh or
    1 teaspoon dried dill weed
1   teaspoon balsamic vinegar
¼   cup chopped seeded cucumber
    Sliced cucumber, tomato and red
    onion and/or fresh spinach leaves,
    if desired

1. Set oven control to broil. In large bowl, mix chopped onion, parsley, garlic and salt. Add beef; mix well. Shape mixture into 4 patties, ¾ inch thick.

2. Place patties on broiler pan. Broil with tops 3 to 4 inches from heat 12 to 14 minutes, turning once, until meat thermometer inserted in center of patties reads 160°F.

3. Meanwhile, in small bowl, stir yogurt, mustard, dill and vinegar. Stir in chopped cucumber.

4. Spoon 2 tablespoons sauce over each burger. Serve with sliced cucumber, tomato and red onion and/or spinach leaves.

1 Burger: Calories 200 (Calories from Fat 80); Total Fat 9g (Saturated Fat 3.5g; Trans Fat 0.5g);
Cholesterol 70mg; Sodium 310mg; Total Carbohydrate 5g (Dietary Fiber 0g); Protein 23g **% Daily Value:** Vitamin A 8%;
Vitamin C 6%; Calcium 6%; Iron 15% **Exchanges:** ½ Vegetable, 3 Very Lean Meat, 1½ Fat **Carbohydrate Choices:** ½

a little bit more

Dive into these burgers by serving them with the
dill sauce between 2 (½-inch) slices of baguette.
You'll add only 70 calories per burger.

grilled chicken sandwiches with lime dressing

Prep Time: 35 Minutes   **Start to Finish:** 35 Minutes   **Makes:** 4 sandwiches

290 Calories

¼ cup fat-free mayonnaise or salad dressing

½ teaspoon grated lime or lemon peel

⅛ teaspoon salt

1 medium zucchini or yellow summer squash, or ½ of each, cut lengthwise into ¼-inch-thick slices

3 tablespoons white Worcestershire sauce

1 teaspoon olive oil

4 boneless skinless chicken breasts (1 lb)

4 whole wheat burger buns, split

1 medium tomato, thinly sliced

1. Heat gas or charcoal grill. In small bowl, mix mayonnaise, lime peel and salt. Cover; refrigerate until serving time.

2. Brush zucchini slices with 1 tablespoon of the Worcestershire sauce and the oil; set aside. Brush both sides of chicken with remaining 2 tablespoons Worcestershire sauce.

3. Place chicken on grill over medium heat. Cook uncovered 12 to 15 minutes, turning once, until juice of chicken is clear when center of thickest part is cut (at least 165°F). Add zucchini slices to grill for last 6 minutes of cooking time, turning once, until softened and lightly browned. Place buns, cut side down, on grill 1 to 2 minutes until toasted.

4. Spread mayonnaise mixture on cut sides of buns. Cut zucchini slices crosswise in half, if desired. On bun bottoms, place chicken, tomato and zucchini; cover with bun tops.

1 Sandwich: Calories 290 (Calories from Fat 60); Total Fat 7g (Saturated Fat 2g; Trans Fat 0g); Cholesterol 70mg; Sodium 590mg; Total Carbohydrate 25g (Dietary Fiber 4g); Protein 32g **% Daily Value:** Vitamin A 8%; Vitamin C 10%; Calcium 8%; Iron 15% **Exchanges:** 1 Starch, ½ Other Carbohydrate, ½ Vegetable, 4 Very Lean Meat, 1 Fat **Carbohydrate Choices:** 1½

a little bit more

Top each chicken breast with a 1-ounce slice of reduced-fat Swiss cheese about 1 minute before removing the chicken from the grill for an added 50 calories per serving.

grilled caesar-flank steak sandwiches

Prep Time: 30 Minutes   **Start to Finish:** 30 Minutes   **Makes:** 4 sandwiches

410 Calories

DRESSING

- ½ cup Boursin light cheese with garlic and herbs (from 6.5-oz container)
- 1 tablespoon fresh lemon juice
- 1 teaspoon anchovy paste
- ¾ teaspoon Worcestershire sauce

SANDWICHES

- ¾ lb beef flank steak
- 1 teaspoon salt-free garlic-pepper blend
- 4 pieces (4 inch) French bread, cut in half lengthwise
  Olive oil cooking spray
- 1 heart romaine lettuce, cut in half lengthwise
- ¼ cup freshly shredded Parmesan cheese (1 oz)

1. Heat gas or charcoal grill. In small bowl, mix all dressing ingredients; set aside.

2. Sprinkle each side of steak with ½ teaspoon garlic-pepper blend. Place steak on grill over medium-high heat. Cover grill; cook about 12 minutes, turning once, for medium doneness. Place steak on cutting board; cover with foil. Reduce grill heat to medium.

3. Spray cut sides of bread with olive oil cooking spray. Place bread and lettuce, cut sides down, on grill. Cover grill; cook 1 to 2 minutes or until bread is toasted and grill marks appear on lettuce and it becomes slightly wilted. Cut lettuce crosswise into 1-inch strips; discard root end.

4. Cut steak across grain into thin slices. For each sandwich, spread 1 tablespoon dressing on cut sides of bread bottoms and tops. Divide steak slices evenly over bread bottoms; top with grilled lettuce and 1 tablespoon Parmesan cheese. Cover with bread tops.

1 Sandwich: Calories 410 (Calories from Fat 90); Total Fat 10g (Saturated Fat 4.5g; Trans Fat 0g); Cholesterol 75mg; Sodium 740mg; Total Carbohydrate 40g (Dietary Fiber 2g); Protein 39g **% Daily Value:** Vitamin A 20%; Vitamin C 2%; Calcium 15%; Iron 25% **Exchanges:** 2½ Starch, 4 Very Lean Meat, ½ Lean Meat, 1 Fat **Carbohydrate Choices:** 2½

grilled fajita pitas

Prep Time: 30 Minutes **Start to Finish:** 24 Hours 30 Minutes **Makes:** 6 sandwiches

230 Calories

¾ lb beef flank steak
½ cup fat-free Italian dressing
½ teaspoon grated lime peel
¼ cup fresh lime juice
2 tablespoons chopped fresh cilantro
1 small onion, finely chopped (¼ cup)
¼ teaspoon salt

¼ teaspoon pepper
4 cups mixed spring greens
1 medium red bell pepper, cut into bite-size strips
1 medium avocado, pitted, peeled and thinly sliced
3 whole wheat pita (pocket) breads (6 inch), cut in half to form pockets

1. On both sides of steak, make cuts about 1 inch apart and ¼ inch deep in crisscross pattern. Place steak in resealable food-storage plastic bag.

2. In small bowl, mix dressing, lime peel, lime juice and cilantro. Pour half of the dressing mixture over steak. Seal bag; turn to coat steak. Refrigerate up to 24 hours to marinate, turning bag occasionally. Add onion to remaining dressing mixture in bowl. Cover; refrigerate until serving time.

3. Heat gas or charcoal grill. Drain steak, discarding marinade. Sprinkle steak with salt and pepper. Place on grill over medium heat. Cover grill; cook 17 to 21 minutes for medium doneness (160°F), turning once.

4. Transfer steak from grill to cutting board; thinly slice across grain. In large bowl, gently toss steak, mixed greens, bell pepper, avocado and reserved dressing mixture. Divide mixture evenly among pita halves.

1 Sandwich: Calories 230 (Calories from Fat 60); Total Fat 7g (Saturated Fat 1.5g; Trans Fat 0g); Cholesterol 40mg; Sodium 500mg; Total Carbohydrate 22g (Dietary Fiber 5g); Protein 20g **% Daily Value:** Vitamin A 60%; Vitamin C 30%; Calcium 4%; Iron 15% **Exchanges:** 1 Starch, 1½ Vegetable, 2 Lean Meat **Carbohydrate Choices:** 1½

veggie salad pitas

Prep Time: 20 Minutes   **Start to Finish:** 2 Hours 20 Minutes   **Makes:** 4 sandwiches

160 Calories

1   cup chopped yellow summer squash or zucchini or ½ cup of each
¾   cup chopped fresh broccoli
2   plum (Roma) tomatoes, seeded, chopped (⅔ cup)
2   tablespoons chopped pitted kalamata or ripe olives
2   tablespoons chopped fresh Italian (flat-leaf) parsley

¼   cup fat-free Italian dressing
¾   cup cannellini beans (from 15-oz can), drained, rinsed
1½ teaspoons spicy brown mustard
¼   teaspoon salt
2   whole wheat pita (pocket) breads (6 inch), cut in half to form pockets

1. In medium bowl, toss squash, broccoli, tomatoes, olives and parsley with 2 tablespoons of the dressing. Cover; refrigerate at least 2 hours or up to 24 hours.

2. In food processor, place beans, mustard, salt and remaining 2 tablespoons dressing. Cover; process until smooth and spreadable.

3. Spread bean mixture inside each pita half; fill with chilled vegetable mixture.

1 Sandwich: Calories 160 (Calories from Fat 15); Total Fat 1.5g (Saturated Fat 0g; Trans Fat 0g); Cholesterol 0mg; Sodium 650mg; Total Carbohydrate 28g (Dietary Fiber 5g); Protein 7g **% Daily Value:** Vitamin A 10%; Vitamin C 45%; Calcium 6%; Iron 15% **Exchanges:** 1½ Starch, 1 Vegetable **Carbohydrate Choices:** 2

a little bit more

Beef up this sandwich by adding 2 ounces thinly sliced deli roast beef in each pita half for an additional 65 calories per serving.

chicken salad sandwiches

Prep Time: 10 Minutes **Start to Finish:** 10 Minutes **Makes:** 4 sandwiches

270 Calories

1	cup chopped cooked chicken breast
⅓	cup chopped apple or celery
1	hard-cooked egg, chopped
2	tablespoons plain fat-free yogurt
2	tablespoons reduced-fat mayonnaise or salad dressing
¼	teaspoon salt
¼	teaspoon pepper
8	slices whole wheat bread
4	leaves romaine or leaf lettuce
1	medium tomato, thinly sliced
¾	cup thinly sliced cucumber

1. In medium bowl, stir together chicken, apple and egg. Add yogurt, mayonnaise, salt and pepper; stir to combine.

2. On 4 bread slices, place lettuce, tomato and cucumber. Divide chicken salad among sandwiches. Top with remaining 4 bread slices. Cut each sandwich in half to serve.

1 Sandwich: Calories 270 (Calories from Fat 70); Total Fat 7g (Saturated Fat 1.5g; Trans Fat 0.5g); Cholesterol 85mg; Sodium 520mg; Total Carbohydrate 29g (Dietary Fiber 5g); Protein 20g **% Daily Value:** Vitamin A 60%; Vitamin C 20%; Calcium 10%; Iron 15% **Exchanges:** 2 Starch, ½ Vegetable, 2 Very Lean Meat, 1 Fat **Carbohydrate Choices:** 2

a little bit less

Want an even "skinnier" sandwich? Omit the egg and use fat-free mayonnaise to save 40 calories per serving.

turkey-apple salad wraps

Prep Time: 20 Minutes   **Start to Finish:** 20 Minutes   **Makes:** 4 servings (3 wraps each)

260 Calories

¾   lb cooked turkey breast, shredded
1   cup chopped green apple
½   cup chopped celery
½   cup sliced green onions (8 medium)
½   cup chopped fresh Italian (flat-leaf) parsley
¼   cup chopped walnuts, toasted*
¼   cup dried tart cherries

1   container (6 oz) fat-free Greek plain yogurt
2   tablespoons fresh lemon juice
½   to 1 teaspoon red pepper sauce
¼   teaspoon salt
¼   teaspoon freshly ground black pepper
12   leaves Boston or Bibb lettuce

1. In large bowl, toss turkey, apple, celery, onions, parsley, walnuts and cherries.

2. In small bowl, mix yogurt, lemon juice, pepper sauce, salt and pepper until blended. Pour over turkey mixture; toss to coat.

3. Spoon salad into center of each lettuce leaf. Serve immediately.

*To toast nuts, cook in an ungreased skillet over medium heat for 5 to 7 minutes, stirring frequently, until nuts begin to brown, then stirring constantly until nuts are light brown.

1 Serving: Calories 260 (Calories from Fat 50); Total Fat 6g (Saturated Fat 1g; Trans Fat 0g); Cholesterol 75mg; Sodium 250mg; Total Carbohydrate 19g (Dietary Fiber 3g); Protein 31g **% Daily Value:** Vitamin A 35%; Vitamin C 30%; Calcium 15%; Iron 15% **Exchanges:** 1 Other Carbohydrate, 1 Vegetable, 4 Very Lean Meat, 1 Fat **Carbohydrate Choices:** 1

a little bit less

Serve only 2 wraps per serving, for a savings of 90 calories. Wrap leftover turkey mixture and lettuce leaves separately and refrigerate. Then, later, enjoy the third wrap as a bedtime snack when the hungries strike!

pineapple-seafood rolls

Prep Time: 20 Minutes   **Start to Finish:** 20 Minutes   **Makes:** 5 sandwiches

230 Calories

DRESSING
- ¼ cup reduced-fat mayonnaise
- 2 tablespoons plain fat-free yogurt
- 2 tablespoons rice vinegar
- ½ teaspoon seafood seasoning
- ⅛ teaspoon red pepper sauce, if desired

SANDWICHES
- 12 oz refrigerated flake-style imitation crabmeat, large pieces broken up (about 1¾ cups)
- 2 cups coleslaw mix (from 14- to 16-oz bag)
- 1 can (8 oz) pineapple chunks in juice, drained, cut in half
- 5 whole wheat sandwich thin hot dog buns (from 12-oz package)
- 5 leaves romaine lettuce

1. In small bowl, stir all dressing ingredients with whisk. In large bowl, toss imitation crabmeat, coleslaw mix and pineapple. Pour dressing over mixture and mix well.

2. Using serrated knife, carefully cut each bun to open more, but do not cut entirely through bun. Line each bun with 1 lettuce leaf; top with about ¾ cup crabmeat mixture. Serve immediately.

1 Sandwich: Calories 230 (Calories from Fat 50); Total Fat 6g (Saturated Fat 1g; Trans Fat 0g); Cholesterol 20mg; Sodium 710mg; Total Carbohydrate 30g (Dietary Fiber 4g); Protein 14g **% Daily Value:** Vitamin A 60%; Vitamin C 15%; Calcium 10%; Iron 10% **Exchanges:** 2 Starch, ½ Vegetable, 1 Medium-Fat Meat **Carbohydrate Choices:** 2

a little bit more
For an additional 55 calories, add half of a 1-ounce slice of Colby cheese to each sandwich.

veggie-ranch turkey wraps

Prep Time: 30 Minutes   **Start to Finish:** 30 Minutes   **Makes:** 6 servings (½ wrap each)

180 Calories

1	large red or green bell pepper, cut into ½-inch-wide strips
1	medium yellow summer squash, cut lengthwise into ¼-inch-thick slices
1	small red onion, cut into 1-inch-wide wedges
2	teaspoons canola oil
3	tablespoons fat-free ranch dressing
3	spinach-flavor or whole wheat flour tortillas (10 inch)
6	oz thinly sliced cooked turkey breast
2	oz reduced-fat Monterey Jack or pepper Jack cheese, cut into thin slices
¼	cup chopped fresh cilantro

1. Heat gas or charcoal grill. Spray grill basket (grill "wok") with cooking spray. Brush bell pepper, squash and onion with oil; place in basket. Place basket on grill over medium heat. Cover grill; cook 6 to 12 minutes, turning or stirring occasionally, until vegetables are tender. Remove from grill; cover to keep warm.

2. To assemble wraps, spread ranch dressing on one side of each tortilla. Divide turkey and cheese among tortillas. Spoon grilled vegetables over cheese just below center of each tortilla. Sprinkle with cilantro. Fold bottom third of tortilla partially over vegetables; fold in sides and roll up. Cut wraps in half.

1 Serving: Calories 180 (Calories from Fat 45); Total Fat 5g (Saturated Fat 2g; Trans Fat 0g); Cholesterol 30mg; Sodium 300mg; Total Carbohydrate 19g (Dietary Fiber 3g); Protein 14g **% Daily Value:** Vitamin A 6%; Vitamin C 25%; Calcium 10%; Iron 8% **Exchanges:** 1 Starch, 1 Vegetable, 1 Very Lean Meat, ½ Lean Meat, ½ Fat **Carbohydrate Choices:** 1

a little bit more

Pair this sandwich with a medium nectarine for an added 60 calories. If you slice it, you can trick yourself into thinking you are eating more, as the slices take up more space on your plate than a whole piece of fruit.

lemony asparagus and smoked salmon wraps

Prep Time: 30 Minutes   **Start to Finish:** 30 Minutes   **Makes:** 4 wraps

190 Calories

8 oz fresh asparagus spears, trimmed	8 oz smoked salmon, cut or flaked into ½-inch pieces
4 oz fat-free cream cheese spread (from 8-oz container)	¼ cup chopped fresh or 2 teaspoons dried basil leaves
2 teaspoons grated lemon peel	4 whole wheat flour tortillas (7 to 8 inch)
2 tablespoons fresh lemon juice	1 medium red bell pepper, cut into thin bite-size strips
⅛ teaspoon ground red pepper (cayenne)	

1. In 2-quart saucepan, place asparagus and enough water just to cover. Heat to boiling; boil 3 to 5 minutes or until crisp-tender. Drain and plunge asparagus into ice water to cool quickly. Drain again; pat dry with paper towels.

2. In medium bowl, mix cream cheese spread, lemon peel, lemon juice and red pepper. Fold in salmon and basil. Spread mixture on one side of each tortilla. Arrange asparagus and bell pepper on salmon mixture. Roll up tortillas; secure with toothpicks, if necessary.

1 Wrap: Calories 190 (Calories from Fat 35); Total Fat 4g (Saturated Fat 1g; Trans Fat 0g); Cholesterol 15mg; Sodium 790mg; Total Carbohydrate 20g (Dietary Fiber 4g); Protein 19g **% Daily Value:** Vitamin A 35%; Vitamin C 80%; Calcium 15%; Iron 15% **Exchanges:** 1 Starch, ½ Vegetable, 1 Very Lean Meat, 1 Lean Meat **Carbohydrate Choices:** 1

a little bit more

Serve up a juicy side of 1 cup cubed watermelon. It adds 50 calories and is a good source of vitamins A and C.

bacon and edamame wraps

Prep Time: 30 Minutes   Start to Finish: 30 Minutes   Makes: 4 wraps

270 Calories

1 cup frozen shelled edamame (from 10- to 12-oz bag)

1 medium jalapeño chile, seeded, chopped

2 tablespoons chopped fresh cilantro

2 tablespoons fresh lemon juice

2 tablespoons water

1 clove garlic, halved

4 slices frozen soy-protein bacon or refrigerated turkey bacon

4 whole wheat or garden vegetable–flavor flour tortillas (8 inch)

2 cups torn mixed salad greens

2 medium tomatoes, seeded, chopped

¼ cup fat-free ranch dressing

1. Cook edamame as directed on bag. Drain and rinse with cold water; drain again. In food processor, place edamame, chile, cilantro, lemon juice, water and garlic. Cover; process until smooth. Set aside.

2. Meanwhile, cook bacon as directed on package. Drain well on paper towels; chop bacon.

3. To assemble, spread about ¼ cup of the edamame mixture on each tortilla. Top with salad greens, tomatoes, ranch dressing and bacon, placing ingredients on edge of tortilla. Roll up to enclose filling; secure with toothpicks, if necessary.

1 Wrap: Calories 270 (Calories from Fat 60); Total Fat 6g (Saturated Fat 1g; Trans Fat 0g); Cholesterol 0mg; Sodium 560mg; Total Carbohydrate 40g (Dietary Fiber 7g); Protein 13g **% Daily Value:** Vitamin A 45%; Vitamin C 20%; Calcium 10%; Iron 20% **Exchanges:** 2 Starch, 2 Vegetable, ½ Very Lean Meat, 1 Fat **Carbohydrate Choices:** 2½

a little bit more

Turn this sandwich into a lunch on the go by adding an apple. A medium apple will add 95 calories. Eat the peel too—to get all of the fiber.

mexican kiwi tostadas

Prep Time: 40 Minutes   **Start to Finish:** 40 Minutes   **Makes:** 4 tostadas

230 Calories

1 teaspoon ground cumin	Cooking spray
¼ teaspoon crushed red pepper flakes	¼ cup reduced-fat sour cream
⅛ teaspoon salt	2 tablespoons chunky-style salsa
2 boneless skinless chicken breasts (8 oz)	2 cups shredded romaine lettuce
1 teaspoon canola oil	3 kiwifruit, peeled, sliced
4 soft corn tortillas (6 inch) or tostada shells	¼ cup shredded pepper Jack cheese (1 oz)
	Additional chunky-style salsa, if desired

1. Heat gas or charcoal grill. In small bowl, mix cumin, pepper flakes and salt. Brush both sides of chicken with oil; sprinkle evenly with cumin mixture.

2. Place chicken on grill over medium heat. Cover grill; cook 12 to 15 minutes, turning once, until juice of chicken is clear when center of thickest part is cut (at least 165°F).

3. Meanwhile, heat oven to 400°F. Spray tortillas with cooking spray; place on cookie sheet. Bake 10 to 15 minutes, turning once, until crisp. (If using tostada shells, heat as directed on package.)

4. Transfer chicken from grill to cutting board; cut into bite-size strips. In small bowl, mix sour cream and 2 tablespoons salsa. Spread mixture on warmed tortillas. Top evenly with lettuce, kiwifruit, chicken and cheese. Serve with additional salsa.

1 Tostada: Calories 230 (Calories from Fat 80); Total Fat 8g (Saturated Fat 3g; Trans Fat 0g); Cholesterol 45mg; Sodium 240mg; Total Carbohydrate 21g (Dietary Fiber 3g); Protein 17g **% Daily Value:** Vitamin A 45%; Vitamin C 50%; Calcium 10%; Iron 8% **Exchanges:** ½ Starch, ½ Fruit, ½ Vegetable, 2 Very Lean Meat, 1½ Fat **Carbohydrate Choices:** 1½

a little bit more

You can make a super-quick cucumber-tomato salad (below) to go with the tostadas for only 20 calories per serving.

cucumber-tomato salad In medium bowl, toss 3 medium plum (Roma) tomatoes, each cut into 6 wedges, 1 medium cucumber, thickly sliced, 1 tablespoon cider vinegar, ½ teaspoon sugar and ¼ teaspoon each garlic powder and pepper. Let stand at room temperature for flavors to blend while grilling the chicken.

grilled fish tacos

Prep Time: 20 Minutes **Start to Finish:** 20 Minutes **Makes:** 8 tacos

150 Calories

TACOS

- 1 lb sea bass, red snapper or other medium-firm fish fillets
- 1 tablespoon olive oil
- 1 teaspoon ground cumin or chili powder
- ½ teaspoon salt
- ¼ teaspoon pepper
- 8 soft corn tortillas (6 inch), heated as directed on package
- ¼ cup sour cream
- ½ cup chunky-style salsa

TOPPINGS, IF DESIRED

Shredded lettuce
Chopped avocado
Chopped tomato
Chopped onion
Chopped fresh cilantro
Fresh lime wedges

1. Heat gas or charcoal grill. Brush fish with oil; sprinkle with cumin, salt and pepper.

2. Carefully brush additional oil on grill rack. Place fish on grill over medium heat. Cover grill; cook 5 to 7 minutes, turning once, until fish flakes easily with fork.

3. Spread one side of each tortilla with sour cream; top with fish, salsa and choice of toppings. Squeeze lime juice over tacos. Serve immediately.

1 Taco: Calories 150 (Calories from Fat 50); Total Fat 6g (Saturated Fat 2g; Trans Fat 0g); Cholesterol 30mg; Sodium 290mg; Total Carbohydrate 12g (Dietary Fiber 1g); Protein 12g **% Daily Value:** Vitamin A 4%; Vitamin C 0%; Calcium 4%; Iron 6% **Exchanges:** ½ Starch, ½ Other Carbohydrate, 1½ Very Lean Meat, 1 Fat **Carbohydrate Choices:** 1

a little bit more

Make it a Mexican meal by serving these tacos with cooked brown rice tossed with chopped fresh cilantro. A ½-cup serving adds 110 calories.

taco mac and cheese

Prep Time: 35 Minutes **Start to Finish:** 55 Minutes **Makes:** 5 servings

360 Calories

3 cups uncooked multigrain or whole-grain rotini pasta (9 oz)

1½ cups cubed (about ¾ inch) peeled butternut squash

¾ cup fat-free chicken broth with ⅓ less sodium

½ cup evaporated low-fat milk (from 12-oz can)

4 teaspoons taco seasoning mix (from 1-oz package)

1¼ cups shredded reduced-fat taco-flavored Mexican cheese blend (5 oz)

2 plum (Roma) tomatoes, sliced

¼ cup low-sodium refrigerated salsa

¼ cup reduced-fat sour cream

12 baked tortilla chips
Fresh cilantro sprigs, if desired

1. Heat oven to 375°F. Spray 1½-quart casserole with cooking spray. Cook pasta as directed on package, omitting salt and oil and using minimum cook time. Drain and return to saucepan.

2. Meanwhile, in 2-quart saucepan, heat squash and broth to boiling over high heat; reduce heat. Cover; simmer 15 minutes or until squash is tender. Stir in milk and taco seasoning. Return to boiling; remove from heat. Place squash mixture in blender. Cover; blend on medium speed 20 seconds or until smooth. Return to saucepan. Stir in 1 cup of the cheese until melted. Pour over pasta; mix well. Pour mixture into casserole. Top with tomato slices.

3. Bake uncovered 15 minutes. Sprinkle with remaining ¼ cup cheese. Bake 4 to 5 minutes longer or until cheese is melted.

4. Divide pasta mixture among 4 plates. Top each serving with 1 tablespoon each salsa and sour cream. Crumble 3 tortilla chips over each. Garnish with cilantro. Serve immediately.

1 Serving: Calories 360 (Calories from Fat 80); Total Fat 8g (Saturated Fat 4.5g; Trans Fat 0g); Cholesterol 25mg; Sodium 640mg; Total Carbohydrate 54g (Dietary Fiber 6g); Protein 18g **% Daily Value:** Vitamin A 90%; Vitamin C 8%; Calcium 45%; Iron 10% **Exchanges:** 3 Starch, ½ Other Carbohydrate, ½ Vegetable, ½ Very Lean Meat, ½ Lean Meat, 1 Fat **Carbohydrate Choices:** 3½

vegetable-cashew noodle bowl

Prep Time: 30 Minutes   **Start to Finish:** 30 Minutes   **Makes:** 4 servings (1¼ cups each)

330 Calories

8 oz uncooked Japanese udon noodles	1 tablespoon grated lemon peel
1 red bell pepper, cut into 2×¼-inch strips	3 cloves garlic
1 yellow bell pepper, cut into 2×¼-inch strips	1 teaspoon fresh lemon juice
2 small carrots, thinly sliced	Salt and pepper to taste
2 cups fresh cilantro leaves	2 tablespoons olive oil
	1 green onion, sliced
	3 tablespoons lightly salted roasted cashews

1. In 6- to 8-quart Dutch oven or stockpot, heat 4 quarts water to boiling. Add noodles; return to boiling. Reduce heat; cook 13 to 14 minutes or until tender. During last 4 minutes of cooking time, add bell peppers and carrots. Drain. Return noodle mixture to pan; cover to keep warm.

2. Meanwhile, in food processor, place cilantro, lemon peel and garlic. Cover; process until very finely chopped. Add lemon juice, salt, pepper and oil. Cover; process until mixture is smooth.

3. Pour cilantro sauce over noodle mixture; toss to coat evenly. Divide among 4 bowls. Sprinkle with onion and cashews.

1 Serving: Calories 330 (Calories from Fat 100); Total Fat 11g (Saturated Fat 1.5g; Trans Fat 0g); Cholesterol 0mg; Sodium 70mg; Total Carbohydrate 49g (Dietary Fiber 6g); Protein 10g **% Daily Value:** Vitamin A 120%; Vitamin C 80%; Calcium 6%; Iron 15% **Exchanges:** 2 Starch, ½ Other Carbohydrate, 2 Vegetable, 2 Fat **Carbohydrate Choices:** 3

a little bit less

Want crunch but fewer calories? Skip the cashews and sprinkle each serving with 1 teaspoon sesame seeds (toasted, if desired), for a savings of 25 calories per serving.

thai beef noodle bowls

Prep Time: 50 Minutes   **Start to Finish:** 50 Minutes   **Makes:** 6 servings (2⅔ cups each)

180 Calories

1	tablespoon canola oil
1	lb beef top sirloin steak, thinly sliced across grain
½	teaspoon freshly ground black pepper
⅛	teaspoon salt
1	medium onion, thinly sliced (1 cup)
2	tablespoons finely chopped gingerroot
2	jalapeño chiles, seeded, chopped
2	large cloves garlic, finely chopped
3	cups water
3	cups reduced-sodium chicken broth (from 32-oz carton)

2	tablespoons reduced-sodium soy sauce
1½	cups thinly sliced Chinese (napa) cabbage
1	package (8 oz) tofu shirataki noodles (spaghetti style), drained, rinsed well
6	fresh mint leaves
2	tablespoons chopped fresh cilantro
6	tablespoons thinly sliced green onions (5 to 6 medium)
1	lime, cut into 6 pieces

1. In 5-quart Dutch oven, heat oil over medium-high heat. Sprinkle beef with pepper and salt. Cook beef in oil, stirring occasionally, until brown on all sides. Using slotted spoon, transfer from pan to bowl (leave juices in pan); cover to keep warm.

2. Reduce heat to medium. Add onion, gingerroot and chiles. Cook 5 to 7 minutes, stirring occasionally, until onion is tender. Add garlic; cook 1 minute, scraping up any beef bits from bottom of pan. Add water, broth and soy sauce; heat to boiling. Add cabbage and noodles, stirring well to separate noodles. Return beef to pan; cook uncovered, stirring occasionally, until hot.

3. Divide mixture among 6 bowls. Top each serving with 1 mint leaf, 1 teaspoon cilantro, 1 tablespoon green onions and 1 lime piece.

1 Serving: Calories 180 (Calories from Fat 50); Total Fat 6g (Saturated Fat 1g; Trans Fat 0g); Cholesterol 55mg; Sodium 550mg; Total Carbohydrate 8g (Dietary Fiber 2g); Protein 24g **% Daily Value:** Vitamin A 4%; Vitamin C 10%; Calcium 8%; Iron 15% **Exchanges:** 1 Vegetable, 2 Very Lean Meat, 1 Lean Meat, ½ Fat **Carbohydrate Choices:** ½

a little bit more

Light on calories but big on flavor, a simple Asian salad makes a great side to these noodle bowls. Toss 1 cup salad greens, ¼ cup sliced fresh mushrooms and 1 tablespoon chopped red onion with 1 tablespoon reduced-fat Asian toasted sesame dressing. It will add about 40 calories per serving.

mediterranean beef pita pizzas

Prep Time: 25 Minutes   **Start to Finish:** 35 Minutes   **Makes:** 4 pizzas

250 Calories

6   oz lean (at least 80%) ground beef
1   small onion, finely chopped
     (¼ cup)
2   cloves garlic, finely chopped
1   can (8 oz) no-salt-added
     tomato sauce
1   teaspoon chopped fresh
     rosemary leaves or ¼ teaspoon
     dried rosemary leaves, crushed
2   whole wheat pita (pocket) breads
     (6 inch)

½   cup shredded reduced-fat
     mozzarella cheese (2 oz)
½   cup shredded fresh spinach
1   medium tomato, chopped (¾ cup)
¼   cup crumbled reduced-fat feta
     cheese (1 oz)
12   pitted kalamata or ripe
     olives, quartered

1. Heat oven to 400°F. In 8-inch nonstick skillet, cook beef, onion and garlic over medium-high heat 5 to 7 minutes, stirring occasionally, until beef is thoroughly cooked; drain. Stir in tomato sauce and rosemary. Heat to boiling; reduce heat. Simmer uncovered 2 minutes.

2. Carefully split pita breads in half horizontally. Place pita halves, rough sides up, on ungreased large cookie sheet. Bake 3 to 4 minutes or until lightly toasted.

3. Divide beef mixture among toasted pita halves; sprinkle with mozzarella cheese. Bake 2 to 3 minutes or until cheese is melted. Top with spinach, tomato, feta cheese and olives. Serve immediately.

1 Pizza: Calories 250 (Calories from Fat 90); Total Fat 11g (Saturated Fat 4g; Trans Fat 0g); Cholesterol 40mg; Sodium 450mg; Total Carbohydrate 24g (Dietary Fiber 3g); Protein 16g **% Daily Value:** Vitamin A 20%; Vitamin C 10%; Calcium 15%; Iron 15% **Exchanges:** 1 Starch, ½ Other Carbohydrate, 1 Vegetable, 1½ Lean Meat, 1 Fat **Carbohydrate Choices:** 1½

buffalo chicken pizza

Prep Time: 10 Minutes   **Start to Finish:** 20 Minutes   **Makes:** 6 servings

250 Calories

1	package (10 oz) prebaked whole wheat thin Italian pizza crust (12 inch)
¼	cup fat-free ranch dressing
¼	cup finely chopped celery
1	cup chopped cooked chicken breast
3	tablespoons Buffalo wing sauce
¾	cup green and red bell pepper strips
¾	cup shredded reduced-fat mozzarella cheese (3 oz)
1	tablespoon crumbled blue cheese

1. Heat oven to 400°F. Place pizza crust on ungreased cookie sheet. Spread ranch dressing over crust. Sprinkle with celery.

2. In small bowl, stir together chicken and Buffalo wing sauce; arrange over crust. Top with bell peppers and cheeses.

3. Bake 10 minutes or until mozzarella is melted and just beginning to brown.

1 Serving: Calories 250 (Calories from Fat 60); Total Fat 7g (Saturated Fat 2.5g; Trans Fat 0g); Cholesterol 30mg; Sodium 470mg; Total Carbohydrate 30g (Dietary Fiber 3g); Protein 15g **% Daily Value:** Vitamin A 4%; Vitamin C 8%; Calcium 15%; Iron 10% **Exchanges:** 1½ Starch, ½ Other Carbohydrate, 1 Very Lean Meat, ½ Lean Meat, 1 Fat **Carbohydrate Choices:** 2

a little bit more

Serve this tasty pizza with additional fresh veggies and fat-free ranch dressing to dip them in. One cup carrot strips and 1 tablespoon dressing will add 70 calories.

pesto shrimp pizza

Prep Time: 20 Minutes   **Start to Finish:** 1 Hour 40 Minutes   **Makes:** 16 servings

180 Calories

2	teaspoons active dry yeast
½	cup warm water (105°F to 115°F)
2	teaspoons honey
2	teaspoons olive oil
½	cup whole wheat flour
2	tablespoons yellow cornmeal
¼	teaspoon salt
½	to 1 cup all-purpose flour

½	lb cooked deveined peeled medium shrimp, thawed if frozen, tail shells removed
6	tablespoons refrigerated reduced-fat basil pesto
½	cup shredded reduced-fat mozzarella cheese (2 oz)

1. In small bowl, dissolve yeast in warm water. Let stand 5 minutes. Stir in honey and oil. In medium bowl, mix whole wheat flour, cornmeal and salt. Stir in yeast mixture. Using a wooden spoon, stir in as much of the all-purpose flour as you can.

2. Place dough on lightly floured surface; knead in enough of the remaining all-purpose flour to make a moderately stiff dough that is smooth and elastic (3 to 4 minutes total). Shape dough into a ball. Cover; let rise in warm place (80°F to 85°F) 30 to 45 minutes or until nearly doubled in size.

3. Heat oven to 425°F. Grease 2 small cookie sheets. Punch down dough; divide dough in half. Let rest 10 minutes.

4. On lightly floured surface, roll each dough half to 10- to 12-inch oval. Transfer dough to cookie sheets. Prick dough with fork. Bake 6 to 8 minutes or until lightly browned.

5. Toss shrimp with 2 tablespoons of the pesto. Spread remaining 4 tablespoons pesto over baked crusts. Top with shrimp; sprinkle with cheese. Bake 5 to 8 minutes longer or until cheese is melted.

1 Serving: Calories 180 (Calories from Fat 60); Total Fat 7g (Saturated Fat 1.5g; Trans Fat 0g); Cholesterol 65mg; Sodium 480mg; Total Carbohydrate 17g (Dietary Fiber 2g); Protein 12g **% Daily Value:** Vitamin A 2%; Vitamin C 0%; Calcium 8%; Iron 4% **Exchanges:** 1 Starch, 1½ Very Lean Meat, 1 Fat **Carbohydrate Choices:** 1

fresh mozzarella and tomato pizza

Prep Time: 35 Minutes   **Start to Finish:** 3 Hours 15 Minutes   **Makes:** 8 servings

140 Calories

ITALIAN-STYLE PIZZA DOUGH

1	package regular active or fast-acting dry yeast
½	cup warm water (105°F to 115°F)
1¼ to 1½ cups all-purpose flour	
1	teaspoon olive oil
½	teaspoon salt
½	teaspoon sugar

TOPPINGS

4	oz fresh mozzarella cheese, well drained
2	plum (Roma) tomatoes, thinly sliced
¼	teaspoon salt
	Freshly cracked pepper
¼	cup thin strips fresh basil leaves
1	tablespoon chopped fresh oregano leaves
1	tablespoon small capers, if desired
1	tablespoon olive oil

1. In large bowl, dissolve yeast in warm water. Stir in half of the flour, 1 teaspoon oil, ½ teaspoon salt and the sugar. Stir in enough of the remaining flour to make dough easy to handle. On lightly floured surface, knead dough about 10 minutes or until smooth and springy.

2. Grease large bowl with shortening. Place dough in bowl, turning dough to grease all sides. Cover; let rise in warm place (80°F to 85°F) 20 minutes. Gently push fist into dough to deflate. Cover; refrigerate at least 2 hours but no longer than 48 hours. (If dough doubles in size during refrigeration, gently push fist into dough to deflate.)

3. Move oven rack to lowest position. Heat oven to 425°F. Grease cookie sheet or 12-inch pizza pan with oil. Using floured fingers, press dough into 12-inch round on cookie sheet or pat in pizza pan, pressing dough from center to edge so edge is slightly thicker than center.

4. Cut cheese into ¼-inch slices. Place cheese on crust to within ½ inch of edge. Arrange tomatoes on cheese. Sprinkle with ¼ teaspoon salt, pepper, 2 tablespoons of the basil, the oregano and capers. Drizzle with 1 tablespoon oil.

5. Bake about 20 minutes or until crust is golden brown and cheese is melted. Sprinkle with remaining 2 tablespoons basil.

1 Serving: Calories 140 (Calories from Fat 50); Total Fat 6g (Saturated Fat 2.5g; Trans Fat 0g); Cholesterol 15mg; Sodium 280mg; Total Carbohydrate 17g (Dietary Fiber 1g); Protein 5g **% Daily Value:** Vitamin A 6%; Vitamin C 0%; Calcium 10%; Iron 6% **Exchanges:** ½ Starch, ½ Other Carbohydrate, ½ Medium-Fat Meat, ½ Fat **Carbohydrate Choices:** 1

a little bit more

Warm up on a cold night by pairing this Italian-inspired pizza with Italian Bean Soup with Greens (page 134), for an additional 220 calories.

white bean and spinach pizza

Prep Time: 10 Minutes   **Start to Finish:** 30 Minutes   **Makes:** 8 servings

190 Calories

½ cup dry-pack sun-dried tomato halves

1 can (15 to 16 oz) Great Northern or navy beans, drained, rinsed

2 cloves garlic

1 package (10 oz) prebaked thin Italian pizza crust (12 inch)

¼ teaspoon dried oregano leaves

1 cup firmly packed fresh spinach leaves, shredded

½ cup shredded reduced-fat Colby–Monterey Jack cheese blend (2 oz)

1. Heat oven to 425°F. In small bowl, place sun-dried tomatoes. Pour enough boiling water over tomatoes to cover; let stand 10 minutes. Drain. Cut into thin strips; set aside.

2. In food processor, place beans and garlic. Cover; process until smooth. Place pizza crust on ungreased cookie sheet. Spread bean mixture over crust. Sprinkle with oregano, tomatoes, spinach and cheese.

3. Bake about 10 minutes or until cheese is melted.

1 Serving: Calories 190 (Calories from Fat 35); Total Fat 4g (Saturated Fat 1g; Trans Fat 0g); Cholesterol 0mg; Sodium 410mg; Total Carbohydrate 30g (Dietary Fiber 4g); Protein 8g **% Daily Value:** Vitamin A 8%; Vitamin C 0%; Calcium 10%; Iron 15% **Exchanges:** 2 Other Carbohydrate, ½ Vegetable, 1 Very Lean Meat, ½ Fat **Carbohydrate Choices:** 2

a little bit more

Hard to stop at just 1 slice? It's no problem with this pizza—2 slices are still reasonable at only 380 calories, so enjoy!

chicken minestrone soup

Prep Time: 30 Minutes **Start to Finish:** 45 Minutes **Makes:** 8 servings (1⅓ cups each)

250
Calories

1	tablespoon olive oil	1	cup ½-inch pieces fresh green beans
1	cup sliced carrots	¼	teaspoon pepper
½	cup chopped celery	1	cup uncooked multigrain bow-tie (farfalle) pasta (2 oz)
1	medium onion, chopped (½ cup)	1	medium zucchini, quartered lengthwise, cut into ½-inch slices
1	carton (32 oz) reduced-sodium chicken broth (4 cups)	1	can (14.5 oz) diced tomatoes with basil and garlic, undrained
1¼	cups water		
2	cans (15 oz each) cannellini beans, drained, rinsed		
8	oz boneless skinless chicken breast, cut into bite-size pieces		

1. In 5- to 6-quart Dutch oven, heat oil over medium heat. Add carrots, celery and onion; cook 5 minutes, stirring frequently. Add broth, water, cannellini beans, chicken, green beans and pepper. Heat to boiling; stir in pasta. Reduce heat. Simmer uncovered 5 minutes.

2. Stir in zucchini. Return to boiling; reduce heat. Simmer uncovered 8 to 10 minutes longer or until pasta is tender and green beans are crisp-tender. Stir in tomatoes; cook until thoroughly heated.

1 Serving: Calories 250 (Calories from Fat 30); Total Fat 3.5g (Saturated Fat 0.5g; Trans Fat 0g); Cholesterol 25mg; Sodium 670mg; Total Carbohydrate 33g (Dietary Fiber 7g); Protein 20g **% Daily Value:** Vitamin A 60%; Vitamin C 15%; Calcium 10%; Iron 25% **Exchanges:** 1½ Starch, 2 Vegetable, 1½ Very Lean Meat, ½ Fat **Carbohydrate Choices:** 2

a little bit more

Sprinkle each serving with 1 tablespoon shredded Parmesan cheese for 20 calories extra.

italian bean soup with greens

Prep Time: 20 Minutes   **Start to Finish:** 1 Hour 10 Minutes   **Makes:** 8 servings (1⅓ cups each)

220 Calories

2 tablespoons olive oil	2 teaspoons dried basil leaves
2 medium carrots, sliced (1 cup)	1 teaspoon dried oregano leaves
1 large onion, chopped (1 cup)	⅛ teaspoon salt
1 stalk celery, chopped (⅓ cup)	¼ teaspoon pepper
2 cloves garlic, finely chopped	1 carton (32 oz) vegetable broth with ⅓ less sodium (4 cups)
2 cans (15 to 15.5 oz each) Great Northern or cannellini beans, drained, rinsed	4 cups packed fresh spinach leaves
1 can (28 oz) diced tomatoes, undrained	½ cup shredded Parmesan cheese (2 oz)

1. In 5-quart Dutch oven, heat oil over medium-high heat. Add carrots, onion, celery and garlic; cook about 5 minutes, stirring frequently, until onion is tender.

2. Stir in beans, tomatoes, basil, oregano, salt, pepper and broth. Reduce heat. Cover; simmer 30 to 45 minutes or until vegetables are tender.

3. Increase heat to medium; stir in spinach. Cover; cook 3 to 5 minutes longer or until spinach is wilted. Sprinkle individual servings with cheese.

1 Serving: Calories 220 (Calories from Fat 50); Total Fat 6g (Saturated Fat 1.5g; Trans Fat 0g); Cholesterol 0mg; Sodium 720mg; Total Carbohydrate 31g (Dietary Fiber 7g); Protein 12g **% Daily Value:** Vitamin A 100%; Vitamin C 20%; Calcium 20%; Iron 25% **Exchanges:** 1½ Starch, 2 Vegetable, ½ Very Lean Meat, 1 Fat **Carbohydrate Choices:** 2

a little bit more

This soup is begging for a piece of crusty bread to be dipped in it. One 2-ounce piece (about 1 inch thick) whole-grain artisan bread would add 140 calories and a whole lot of satisfaction!

soybean-squash soup

Prep Time: 20 Minutes   **Start to Finish:** 1 Hour   **Makes:** 4 servings (1¼ cups each)

280 Calories

1 tablespoon olive oil
1 large onion, chopped (1 cup)
2 cloves garlic, finely chopped
1 small butternut squash (about 1¼ lb), peeled, seeded and cubed (about 3 cups)
1 can (15 oz) black soybeans, drained, rinsed

1 can (14.5 oz) diced tomatoes, undrained
1 tablespoon ground cumin
⅛ teaspoon salt
¼ teaspoon pepper
¼ teaspoon crushed red pepper flakes
1 cup vegetable broth or water

1. In 5-quart Dutch oven, heat oil over medium-high heat. Cook onion and garlic in oil 3 minutes, stirring frequently, until onion is tender.

2. Stir in remaining ingredients. Heat to boiling; reduce heat. Cover; simmer 40 minutes or until squash is tender.

1 Serving: Calories 280 (Calories from Fat 100); Total Fat 11g (Saturated Fat 1.5g; Trans Fat 0g); Cholesterol 0mg; Sodium 740mg; Total Carbohydrate 29g (Dietary Fiber 9g); Protein 15g **% Daily Value:** Vitamin A 250%; Vitamin C 30%; Calcium 15%; Iron 35% **Exchanges:** 1 Starch, 2½ Vegetable, 1 Very Lean Meat, 2 Fat **Carbohydrate Choices:** 2

a little bit more

Top off this soup with a dollop of sour cream. A tablespoon of reduced-fat sour cream adds 20 calories.

lentil and tomato chicken soup

Prep Time: 30 Minutes   **Start to Finish:** 1 Hour   **Makes:** 6 servings

250 Calories

1 tablespoon olive oil	1 tablespoon chopped fresh basil or 1 teaspoon dried basil leaves
1 large onion, chopped (1 cup)	4 cups coarsely chopped fresh kale
1 cup coarsely chopped carrots	¼ teaspoon pepper
2 cloves garlic, finely chopped	2 cups cubed cooked chicken breast
6 cups reduced-sodium chicken broth (from two 32-oz cartons)	1 can (14.5 oz) no-salt-added diced tomatoes, undrained
⅔ cup dried lentils, sorted, rinsed	

1. In 4-quart Dutch oven, heat oil over medium heat. Add onion, carrots and garlic. Cover; cook 5 to 7 minutes, stirring occasionally, until vegetables are nearly tender.

2. Stir in broth, lentils and dried basil (if using). Heat to boiling; reduce heat. Cover; simmer 10 minutes. Stir in kale and pepper. Return to boiling; reduce heat. Cover; simmer 10 minutes.

3. Add chicken and tomatoes. Cover; simmer 5 to 10 minutes longer or until kale and lentils are tender. Stir in fresh basil (if using).

1 Serving: Calories 250 (Calories from Fat 45); Total Fat 5g (Saturated Fat 1g; Trans Fat 0g); Cholesterol 40mg; Sodium 640mg; Total Carbohydrate 26g (Dietary Fiber 6g); Protein 24g **% Daily Value:** Vitamin A 210%; Vitamin C 50%; Calcium 10%; Iron 20% **Exchanges:** 1 Starch, 2 Vegetable, 2½ Very Lean Meat, ½ Fat **Carbohydrate Choices:** 2

a little bit less

Go meatless! This soup is a powerhouse of protein, even without the chicken. Omit the chicken to save 80 calories per serving.

zesty mexican soup

Prep Time: 30 Minutes   **Start to Finish:** 30 Minutes   **Makes:** 6 servings (1 cup each)

160 Calories

2 cups cubed cooked chicken	1 cup chunky-style salsa
1 can (14 oz) chicken broth	1 can (4.5 oz) chopped green chiles
1 can (11.5 oz) vegetable juice	¼ cup chopped fresh cilantro
1 can (11 oz) whole kernel corn with red and green peppers, undrained	

1. In 3-quart saucepan, mix all ingredients except cilantro. Heat to boiling over medium-high heat.

2. Reduce heat to low; simmer uncovered 10 minutes, stirring occasionally, until thoroughly heated. Stir in cilantro.

1 Serving: Calories 160 (Calories from Fat 35); Total Fat 3.5g (Saturated Fat 1g; Trans Fat 0g); Cholesterol 40mg; Sodium 930mg; Total Carbohydrate 17g (Dietary Fiber 1g); Protein 15g **% Daily Value:** Vitamin A 25%; Vitamin C 20%; Calcium 0%; Iron 4% **Exchanges:** 1 Other Carbohydrate, ½ Vegetable, 1 Very Lean Meat, 1 Lean Meat **Carbohydrate Choices:** 1

a little bit more

Crumble 4 baked tortilla chips (½ ounce) over each serving of soup for a little crunch and 60 extra calories.

curried corn soup

Prep Time: 35 Minutes   **Start to Finish:** 45 Minutes   **Makes:** 4 servings (1¾ cups each)

260 Calories

2 teaspoons canola oil	1 cup reduced-sodium chicken broth
1 cup finely chopped green or red bell pepper or ½ cup of each	3 cups fat-free (skim) milk
1 small onion, finely chopped (¼ cup)	½ lb cooked deveined peeled medium shrimp, thawed if frozen, tail shells removed
2 teaspoons curry powder	2 tablespoons chopped fresh cilantro
¼ teaspoon salt	⅓ cup plain fat-free yogurt
¼ teaspoon freshly ground black pepper	Fresh cilantro sprigs, if desired
1 bag (12 oz) frozen whole kernel corn	

1. In 3-quart saucepan, heat oil over medium-high heat. Cook bell pepper and onion in oil about 4 minutes, stirring occasionally, until tender. Add curry powder, salt and pepper; cook 1 minute, stirring constantly.

2. Stir in corn and broth. Heat to boiling; reduce heat. Cover; cook 5 minutes or until corn is tender. Remove from heat; cool about 10 minutes.

3. In blender, place corn mixture and ½ cup of the milk. Cover; blend on medium speed until mixture is nearly smooth. Return mixture to saucepan.

4. Cut each shrimp in half, if desired. Stir shrimp and remaining 2½ cups milk into corn mixture. Cook until thoroughly heated (do not boil). Stir in chopped cilantro. Garnish individual servings with yogurt and cilantro sprigs.

1 Serving: Calories 260 (Calories from Fat 40); Total Fat 4g (Saturated Fat 0.5g; Trans Fat 0g); Cholesterol 125mg; Sodium 920mg; Total Carbohydrate 32g (Dietary Fiber 3g); Protein 23g **% Daily Value:** Vitamin A 20%; Vitamin C 30%; Calcium 35%; Iron 6% **Exchanges:** 1½ Starch, 2 Vegetable, 2 Very Lean Meat, ½ Fat **Carbohydrate Choices:** 2

a little bit more

Serve each serving of soup with 2 Turkey-Apple Salad Wraps (page 111) for an added 180 calories per serving.

ginger chicken noodle soup

Prep Time: 20 Minutes   **Start to Finish:** 50 Minutes   **Makes:** 5 servings (1½ cups each)

220 Calories

1 teaspoon canola oil	2 to 3 teaspoons grated gingerroot or ½ to ¾ teaspoon ground ginger
1 lb boneless skinless chicken breasts, cut into 1-inch pieces	¼ teaspoon pepper
3 medium carrots, sliced	2 oz uncooked soba (buckwheat) noodles, coarsely broken
5¼ cups reduced-sodium chicken broth (from two 32-oz cartons)	1 box (9 oz) frozen sugar snap peas
1 cup water	Additional reduced-sodium soy sauce, if desired
2 tablespoons rice vinegar	
1 tablespoon reduced-sodium soy sauce	

1. In 4-quart Dutch oven, heat oil over medium-high heat. Cook chicken in oil, stirring frequently, just until browned; drain. Add carrots, broth, water, vinegar, 1 tablespoon soy sauce, the gingerroot and pepper. Heat to boiling; reduce heat. Cover; simmer 20 minutes.

2. Stir in noodles. Return to boiling; reduce heat. Simmer uncovered 8 to 10 minutes or until noodles are tender.

3. Meanwhile, cook peas as directed on box. Stir peas into soup just before serving. Serve with additional soy sauce.

Slow Cooker Directions: Spray 3½- to 4½-quart slow cooker with cooking spray. In 12-inch skillet, heat oil over medium-high heat. Cook chicken in oil, stirring frequently, just until browned. Using slotted spoon, transfer chicken to slow cooker. Add carrots, broth, water, vinegar, 1 tablespoon soy sauce, the gingerroot and pepper. Cover; cook on Low heat setting 4 to 6 hours. Increase heat setting to High. Stir in noodles. Cover; cook 10 to 15 minutes longer or until noodles are tender. Cook peas as directed on box. Stir peas into soup just before serving.

1 Serving: Calories 220 (Calories from Fat 40); Total Fat 4g (Saturated Fat 1g; Trans Fat 0g); Cholesterol 55mg; Sodium 790mg; Total Carbohydrate 17g (Dietary Fiber 3g); Protein 27g **% Daily Value:** Vitamin A 130%; Vitamin C 10%; Calcium 6%; Iron 10% **Exchanges:** 1 Starch, 1 Vegetable, 3 Very Lean Meat, ½ Fat **Carbohydrate Choices:** 1

better-than-grandma's chicken and noodles

Prep Time: 20 Minutes   **Start to Finish:** 4 Hours 20 Minutes   **Makes:** 8 servings (1¼ cups each)

330 Calories

3 medium carrots, cut into 1-inch pieces

2 medium parsnips, peeled, cut into 1-inch pieces

1 cup frozen small whole onions (from 1-lb bag), thawed

2 stalks celery, cut into 1-inch pieces

3 whole chicken legs (drumsticks and thighs), about 3 lb, skinned

½ teaspoon dried thyme leaves, crushed

½ teaspoon dried sage leaves, crushed

2 cloves garlic, finely chopped

¼ teaspoon salt

¼ teaspoon pepper

3½ cups reduced-sodium chicken broth (from 32-oz carton)

¼ cup dry sherry or additional reduced-sodium chicken broth

1 package (12 oz) frozen egg noodles

1 box (9 oz) frozen baby sweet peas

4 to 5 fresh sage leaves, if desired

1. Spray 5- to 6-quart slow cooker with cooking spray. In slow cooker, mix carrots, parsnips, onions and celery. Top with chicken; sprinkle with thyme, dried sage, garlic, salt and pepper. Pour broth and sherry over chicken and vegetables.

2. Cover; cook on High heat setting 3 hours or on Low heat setting 7 hours.

3. Stir in noodles. If using Low heat setting, increase heat to High setting. Cover; cook 1 hour to 1 hour 30 minutes longer or until noodles are tender and juice of chicken is clear when thickest part is cut to bone (at least 165°F).

4. Remove chicken. When cool enough to handle, remove chicken from bones; discard bones. Coarsely shred chicken; stir into mixture in slow cooker. Cook peas as directed on box; stir peas into chicken mixture. Garnish with fresh sage leaves.

1 Serving: Calories 330 (Calories from Fat 60); Total Fat 7g (Saturated Fat 1.5g; Trans Fat 0g); Cholesterol 110mg; Sodium 430mg; Total Carbohydrate 38g (Dietary Fiber 4g); Protein 28g **% Daily Value:** Vitamin A 90%; Vitamin C 10%; Calcium 6%; Iron 15% **Exchanges:** 2 Starch, 2 Vegetable, ½ Very Lean Meat, 2 Lean Meat **Carbohydrate Choices:** 2½

a little bit more

This heartwarming dish is perfect served with a 2½-inch multigrain roll spread with 2 teaspoons butter, for an added 170 calories per serving.

southwest corn chowder

Prep Time: 20 Minutes   **Start to Finish:** 40 Minutes   **Makes:** 6 servings

140 Calories

1	large onion, chopped (1 cup)
1	medium leek, rinsed, cut in half lengthwise and chopped
2	bags (12 oz each) frozen whole kernel corn
3½	cups reduced-sodium chicken broth (from 32-oz carton)
1	medium red bell pepper, chopped

⅛	teaspoon freshly ground black pepper
⅛	teaspoon ground red pepper (cayenne)
3	threads saffron, crushed, if desired
	Chopped fresh chives, if desired

1. Spray 4- to 5-quart Dutch oven with cooking spray; heat over medium heat. Add onion and leek; cook about 5 minutes, stirring occasionally, until tender.

2. Add corn. Cook about 5 minutes, stirring occasionally, until corn softens. Add 1¾ cups of the broth. Heat to boiling; reduce heat. Cover; simmer about 20 minutes or until corn is very tender. Remove from heat; cool slightly.

3. Transfer half of the corn mixture to blender or food processor. Cover; blend or process until smooth. Return mixture to Dutch oven.

4. Add remaining 1¾ cups broth, the bell pepper, black pepper, red pepper and saffron; cook until thoroughly heated. Garnish individual servings with chives.

1 Serving: Calories 140 (Calories from Fat 10); Total Fat 1g (Saturated Fat 0g; Trans Fat 0g); Cholesterol 0mg; Sodium 330mg; Total Carbohydrate 28g (Dietary Fiber 3g); Protein 5g **% Daily Value:** Vitamin A 20%; Vitamin C 25%; Calcium 0%; Iron 6% **Exchanges:** ½ Starch, 1 Other Carbohydrate, 1½ Vegetable **Carbohydrate Choices:** 2

a little bit more

If your family includes those who say, "It's not a meal without meat," then stir in 1½ cups of turkey ham cubes with the remaining broth and top each serving with a tablespoon of shredded Cheddar cheese. It adds just 50 calories per serving.

chunky vegetable-beef barley soup

Prep Time: 30 Minutes **Start to Finish:** 2 Hours 15 Minutes **Makes:** 8 servings

210
Calories

1	tablespoon canola oil	¼	teaspoon pepper
¾	lb lean beef stew meat, cut into 1-inch cubes	1	dried bay leaf
7	cups reduced-sodium beef broth (from two 32-oz cartons)	1	cup frozen mixed vegetables (from 12-oz bag)
1	large onion, chopped (1 cup)	1	can (14.5 oz) no-salt-added diced tomatoes, undrained
½	cup chopped celery	1	cup ½-inch slices peeled parsnip or ½-inch cubes peeled potato
1	teaspoon dried oregano or basil leaves, crushed	⅔	cup uncooked quick-cooking barley
2	cloves garlic, finely chopped		

1. In 5- to 6-quart Dutch oven, heat oil over medium heat. Cook beef in oil, stirring frequently, until browned. Stir in broth, onion, celery, oregano, garlic, pepper and bay leaf. Heat to boiling; reduce heat. Cover; simmer 1 hour 30 minutes.

2. Stir in frozen vegetables, tomatoes, parsnip and barley. Heat to boiling; reduce heat. Cover; simmer about 15 minutes longer or until meat and vegetables are tender. Remove and discard bay leaf before serving.

Slow Cooker Directions: Spray 5- to 6-quart slow cooker with cooking spray. Thaw the frozen mixed vegetables, and substitute regular barley for quick-cooking barley. In 12-inch skillet, heat oil over medium heat. Cook beef in oil, stirring frequently, until browned; drain. In slow cooker, mix beef and remaining ingredients. Cover; cook on Low heat setting 8 to 10 hours or on High heat setting 4 to 5 hours.

1 Serving: Calories 210 (Calories from Fat 60); Total Fat 7g (Saturated Fat 2g; Trans Fat 0g); Cholesterol 25mg; Sodium 420mg; Total Carbohydrate 23g (Dietary Fiber 4g); Protein 13g **% Daily Value:** Vitamin A 10%; Vitamin C 8%; Calcium 4%; Iron 10% **Exchanges:** 1½ Starch, ½ Vegetable, 1 Lean Meat, ½ Fat **Carbohydrate Choices:** 1½

a little bit more

A steaming hot bowl of this soup goes great with Bacon and Edamame Wraps (page 116), for an added 270 calories per serving.

bean and barley chili with cilantro sour cream

Prep Time: 15 Minutes   **Start to Finish:** 1 Hour 15 Minutes   **Makes:** 6 servings (1⅓ cups each)

300 Calories

CHILI

1	tablespoon olive oil
1	large onion, chopped (1 cup)
2	cloves garlic, finely chopped
½	cup uncooked pearl barley
2	tablespoons chili powder
1½	teaspoons ground cumin
	Salt and pepper to taste
2	cups water
2	cans (14.5 oz each) diced tomatoes, undrained
1	can (15 oz) black beans, drained, rinsed
1	can (15 oz) dark red kidney beans, drained, rinsed
¾	cup chunky-style salsa

CILANTRO SOUR CREAM

½	cup reduced-fat sour cream
2	tablespoons finely chopped fresh cilantro

1. In 5-quart Dutch oven, heat oil over medium-high heat. Cook onion and garlic in oil 5 minutes, stirring frequently, until tender. Stir in barley, chili powder, cumin, salt, pepper, water and tomatoes. Reduce heat. Cover; simmer 30 minutes.

2. Stir in black beans, kidney beans and salsa. Cover; cook about 30 minutes longer or until barley is tender.

3. In small bowl, mix sour cream and cilantro until blended. Top individual servings with cilantro sour cream.

1 Serving: Calories 300 (Calories from Fat 50); Total Fat 6g (Saturated Fat 2g; Trans Fat 0g); Cholesterol 10mg; Sodium 960mg; Total Carbohydrate 48g (Dietary Fiber 11g); Protein 12g **% Daily Value:** Vitamin A 40%; Vitamin C 20%; Calcium 10%; Iron 25% **Exchanges:** 2 Starch, 1 Other Carbohydrate, 1 Vegetable, ½ Very Lean Meat, 1 Fat **Carbohydrate Choices:** 3

a little bit more

For a change of pace, serve this chili over baked potatoes. Cut 6 baked medium potatoes in half lengthwise; place on plates. Mash potatoes slightly with fork. Spoon 1 cup chili over each potato for 360 calories per serving.

savory white chicken chili

Prep Time: 35 Minutes   **Start to Finish:** 35 Minutes   **Makes:** 6 servings (1 cup each)

330
Calories

2 tablespoons olive oil	¼ teaspoon salt
1 lb boneless skinless chicken breasts, cut into 1-inch pieces	½ teaspoon sugar
1 medium onion, chopped (½ cup)	¼ teaspoon ground red pepper (cayenne)
2 cloves garlic, finely chopped	2 cans (15 oz each) cannellini beans, drained, rinsed
1½ cups reduced-sodium chicken broth	1 can (4.5 oz) chopped green chiles
1 medium red bell pepper, chopped	¼ cup chopped fresh cilantro
1 tablespoon chili powder	1 container (6 oz) fat-free Greek plain yogurt
1 teaspoon ground cumin	

1. In 4-quart saucepan or Dutch oven, heat oil over medium heat. Cook chicken, onion and garlic in oil 5 to 7 minutes, stirring occasionally, until chicken is no longer pink.

2. Stir in remaining ingredients, except cilantro and yogurt. Heat to boiling; reduce heat. Cover; simmer 10 minutes, stirring occasionally.

3. Remove from heat; stir in cilantro and yogurt. Serve with additional yogurt and chopped cilantro, if desired.

1 Serving: Calories 330 (Calories from Fat 70); Total Fat 8g (Saturated Fat 1.5g; Trans Fat 0g); Cholesterol 50mg; Sodium 730mg; Total Carbohydrate 35g (Dietary Fiber 8g); Protein 31g **% Daily Value:** Vitamin A 25%; Vitamin C 30%; Calcium 20%; Iron 30% **Exchanges:** 1½ Starch, 2½ Vegetable, 2 Very Lean Meat, 1 Lean Meat, ½ Fat **Carbohydrate Choices:** 2

a little bit less

This chili is perfect for hearty appetites. If you're not so hungry, serve yourself ¾ cup chili to save 80 calories.

calico bean chili

Prep Time: 20 Minutes   **Start to Finish:** 20 Minutes   **Makes:** 2 servings

1   cup water
1   can (14.5 oz) no-salt-added diced tomatoes, undrained
1   cup no-salt-added black beans (from 15-oz can), drained, rinsed
¾   cup black-eyed peas (from 15-oz can), drained, rinsed

1   large onion, chopped (1 cup)
¼   cup no-salt-added tomato paste
1   tablespoon chili powder
¼   teaspoon ground cumin
¼   cup shredded reduced-fat Cheddar cheese (1 oz), if desired

1. In 2-quart saucepan, stir together all ingredients except cheese. Heat to boiling; reduce heat. Cover; simmer 10 minutes, stirring occasionally, until thoroughly heated.

2. Sprinkle each serving with 2 tablespoons cheese.

1 Serving: Calories 310 (Calories from Fat 20); Total Fat 2g (Saturated Fat 0g; Trans Fat 0g); Cholesterol 0mg; Sodium 280mg; Total Carbohydrate 56g (Dietary Fiber 15g); Protein 16g **% Daily Value:** Vitamin A 45%; Vitamin C 25%; Calcium 15%; Iron 20% **Exchanges:** 2 Starch, 1 Other Carbohydrate, 1½ Vegetable, 1 Very Lean Meat **Carbohydrate Choices:** 4

a little bit more

What's a great side to serve with chili? How about a 100-calorie, low-fat corn muffin top? Look for these enriched breads in the freezer section of your grocery store.

Chapter 3
Dinner

spicy cashew chicken

Prep Time: 30 Minutes   **Start to Finish:** 30 Minutes   **Makes:** 4 servings

370 Calories

2	tablespoons oyster sauce
1	tablespoon reduced-sodium soy sauce
1	tablespoon packed brown sugar
2	teaspoons cornstarch
⅓	cup water
1	tablespoon canola oil
2	medium red or green bell peppers, or 1 of each, cut into bite-size strips
1	medium onion, sliced

3	cups coarsely shredded bok choy or Chinese (napa) cabbage
2	to 4 red Fresno or jalapeño chiles, seeded, finely chopped
1	clove garlic, finely chopped
¾	lb boneless skinless chicken breasts, cut into bite-size strips
2	cups hot cooked brown rice
¼	cup lightly salted roasted cashews, coarsely chopped

1. In small bowl, stir together oyster sauce, soy sauce, brown sugar and cornstarch. Stir in water; set sauce aside.

2. In large wok or nonstick skillet, heat oil over medium-high heat. Add bell peppers and onion; cook 2 minutes, stirring constantly. Add bok choy, chiles and garlic; cook 1 to 2 minutes longer or until peppers and onion are crisp-tender. Remove vegetable mixture from wok; set aside.

3. Add chicken to wok. Cook 3 to 4 minutes, stirring constantly, until no longer pink in center. Push chicken to side of wok. Stir sauce; add to wok. Cook and stir until thickened and bubbly. Return vegetable mixture to wok. Cook 1 minute or until thoroughly heated.

4. To serve, place ½ cup rice in each of 4 bowls. Top with 1¼ cups chicken mixture and 1 tablespoon cashews.

1 Serving: Calories 370 (Calories from Fat 100); Total Fat 11g (Saturated Fat 2g; Trans Fat 0g); Cholesterol 55mg; Sodium 500mg; Total Carbohydrate 41g (Dietary Fiber 5g); Protein 25g **% Daily Value:** Vitamin A 90%; Vitamin C 130%; Calcium 10%; Iron 15% **Exchanges:** 2 Starch, ½ Other Carbohydrate, 1 Vegetable, 2½ Very Lean Meat, 1½ Fat
Carbohydrate Choices: 3

a little bit more

Savor a cup of hot green tea mixed with a teaspoon of honey with your Asian meal, for only 25 additional calories.

chicken and butternut squash pot pie

Prep Time: 20 Minutes   **Start to Finish:** 55 Minutes   **Makes:** 8 servings

250 Calories

FILLING

1½	cups fat-free (skim) milk
¼	cup all-purpose flour
½	teaspoon dried thyme leaves
½	teaspoon dried sage leaves
½	teaspoon salt
⅛	teaspoon pepper
1	medium onion, chopped (½ cup)
1	can (10¾ oz) condensed 98% fat-free cream of chicken soup
¼	cup fat-free sour cream
2	cups cubed cooked chicken
2	cups cubed peeled butternut squash
1	cup frozen sweet peas (from 12-oz bag), thawed

CRUST

1	can (8 oz) refrigerated seamless flaky dough sheet
1	egg white, beaten
⅛	teaspoon dried thyme leaves

1. Heat oven to 375°F. In 3-quart saucepan, mix milk, flour, ½ teaspoon thyme, the sage, salt and pepper with whisk until blended. Stir in onion. Cook over medium-high heat about 5 minutes, stirring constantly, until bubbly and thickened. Reduce heat to medium.

2. Stir in soup, sour cream, chicken, squash and peas; mix well. Cook over medium heat 3 to 4 minutes, stirring occasionally, until thoroughly heated. Spoon hot chicken mixture into ungreased 12×8-inch (2-quart) glass baking dish.

3. Unroll dough on work surface; gently press dough into 12×8-inch rectangle. Place over chicken mixture. Brush dough with egg white; sprinkle with ⅛ teaspoon thyme.

4. Bake 20 to 25 minutes or until crust is golden brown and filling is bubbly. Let stand 10 minutes before serving.

1 Serving: Calories 250 (Calories from Fat 70); Total Fat 8g (Saturated Fat 3g; Trans Fat 0g); Cholesterol 35mg; Sodium 590mg; Total Carbohydrate 29g (Dietary Fiber 2g); Protein 15g **% Daily Value:** Vitamin A 80%; Vitamin C 6%; Calcium 10%; Iron 10% **Exchanges:** 1½ Starch, 1 Vegetable, ½ Very Lean Meat, ½ Lean Meat, 1 Fat **Carbohydrate Choices:** 2

a little bit more

Really hearty appetites? Increase the serving size of this dish to serve 6, for an additional 85 calories.

tangy barbecue chicken

Prep Time: 35 Minutes   **Start to Finish:** 3 Hours 35 Minutes   **Makes:** 6 servings

400 Calories

3   to 4 lb meaty chicken pieces (breasts, thighs and drumsticks), skinned
1½ cups dry sherry
1   large onion, finely chopped (1 cup)
¼   cup fresh lemon juice
2   dried bay leaves
6   cloves garlic, finely chopped
1   cup reduced-sodium chicken broth

1   can (6 oz) tomato paste
¼   cup honey
3   tablespoons mild-flavor (light) molasses
¼   teaspoon salt
½   teaspoon dried thyme leaves, crushed
¼   to ½ teaspoon ground red pepper (cayenne)
¼   teaspoon black pepper
2   tablespoons vinegar

1. Place chicken in large resealable food-storage plastic bag. In medium bowl, stir together sherry, onion, lemon juice, bay leaves and garlic. Pour over chicken; seal bag. Refrigerate 2 to 4 hours to marinate, turning bag occasionally. Drain chicken, reserving marinade. Keep chicken refrigerated until ready to grill.

2. In large saucepan, mix reserved marinade, the broth, tomato paste, honey, molasses, salt, thyme, red pepper and black pepper. Heat to boiling; reduce heat. Simmer uncovered about 30 minutes or until reduced to 2 cups. Remove from heat; remove and discard bay leaves. Stir vinegar into sauce; set aside.

3. Heat gas or charcoal grill for indirect cooking. Place chicken on unheated side of two-burner gas grill or over drip pan on charcoal grill. (If using one-burner gas grill, cook over low heat.) Cover grill; cook 50 to 60 minutes or until juice of chicken is clear when thickest part is cut to bone (at least 165°F), brushing with some of the sauce during the last 15 minutes of cooking time. Reheat remaining sauce; serve with chicken.

1 Serving: Calories 400 (Calories from Fat 70); Total Fat 7g (Saturated Fat 2g; Trans Fat 0g); Cholesterol 85mg; Sodium 500mg; Total Carbohydrate 37g (Dietary Fiber 2g); Protein 30g **% Daily Value:** Vitamin A 10%; Vitamin C 10%; Calcium 8%; Iron 25% **Exchanges:** 1 Starch, 1½ Other Carbohydrate, ½ Vegetable, 3½ Very Lean Meat, 1 Fat **Carbohydrate Choices:** 2½

a little bit more

Cook some frozen sweet peas to serve alongside this chicken. A ½-cup serving adds 60 calories and 4 grams of fiber.

pineapple chicken stir-fry

Prep Time: 30 Minutes   **Start to Finish:** 30 Minutes   **Makes:** 6 servings

290
Calories

¾ cup reduced-sodium chicken broth

3 tablespoons red wine vinegar

2 tablespoons reduced-sodium soy sauce

4 teaspoons sugar

1 tablespoon cornstarch

1 clove garlic, finely chopped

4 teaspoons canola oil

3 medium carrots, thinly sliced

1 large red bell pepper, cut into bite-size strips

3 cups fresh snow pea pods, strings removed, or 2 boxes (6 oz each) frozen snow pea pods, thawed

¾ lb boneless skinless chicken breasts, cut into 1-inch pieces

1 can (8 oz) pineapple chunks in juice, drained

3 cups hot cooked brown rice

1. In small bowl, stir together broth, vinegar, soy sauce, sugar, cornstarch and garlic; set aside.

2. In large wok or nonstick skillet, heat 3 teaspoons of the oil over medium-high heat. Add carrots and bell pepper; cook 3 minutes, stirring constantly. Add pea pods; cook about 1 minute longer, stirring constantly, until vegetables are crisp-tender. Remove vegetable mixture from wok; set aside.

3. Add remaining 1 teaspoon oil and the chicken to wok. Cook 3 to 4 minutes, stirring constantly, until chicken is no longer pink in center. Push chicken to side of wok. Stir sauce; add to center of wok. Cook and stir until thickened and bubbly. Add vegetable mixture and pineapple to wok; cook until thoroughly heated.

4. To serve, place ½ cup rice on each of 6 plates. Top with 1¼ cups chicken mixture.

1 Serving: Calories 290 (Calories from Fat 50); Total Fat 6g (Saturated Fat 1g; Trans Fat 0g); Cholesterol 35mg; Sodium 310mg; Total Carbohydrate 40g (Dietary Fiber 5g); Protein 17g **% Daily Value:** Vitamin A 130%; Vitamin C 50%; Calcium 4%; Iron 10% **Exchanges:** 1½ Starch, 1 Other Carbohydrate, 1 Vegetable, 1½ Very Lean Meat, 1 Fat **Carbohydrate Choices:** 2½

a little bit more

Finish your meal with a fortune cookie. You can purchase them near the Asian ingredients at your supermarket or at an Asian restaurant. One cookie adds about 30 calories.

broccoli and peanut chicken with noodles

Prep Time: 35 Minutes   **Start to Finish:** 35 Minutes   **Makes:** 4 servings

370 Calories

¼ cup very finely chopped green onions (about 4 medium)
1 tablespoon grated gingerroot
6 cloves garlic, finely chopped
4 teaspoons olive oil
¼ teaspoon salt
4 boneless skinless chicken breasts (1 lb)
4 oz uncooked rice noodles
1 bag (12 oz) frozen broccoli florets

1 cup chopped carrots
1 teaspoon grated lime peel
2 tablespoons fresh lime juice
2 to 3 tablespoons chopped fresh cilantro
3 tablespoons coarsely chopped unsalted peanuts
Additional chopped fresh cilantro, if desired

1. Heat gas or charcoal grill. In small bowl, mix onions, gingerroot, garlic, 2 teaspoons of the oil and the salt. Rub mixture on both sides of chicken.

2. Place chicken on grill over medium heat. Cover grill; cook 12 to 15 minutes, turning once, until juice of chicken is clear when center of thickest part is cut (at least 165°F). Transfer chicken from grill to cutting board; cover to keep warm.

3. Fill 3-quart saucepan two-thirds full of water; heat to boiling. Add rice noodles, broccoli and carrots. Cook 3 to 4 minutes or just until noodles are tender; drain. Rinse with cold water; drain again. Using kitchen scissors, cut noodles into short lengths. In medium bowl, mix lime peel, lime juice and remaining 2 teaspoons oil. Add noodle mixture and 2 to 3 tablespoons cilantro; toss gently to coat.

4. Cut chicken into thin diagonal slices. Divide noodle mixture among 4 bowls; top with chicken. Sprinkle with peanuts and additional cilantro. Serve immediately.

1 Serving: Calories 370 (Calories from Fat 110); Total Fat 12g (Saturated Fat 2g; Trans Fat 0g); Cholesterol 70mg; Sodium 260mg; Total Carbohydrate 35g (Dietary Fiber 5g); Protein 31g **% Daily Value:** Vitamin A 120%; Vitamin C 30%; Calcium 8%; Iron 10% **Exchanges:** 2 Starch, 1 Vegetable, 3 Very Lean Meat, 2 Fat **Carbohydrate Choices:** 2

a little bit less

You can use less chicken in this recipe and still get plenty of protein and feel full. Reduce the chicken to ½ pound for a dish that's 280 calories per serving.

chicken, rice and bean bake

Prep Time: 30 Minutes   **Start to Finish:** 1 Hour 20 Minutes   **Makes:** 6 servings

450 Calories

¼	cup all-purpose flour
1½	teaspoons chili powder
¼	teaspoon salt
¼	teaspoon freshly ground black pepper
2½	to 3 lb meaty chicken pieces (breast, thighs and drumsticks), skinned
2	tablespoons canola oil
1	can (15 oz) black beans, drained, rinsed

1	can (14.5 oz) diced tomatoes, undrained
1	cup tomato juice
1	box (9 oz) frozen corn
⅔	cup uncooked long-grain white rice
⅛	to ¼ teaspoon ground red pepper (cayenne)
2	cloves garlic, finely chopped

1. Heat oven to 375°F. In large resealable food-storage plastic bag, mix flour, 1 teaspoon of the chili powder, the salt and black pepper. Add half of the chicken pieces. Seal bag; shake to coat. Repeat with remaining chicken pieces.

2. In very large skillet, heat oil over medium heat. Cook chicken in oil on all sides about 10 minutes, turning occasionally, until browned. Remove chicken from skillet and set aside; discard drippings in skillet.

3. Add beans, tomatoes, tomato juice, corn, rice, remaining ½ teaspoon chili powder, the red pepper and garlic to skillet. Heat to boiling; remove from heat. Spoon rice mixture into ungreased 13×9-inch (3-quart) glass baking dish. Arrange chicken pieces on top of rice mixture.

4. Cover; bake 45 to 50 minutes or until rice is tender and juice of chicken is clear when thickest pieces are cut to bone (at least 165°F).

1 Serving: Calories 450 (Calories from Fat 100); Total Fat 11g (Saturated Fat 2.5g; Trans Fat 0g); Cholesterol 70mg; Sodium 430mg; Total Carbohydrate 54g (Dietary Fiber 10g); Protein 33g **% Daily Value:** Vitamin A 20%; Vitamin C 20%; Calcium 10%; Iron 30% **Exchanges:** 3 Starch, 1 Vegetable, 3 Very Lean Meat, 1½ Fat **Carbohydrate Choices:** 3½

chicken curry with couscous

Prep Time: 25 Minutes   **Start to Finish:** 30 Minutes   **Makes:** 6 servings

270 Calories

1	large onion, chopped (1 cup)
2	teaspoons curry powder
1⅓	cups water
⅔	cup uncooked whole wheat couscous
1	cup frozen sweet peas (from 12-oz bag), thawed
2	cups chopped cooked chicken breast
1	large red bell pepper, chopped (1½ cups)
½	cup reduced-fat mayonnaise
3	tablespoons mango chutney

1. Lightly spray 12-inch skillet with cooking spray; heat over medium heat. Add onion; cook, stirring occasionally, until crisp-tender. Stir in curry powder; cook 1 minute longer.

2. Add water, couscous and peas; heat to boiling. Stir in remaining ingredients; return to boiling. Remove from heat. Cover; let stand 5 minutes.

1 Serving: Calories 270 (Calories from Fat 80); Total Fat 9g (Saturated Fat 1.5g; Trans Fat 0g); Cholesterol 45mg; Sodium 210mg; Total Carbohydrate 28g (Dietary Fiber 3g); Protein 18g **% Daily Value:** Vitamin A 35%; Vitamin C 45%; Calcium 4%; Iron 8% **Exchanges:** 1½ Starch, ½ Vegetable, 2 Very Lean Meat, 1½ Fat **Carbohydrate Choices:** 2

a little bit more

The addition of raisins—a common ingredient in curries—will increase the sweet flavor of this dish. Stir ½ cup raisins into the recipe along with the remaining ingredients for an additional 40 calories per serving.

chicken, broccoli and parmesan pasta

Prep Time: 30 Minutes   **Start to Finish:** 30 Minutes   **Makes:** 6 servings

330 Calories

2⅔ cups uncooked whole wheat penne pasta (8 oz)

3 cups fresh broccoli florets

1 lb boneless skinless chicken breasts, cut into bite-size pieces

1 teaspoon adobo seasoning

2 tablespoons olive oil

1 clove garlic, finely chopped

¼ cup reduced-fat mayonnaise

⅛ teaspoon pepper

2 tablespoons shaved Parmesan cheese

1. In 4-quart Dutch oven, cook pasta as directed on package, omitting salt and oil, and adding broccoli during last 5 minutes of cooking time. Drain and return to Dutch oven; cover to keep warm.

2. Meanwhile, in medium bowl, toss chicken with adobo seasoning until coated. In 12-inch skillet, heat oil over medium-high heat. Add garlic; cook and stir 30 seconds. Add chicken; cook 3 to 4 minutes, stirring occasionally, until chicken is no longer pink in center.

3. Add chicken to pasta and broccoli in Dutch oven. Stir in mayonnaise and pepper. Cook over low heat, stirring occasionally, until hot. Sprinkle individual servings with cheese.

1 Serving: Calories 330 (Calories from Fat 100); Total Fat 11g (Saturated Fat 2.5g; Trans Fat 0g); Cholesterol 50mg; Sodium 160mg; Total Carbohydrate 32g (Dietary Fiber 4g); Protein 23g **% Daily Value:** Vitamin A 6%; Vitamin C 35%; Calcium 8%; Iron 10% **Exchanges:** 2 Starch, 1 Vegetable, 2 Very Lean Meat, 2 Fat **Carbohydrate Choices:** 2

a little bit more

A crisp red apple will add color to your plate and fiber to this meal—1 apple, cut into slices, will add 95 calories for each serving.

tarragon chicken linguine

Prep Time: 25 Minutes   **Start to Finish:** 25 Minutes   **Makes:** 4 servings

310
Calories

6 oz uncooked whole wheat linguine or fettuccine	2 teaspoons olive oil
1 bag (12 oz) frozen broccoli florets	¾ lb boneless skinless chicken breasts, cut into bite-size strips
½ cup reduced-sodium chicken broth	1 tablespoon chopped fresh or 1 teaspoon dried tarragon leaves
2 teaspoons cornstarch	
¼ teaspoon salt-free lemon-pepper seasoning	

1. In 4-quart Dutch oven, cook linguine as directed on package, omitting salt and oil, and adding broccoli during last 3 to 5 minutes of cooking time. Drain and return to Dutch oven; cover to keep warm.

2. Meanwhile, in small bowl, mix broth, cornstarch and lemon-pepper seasoning; set aside. In 12-inch nonstick skillet, heat oil over medium heat. Cook chicken in oil about 4 minutes, stirring frequently, until no longer pink in center.

3. Stir cornstarch mixture and stir into skillet. Cook and stir until thickened. Stir in tarragon; cook 2 minutes longer. Serve chicken mixture over linguine and broccoli.

1 Serving: Calories 310 (Calories from Fat 50); Total Fat 6g (Saturated Fat 1g; Trans Fat 0g); Cholesterol 55mg; Sodium 125mg; Total Carbohydrate 36g (Dietary Fiber 7g); Protein 28g **% Daily Value:** Vitamin A 15%; Vitamin C 25%; Calcium 6%; Iron 20% **Exchanges:** 2 Starch, ½ Vegetable, 3 Very Lean Meat, ½ Fat **Carbohydrate Choices:** 2½

a little bit more

Serve up a side of red grapes. Nutritionally, red grapes have about the same nutrients as green grapes, but red ones will provide eye-catching color contrast to the green broccoli in this dish. Add ½ cup of grapes for 50 more calories.

chicken breast cacciatore

Prep Time: 25 Minutes   **Start to Finish:** 1 Hour   **Makes:** 6 servings

370 Calories

1 tablespoon olive oil	½ cup dry white wine
6 small bone-in chicken breasts (about 2½ lb), skinned	1 teaspoon Italian seasoning
1 package (8 oz) sliced fresh mushrooms (about 3 cups)	½ teaspoon salt
1 medium onion, sliced	⅛ teaspoon pepper
1 clove garlic, finely chopped	6 oz uncooked whole wheat fettuccine or linguine
1 can (14.5 oz) no-salt-added diced tomatoes, undrained	2 tablespoons small fresh basil leaves
1 can (6 oz) no-salt-added tomato paste	

1. In very large skillet, heat oil over medium heat. Cook chicken in oil on all sides, turning occasionally, until browned. Remove chicken and set aside; reserve drippings in skillet.

2. Add mushrooms, onion and garlic to drippings in skillet. Cook about 5 minutes, stirring frequently, just until vegetables are tender. Return chicken to skillet.

3. In medium bowl, stir tomatoes, tomato paste, wine, Italian seasoning, salt and pepper. Pour over chicken and vegetables. Heat to boiling; reduce heat. Cover; simmer 30 to 35 minutes, turning chicken once, until juice of chicken is clear when thickest part is cut to bone (at least 165°F).

4. Meanwhile, cook fettuccine as directed on package, omitting salt and oil; drain. Serve fettuccine with chicken and sauce; sprinkle with basil.

1 Serving: Calories 370 (Calories from Fat 70); Total Fat 8g (Saturated Fat 1.5g; Trans Fat 0g); Cholesterol 85mg; Sodium 310mg; Total Carbohydrate 33g (Dietary Fiber 5g); Protein 38g **% Daily Value:** Vitamin A 15%; Vitamin C 10%; Calcium 6%; Iron 25% **Exchanges:** 2 Starch, 1 Vegetable, 4 Very Lean Meat, 1 Fat **Carbohydrate Choices:** 2

a little bit more

Fill your plate by serving steamed broccoli with this dish. For a spark of flavor, sprinkle fresh lemon juice over the cooked broccoli. A ½-cup serving adds just 30 calories.

easy chicken with tomatoes and spinach

Prep Time: 30 Minutes   **Start to Finish:** 30 Minutes   **Makes:** 4 servings

230 Calories

1	tablespoon olive oil	¼	teaspoon pepper
4	boneless skinless chicken breasts (about 1¼ lb)	¼	cup dry white wine or water
1	clove garlic, finely chopped	2	medium plum (Roma) tomatoes, sliced (about 1 cup)
½	teaspoon dried oregano leaves	1	bag (6 oz) fresh baby spinach leaves
½	teaspoon seasoned salt		

1. In 12-inch nonstick skillet, heat oil over medium heat. Sprinkle chicken with garlic, oregano, seasoned salt and pepper. Add chicken to skillet; cook 10 to 15 minutes, turning once, until juice of chicken is clear when center of thickest part is cut (at least 165°F).

2. Stir in wine. Arrange tomato slices on chicken. Cover; cook 2 to 3 minutes or until tomatoes are thoroughly heated.

3. Add spinach. Cover; cook 2 to 3 minutes longer or until spinach is wilted.

1 Serving: Calories 230 (Calories from Fat 70); Total Fat 8g (Saturated Fat 2g; Trans Fat 0g); Cholesterol 90mg; Sodium 290mg; Total Carbohydrate 3g (Dietary Fiber 1g); Protein 33g **% Daily Value:** Vitamin A 80%; Vitamin C 15%; Calcium 6%; Iron 15% **Exchanges:** 1 Vegetable, 4½ Very Lean Meat, 1 Fat **Carbohydrate Choices:** 0

a little bit more

A natural side dish choice for this recipe would be brown rice. Add ½ cup cooked brown rice for 100 calories per serving.

spicy ginger chicken

Prep Time: 20 Minutes   **Start to Finish:** 6 Hours 20 Minutes   **Makes:** 6 servings

300 Calories

12 chicken drumsticks or thighs, or 6 of each (2½ to 3 lb), skinned
2 cans (14.5 oz each) no-salt-added diced tomatoes
2 tablespoons quick-cooking tapioca
1 tablespoon grated gingerroot
1 tablespoon chopped fresh cilantro or Italian (flat-leaf) parsley

4 cloves garlic, finely chopped
2 teaspoons packed brown sugar
½ teaspoon salt
½ teaspoon crushed red pepper flakes
3 cups hot cooked whole-grain couscous
2 tablespoons chopped fresh Italian (flat-leaf) parsley

1. Spray 3½- to 4-quart slow cooker with cooking spray. Place chicken pieces in slow cooker.

2. Drain tomatoes, reserving juice from 1 can. In medium bowl, mix tomatoes, reserved juice, the tapioca, gingerroot, cilantro, garlic, brown sugar, salt and pepper flakes. Pour over chicken.

3. Cover; cook on Low heat setting 6 to 7 hours (or on High heat setting 3 hours to 3 hours 30 minutes).

4. Skim fat from sauce. Serve chicken and sauce with couscous in shallow bowls. Sprinkle with parsley.

1 Serving: Calories 300 (Calories from Fat 50); Total Fat 6g (Saturated Fat 2g; Trans Fat 0g); Cholesterol 70mg; Sodium 280mg; Total Carbohydrate 33g (Dietary Fiber 2g); Protein 28g **% Daily Value:** Vitamin A 15%; Vitamin C 10%; Calcium 6%; Iron 15% **Exchanges:** 1½ Starch, ½ Other Carbohydrate, 3½ Very Lean Meat, ½ Fat **Carbohydrate Choices:** 2

fresh citrus chicken

Prep Time: 25 Minutes   **Start to Finish:** 25 Minutes   **Makes:** 4 servings

190 Calories

1	tablespoon canola oil
4	boneless skinless chicken breasts (1 to 1¼ lb)
3	cloves garlic, thinly sliced
1	teaspoon grated lime peel
2	tablespoons fresh lime juice

2	teaspoons chopped fresh cilantro
⅛	teaspoon crushed red pepper flakes
1	medium orange, peeled, coarsely chopped

1. In 12-inch skillet, heat oil over medium heat. Add chicken and garlic; cook 8 to 10 minutes, turning chicken once and stirring garlic occasionally, until juice of chicken is clear when center of thickest part is cut (at least 165°F).

2. In small bowl, stir lime peel, lime juice, cilantro and pepper flakes. Pour into skillet. Place chopped orange on chicken. Cover; cook 1 to 2 minutes longer or until thoroughly heated. Serve any pan juices with chicken and orange pieces.

1 Serving: Calories 190 (Calories from Fat 60); Total Fat 7g (Saturated Fat 1.5g; Trans Fat 0g); Cholesterol 70mg; Sodium 65mg; Total Carbohydrate 5g (Dietary Fiber 1g); Protein 26g **% Daily Value:** Vitamin A 2%; Vitamin C 20%; Calcium 4%; Iron 6% **Exchanges:** ½ Starch, 3½ Very Lean Meat, 1 Fat **Carbohydrate Choices:** ½

a little bit more

Asparagus would be a great accompaniment to this citrus-flavored dish. A 1 cup serving of steamed asparagus adds 30 calories. Or, grill the asparagus for even more flavor.

crispy-coated chicken

Prep Time: 10 Minutes **Start to Finish:** 35 Minutes **Makes:** 4 servings

250 Calories

1	cup finely crushed multigrain tortilla chips
½	teaspoon dried oregano leaves, crushed
¼	teaspoon ground cumin
¼	teaspoon freshly ground black pepper

1	egg
4	boneless skinless chicken breasts (1 to 1¼ lb)
	Shredded romaine lettuce, if desired
	Chunky-style salsa, if desired
	Sliced avocado, if desired

1. Heat oven to 375°F. Spray 15×10×1-inch pan with cooking spray. In shallow bowl, mix tortilla chips, oregano, cumin and pepper. In another shallow bowl, beat egg slightly. Dip chicken in egg, then coat with tortilla chip mixture. Place in pan.

2. Bake about 25 minutes or until juice of chicken is clear when center of thickest part is cut (at least 165°F). Serve chicken on lettuce with salsa and avocado.

1 Serving: Calories 250 (Calories from Fat 90); Total Fat 10g (Saturated Fat 2g; Trans Fat 0g); Cholesterol 115mg; Sodium 150mg; Total Carbohydrate 11g (Dietary Fiber 0g); Protein 28g **% Daily Value:** Vitamin A 2%; Vitamin C 0%; Calcium 2%; Iron 10% **Exchanges:** ½ Starch, 4 Very Lean Meat, 1½ Fat **Carbohydrate Choices:** 1

a little bit more

Need dinner on the run? Serve the baked chicken on a whole-grain burger bun. Top each with a thin slice of avocado and 1 tablespoon salsa for about 180 additional calories per serving.

chicken with creamy cucumber sauce

Prep Time: 35 Minutes **Start to Finish:** 35 Minutes **Makes:** 4 servings

170 Calories

¾ cup plain fat-free yogurt

4 medium green onions, thinly sliced (¼ cup)

2 teaspoons chopped fresh mint leaves or ½ teaspoon mint flakes

½ teaspoon ground cumin

¼ teaspoon salt

¼ teaspoon pepper

1 cup chopped seeded cucumber

4 boneless skinless chicken breasts (1 to 1¼ lb)

Fresh mint leaves, if desired

1. In medium bowl, stir yogurt, onions, chopped mint, cumin, salt and ⅛ teaspoon of the pepper. Transfer half of the yogurt mixture to small bowl; set aside. Stir cucumber into remaining yogurt mixture; refrigerate sauce until serving time.

2. Set oven control to broil. Sprinkle chicken with remaining ⅛ teaspoon pepper. Place chicken on broiler pan. Broil with tops 4 to 5 inches from heat 12 to 15 minutes, turning once, until juice of chicken is clear when center of thickest part is cut (at least 165°F) and brushing with reserved yogurt mixture toward end of cooking time.

3. Serve chicken with cucumber-yogurt sauce. Garnish with mint leaves.

1 Serving: Calories 170 (Calories from Fat 35); Total Fat 4g (Saturated Fat 1g; Trans Fat 0g); Cholesterol 70mg; Sodium 250mg; Total Carbohydrate 6g (Dietary Fiber 0g); Protein 28g **% Daily Value:** Vitamin A 2%; Vitamin C 0%; Calcium 10%; Iron 8% **Exchanges:** ½ Other Carbohydrate, 4 Very Lean Meat, ½ Fat **Carbohydrate Choices:** ½

a little bit more

Fruited Tabbouleh with Walnuts and Feta (page 84) will complement this chicken recipe beautifully. One ½ cup serving of the tabbouleh together with a serving of the chicken and sauce is only 330 calories.

asian chicken and rice

Prep Time: 15 Minutes   **Start to Finish:** 15 Minutes   **Makes:** 4 servings (1 cup each)

270
Calories

1 package (8.8 oz) microwavable brown rice	½ cup frozen sweet peas (from 12-oz bag)
1 tablespoon canola oil	¼ cup stir-fry sauce
1 lb uncooked chicken breast tenders (not breaded), cut in half crosswise	2 tablespoons sliced almonds, toasted*

1. Cook rice in microwave as directed on package.

2. Meanwhile, in 12-inch skillet, heat oil over medium-high heat. Add chicken and peas; cook 2 to 3 minutes, stirring frequently, until chicken is no longer pink in center and peas are crisp-tender.

3. Stir hot rice into skillet. Add stir-fry sauce; cook and stir until hot. Sprinkle individual servings with almonds.

*To toast almonds, cook in an ungreased skillet over medium heat for 5 to 7 minutes, stirring frequently, until almonds begin to brown, then stirring constantly until light brown.

1 Serving: Calories 270 (Calories from Fat 60); Total Fat 7g (Saturated Fat 1.5g; Trans Fat 0g); Cholesterol 50mg; Sodium 670mg; Total Carbohydrate 23g (Dietary Fiber 2g); Protein 27g **% Daily Value:** Vitamin A 6%; Vitamin C 0%; Calcium 0%; Iron 4% **Exchanges:** 1 Starch, ½ Other Carbohydrate, 3½ Very Lean Meat, 1 Fat **Carbohydrate Choices:** 1½

a little bit more

Add a bit of sweetness to your meal by serving pineapple on the side. A 1 cup portion of cubed fresh pineapple adds 80 calories per serving.

stuffed chicken parmesan

Prep Time: 20 Minutes   **Start to Finish:** 55 Minutes   **Makes:** 6 servings

280
Calories

6   boneless skinless chicken breasts (1¾ to 2 lb)

1   box (10 oz) frozen cut spinach, thawed, well drained

2   oz ⅓-less-fat cream cheese (Neufchâtel), softened

¼   cup shredded Parmesan cheese (1 oz)

1½   teaspoons dried basil leaves

1   clove garlic, finely chopped

¼   cup fat-free egg product

12   stone-ground wheat crackers, crushed (about ½ cup)

½   teaspoon pepper

1   cup Italian herb pasta sauce (from 25.5-oz jar)

¼   cup shredded mozzarella cheese (1 oz)

1. Heat oven to 375°F. Spray 13×9-inch (3-quart) glass baking dish with cooking spray. Between pieces of plastic wrap or waxed paper, place each chicken breast smooth side down; gently pound with flat side of meat mallet or rolling pin until about ¼ inch thick.

2. In medium bowl, mix spinach, cream cheese, Parmesan cheese, ½ teaspoon of the basil and all the garlic until blended. Spread about 1 tablespoon spinach mixture over each chicken breast; roll up tightly. Secure with toothpicks, if necessary.

3. In small shallow bowl, place egg product. In another small shallow bowl, mix cracker crumbs, remaining 1 teaspoon basil and the pepper. Dip chicken roll-ups in egg product, then coat with crumb mixture. Place seam side down in baking dish.

4. Bake uncovered 20 minutes. Pour pasta sauce over chicken; sprinkle with mozzarella cheese. Bake 10 to 15 minutes longer or until thermometer inserted in center of chicken reads at least 165°F. Remove toothpicks before serving.

1 Serving: Calories 280 (Calories from Fat 90); Total Fat 10g (Saturated Fat 4g; Trans Fat 0g); Cholesterol 95mg; Sodium 440mg; Total Carbohydrate 10g (Dietary Fiber 2g); Protein 37g **% Daily Value:** Vitamin A 90%; Vitamin C 2%; Calcium 20%; Iron 15% **Exchanges:** ½ Starch, 5 Very Lean Meat, 1½ Fat **Carbohydrate Choices:** ½

easy green enchiladas

Prep Time: 10 Minutes   **Start to Finish:** 35 Minutes   **Makes:** 4 servings

410 Calories

8 soft corn tortillas (6 inch)
2 cups shredded cooked chicken
1¾ cups green tomatillo salsa
1 cup crumbled or shredded Manchego or Chihuahua cheese or Mexican cheese blend (4 oz)

¼ cup sour cream
1 medium onion, finely chopped (½ cup)
Fresh cilantro leaves, if desired

1. Heat oven to 350°F. Wrap 4 tortillas at a time in microwavable paper towels. Microwave on High 20 to 30 seconds or until they can be folded without cracking.

2. Spoon chicken evenly in center of each tortilla; roll up. Place in ungreased 9-inch square or 11×7-inch (2-quart) glass baking dish. Pour salsa over enchiladas. Sprinkle with cheese, sour cream and onion.

3. Bake uncovered 15 to 25 minutes or until thoroughly heated. Garnish with cilantro. Serve immediately.

1 Serving: Calories 410 (Calories from Fat 160); Total Fat 18g (Saturated Fat 9g; Trans Fat 0g); Cholesterol 95mg; Sodium 610mg; Total Carbohydrate 32g (Dietary Fiber 4g); Protein 30g **% Daily Value:** Vitamin A 10%; Vitamin C 60%; Calcium 25%; Iron 15% **Exchanges:** 1½ Starch, 2 Vegetable, 2 Lean Meat, 1 High-Fat Meat, ½ Fat **Carbohydrate Choices:** 2

a little bit more

Serve the enchiladas with a side of fat-free refried black beans for an additional 90 calories per ½-cup serving.

roasted maple-rum turkey breast with sweet potato stuffing

Prep Time: 25 Minutes   **Start to Finish:** 3 Hours 15 Minutes   **Makes:** 10 servings

320 Calories

STUFFING

- 12 slices white whole-grain bread, cut into ½-inch cubes (7 cups)
- 1 tablespoon olive oil
- ¾ cup chopped onion
- ½ cup sliced celery
- 1 large sweet potato (about 12 oz), peeled, cut into ½-inch cubes (2 cups)
- ⅓ cup sweetened dried cranberries
- 1 can (14 oz) reduced-sodium chicken broth
- 1 tablespoon chopped fresh or 1 teaspoon dried sage leaves
- 1½ teaspoons chopped fresh or ½ teaspoon dried thyme leaves
- ¼ teaspoon salt
- ¼ teaspoon pepper

TURKEY AND GLAZE

- 1 whole turkey breast (4½ to 5 lb), thawed if frozen
- ⅓ cup real maple syrup
- 2 tablespoons dark rum
- ¼ teaspoon salt

1. Heat oven to 350°F. Spray 13×9-inch (3-quart) glass baking dish with cooking spray. On ungreased large cookie sheet with sides, place bread cubes. Bake 15 minutes, stirring once, until light golden brown.

2. Meanwhile, in 12-inch nonstick skillet, heat oil over medium-high heat. Cook onion and celery in oil 4 to 5 minutes, stirring frequently, until crisp-tender. In large bowl, toss onion mixture, toasted bread cubes and remaining stuffing ingredients until well mixed. Spoon into baking dish.

3. Place turkey breast, skin side up, on top of stuffing in center of baking dish. Insert ovenproof meat thermometer so tip is in thickest part of breast and does not touch bone. Cover stuffing with 2 pieces of foil, leaving turkey uncovered. Roast 1 hour.

4. In 1-quart saucepan, heat syrup, rum and ¼ teaspoon salt to boiling; do not stir. Boil uncovered 3 to 4 minutes or until mixture coats and runs off spoon.

5. Brush turkey with half of the glaze. Roast 30 minutes. Brush with remaining glaze. Roast 15 to 45 minutes longer or until thermometer reads at least 165°F. Transfer turkey to serving platter; tent with foil. Let stand 15 minutes for easier carving. Meanwhile, stir stuffing; bake uncovered 15 to 20 minutes longer.

1 Serving: Calories 320 (Calories from Fat 35); Total Fat 4g (Saturated Fat 1g; Trans Fat 0g); Cholesterol 105mg; Sodium 440mg; Total Carbohydrate 29g (Dietary Fiber 3g); Protein 41g **% Daily Value:** Vitamin A 80%; Vitamin C 0%; Calcium 8%; Iron 15% **Exchanges:** ½ Starch, 1½ Other Carbohydrate, 5 Very Lean Meat, ½ Lean Meat **Carbohydrate Choices:** 2

tandoori turkey tenderloins

Prep Time: 25 Minutes   **Start to Finish:** 6 Hours 25 Minutes   **Makes:** 4 servings

170 Calories

4 cloves garlic, finely chopped	¼ teaspoon salt
1 tablespoon grated gingerroot	2 turkey breast tenderloins (8 oz each), halved lengthwise
1 tablespoon curry powder	¾ cup plain fat-free yogurt
2 teaspoons olive oil	
1 teaspoon ground cumin	

1. In small bowl, mix garlic, gingerroot, curry powder, oil, cumin and salt. Spread mixture evenly on all sides of turkey. If desired, wear disposable gloves so the spices don't stain your hands. Place turkey in glass baking dish. Cover; refrigerate 6 hours or up to 24 hours.

2. Heat gas or charcoal grill. Place turkey on grill over medium heat. Cook uncovered 12 to 15 minutes, turning once, until juice of turkey is clear when center of thickest part is cut (at least 165°F). Slice turkey; serve with yogurt.

1 Serving: Calories 170 (Calories from Fat 35); Total Fat 3.5g (Saturated Fat 0.5g; Trans Fat 0g); Cholesterol 75mg; Sodium 230mg; Total Carbohydrate 6g (Dietary Fiber 0g); Protein 29g **% Daily Value:** Vitamin A 0%; Vitamin C 0%; Calcium 10%; Iron 15% **Exchanges:** ½ Starch, 4 Very Lean Meat **Carbohydrate Choices:** ½

a little bit more

Vegetable Confetti (below) makes a terrific serve-with for this grilled turkey. One serving adds only 30 calories and is a great source of vitamins A and C.

Vegetable Confetti Mix 1½ cups shredded carrots (2 medium), 1 cup shredded zucchini (1 small), 1 cup chopped bell pepper (1 medium), ¼ cup fat-free Italian dressing, and ¼ teaspoon pepper in a nonmetal bowl. Makes 4 servings.

cilantro-orange marinated flank steak

Prep Time: 40 Minutes **Start to Finish:** 4 Hours 40 Minutes **Makes:** 4 servings

250 Calories

1 lb beef flank steak, trimmed of fat	1 teaspoon ground coriander
⅓ cup orange juice	¼ teaspoon salt
¼ cup chopped fresh cilantro	¼ teaspoon crushed red pepper flakes
2 tablespoons red wine vinegar	
1 tablespoon olive oil	2 bell peppers (any color), cut in half, seeded
4 cloves garlic, finely chopped	
2 teaspoons ground cumin	1 red onion, cut into ½-inch-thick slices

1. On both sides of steak, make cuts about 1 inch apart and ¼ inch deep in crisscross pattern. Place steak in resealable food-storage plastic bag. In small bowl, stir orange juice, cilantro, vinegar, oil, garlic, cumin, coriander, salt and pepper flakes. Pour over steak. Seal bag; turn to coat. Refrigerate 4 to 6 hours to marinate, turning bag occasionally.

2. Heat gas or charcoal grill. Drain steak, reserving marinade. Brush bell pepper halves and onion slices with reserved marinade; set aside. Discard any remaining marinade.

3. Place steak on grill over medium heat. Cover grill; cook 8 minutes. Turn steak. Place vegetables, cut sides down, on grill. Cover grill; cook 9 to 13 minutes, turning vegetables occasionally, until steak is of desired doneness (160°F for medium) and vegetables are crisp-tender.

4. Thinly slice steak across grain; cut bell peppers into strips. Serve with grilled onion.

1 Serving: Calories 250 (Calories from Fat 80); Total Fat 8g (Saturated Fat 2g; Trans Fat 0g); Cholesterol 85mg; Sodium 200mg; Total Carbohydrate 9g (Dietary Fiber 1g); Protein 34g **% Daily Value:** Vitamin A 8%; Vitamin C 50%; Calcium 4%; Iron 25% **Exchanges:** ½ Starch, ½ Vegetable, 2½ Very Lean Meat, 2 Lean Meat **Carbohydrate Choices:** ½

a little bit more

Splurging once in a while, believe it or not, can help you keep from backsliding when on a diet! Enjoy a 12 ounce serving of a light Mexican beer with this entrée for approximately 110 added calories.

argentinean pork and grilled greens with chimichurri sauce

Prep Time: 35 Minutes   **Start to Finish:** 55 Minutes   **Makes:** 4 servings

260 Calories

¼ cup red wine vinegar	1 clove garlic, finely chopped
¼ cup olive oil	1 pork tenderloin (1 lb)
2 teaspoons grated lemon peel	2 hearts romaine lettuce, cut lengthwise in half
2 tablespoons fresh lemon juice	½ cup finely chopped fresh Italian (flat-leaf) parsley
½ teaspoon salt	
¼ teaspoon crushed red pepper flakes	

1. In small bowl, mix vinegar, oil, lemon peel, lemon juice, salt, pepper flakes and garlic with whisk. Place pork in large resealable food-storage plastic bag. Pour ¼ cup of the marinade over pork. Seal bag and turn to coat pork with marinade. Refrigerate at least 20 minutes but no longer than 2 hours. Reserve remaining marinade for sauce; refrigerate until serving time.

2. Spray grill rack with cooking spray. Heat gas or charcoal grill. Remove pork from marinade; discard marinade. Place pork on grill over medium heat. Cover grill; cook about 20 minutes, turning occasionally, until meat thermometer inserted in center reads 145°F. Add lettuce to grill for last 2 minutes of cooking time, turning once, until slightly wilted and grill marks appear. Transfer pork and greens to serving platter. Tent with foil and let rest 3 minutes.

3. Meanwhile, stir parsley into reserved marinade. Cut tenderloin into 12 slices. On each of 4 plates, place 3 slices pork and half a romaine heart. Drizzle about 2 tablespoons chimichurri sauce over pork and greens.

1 Serving: Calories 260 (Calories from Fat 160); Total Fat 18g (Saturated Fat 3.5g; Trans Fat 0g); Cholesterol 50mg; Sodium 360mg; Total Carbohydrate 2g (Dietary Fiber 0g); Protein 22g **% Daily Value:** Vitamin A 40%; Vitamin C 15%; Calcium 2%; Iron 6% **Exchanges:** ½ Vegetable, ½ Very Lean Meat, 2½ Lean Meat, 2 Fat **Carbohydrate Choices:** 0

a little bit more

Enjoy a 5 ounce glass of South American red wine with this flavorful meal for an additional 125 calories per serving.

sesame beef and green beans

Prep Time: 30 Minutes   **Start to Finish:** 30 Minutes   **Makes:** 4 servings

360 Calories

1   bag (12 oz) frozen whole green beans
½   cup orange juice
2   tablespoons reduced-sodium soy sauce
1   tablespoon sesame oil
1   teaspoon cornstarch
½   teaspoon grated orange peel
½   cup diagonally sliced green onions (about 8 medium)

1   tablespoon grated gingerroot or 1 teaspoon ground ginger
2   cloves garlic, finely chopped
1   teaspoon canola oil
¾   lb boneless beef sirloin steak, trimmed of fat, thinly sliced
2   cups hot cooked brown rice
2   teaspoons sesame seed, toasted*
2   oranges, peeled and sectioned or thinly sliced crosswise

1. In 2-quart saucepan, heat small amount of water to boiling. Add green beans. Cover; cook 5 to 7 minutes or until crisp-tender. (If desired, partially thaw and cut in half crosswise before cooking.) Drain; set aside.

2. Meanwhile, in small bowl, stir orange juice, soy sauce, sesame oil, cornstarch and orange peel; set aside.

3. Spray 12-inch skillet with cooking spray; heat over medium-high heat. Add onions, gingerroot and garlic; cook 1 minute, stirring constantly. Add green beans; cook 2 minutes. Remove vegetables from skillet.

4. Carefully add canola oil to hot skillet. Add beef; cook about 3 minutes, stirring frequently, to the desired doneness. Remove from skillet. Stir sauce; add to skillet. Cook and stir until thickened and bubbly; cook and stir 2 minutes longer. Return meat and vegetables to skillet; cook until thoroughly heated, stirring to coat all ingredients with sauce.

5. To serve, place ½ cup rice on each of 4 plates. Top with 1¼ cups beef mixture. Sprinkle with sesame seed. Serve with orange sections.

   *To toast sesame seed, sprinkle in ungreased skillet. Cook over medium-low heat 5 to 7 minutes, stirring frequently until browning begins, then stirring constantly until golden brown.

1 Serving: Calories 360 (Calories from Fat 80); Total Fat 9g (Saturated Fat 2g; Trans Fat 0g); Cholesterol 55mg; Sodium 310mg; Total Carbohydrate 42g (Dietary Fiber 7g); Protein 27g **% Daily Value:** Vitamin A 15%; Vitamin C 40%; Calcium 8%; Iron 20% **Exchanges:** 2 Starch, ½ Fruit, 1 Vegetable, 2½ Very Lean Meat, 1½ Fat **Carbohydrate Choices:** 3

beef with mint-cucumber sauce

Prep Time: 35 Minutes   **Start to Finish:** 35 Minutes   **Makes:** 4 servings

180 Calories

1   container (6 oz) fat-free Greek plain yogurt
¼   cup coarsely shredded unpeeled cucumber
1   tablespoon finely chopped red onion
1   tablespoon chopped fresh mint

¼   teaspoon sugar
¼   teaspoon salt
⅛   teaspoon pepper
1   lb boneless beef sirloin steak, 1 inch thick, trimmed of fat
½   teaspoon Greek seasoning

1. Heat gas or charcoal grill. In small bowl, stir yogurt, cucumber, onion, mint, sugar, salt and pepper; refrigerate until serving time.

2. Sprinkle steak with Greek seasoning. Place steak on grill over medium heat. Cover grill; cook 15 to 17 minutes for medium-rare (145°F), 20 to 22 minutes for medium (160°F), turning once.

3. Thinly slice steak across grain. Serve with sauce.

1 Serving: Calories 180 (Calories from Fat 35); Total Fat 4g (Saturated Fat 1.5g; Trans Fat 0g); Cholesterol 75mg; Sodium 330mg; Total Carbohydrate 3g (Dietary Fiber 0g); Protein 33g **% Daily Value:** Vitamin A 4%; Vitamin C 0%; Calcium 10%; Iron 15% **Exchanges:** 3½ Very Lean Meat, 1 Lean Meat **Carbohydrate Choices:** 0

a little bit more

It's a snap—sugar snap peas, that is. Add a 1 cup serving, fresh or steamed, for an additional 80 calories.

mexican ground beef and noodles

Prep Time: 25 Minutes   **Start to Finish:** 1 Hour   **Makes:** 6 servings (1 cup each)

330 Calories

1⅓ cups uncooked whole wheat or regular rotini pasta (4 oz)

¾ lb extra-lean (at least 90%) ground beef

2 cloves garlic, finely chopped

1 can (15 oz) black beans, drained, rinsed

1 can (14.5 oz) no-salt-added diced tomatoes, undrained

¾ cup mild or medium salsa

1 teaspoon dried oregano leaves

½ teaspoon ground cumin

½ teaspoon chili powder

½ cup shredded reduced-fat Colby–Monterey Jack cheese blend (2 oz)

⅓ cup reduced-fat sour cream

3 medium green onions, sliced (3 tablespoons)

2 teaspoons coarsely chopped fresh cilantro

½ teaspoon grated lime peel

1. Heat oven to 350°F. Cook pasta as directed on package, omitting salt and oil and using minimum cook time; drain and return to saucepan.

2. Meanwhile, in large skillet, cook beef and garlic over medium-high heat 5 to 7 minutes, stirring occasionally, until beef is thoroughly cooked; drain. Stir beef into pasta in saucepan. Stir in beans, tomatoes, salsa, oregano, cumin and chili powder. Spoon mixture evenly into ungreased 1½- or 2-quart casserole.

3. Cover; bake about 30 minutes or until thoroughly heated. Uncover and sprinkle with cheese. Bake about 3 minutes longer or until cheese is melted.

4. In small bowl, stir sour cream, 2 tablespoons of the onions, the cilantro and lime peel. Top each serving with a spoonful of sour cream mixture. Sprinkle with remaining 1 tablespoon onions.

1 Serving: Calories 330 (Calories from Fat 70); Total Fat 8g (Saturated Fat 3.5g; Trans Fat 0g); Cholesterol 40mg; Sodium 260mg; Total Carbohydrate 42g (Dietary Fiber 9g); Protein 23g **% Daily Value:** Vitamin A 10%; Vitamin C 10%; Calcium 15%; Iron 25% **Exchanges:** 2½ Starch, ½ Vegetable, 2 Lean Meat **Carbohydrate Choices:** 3

beef and noodle layered casserole

Prep Time: 30 Minutes   **Start to Finish:** 1 Hour 35 Minutes   **Makes:** 6 servings (1 cup each)

400 Calories

3 cups uncooked medium egg noodles (6 oz)	1 cup plain fat-free yogurt
1 lb extra-lean (at least 90%) ground beef	1 package (8 oz) ⅓-less-fat cream cheese (Neufchâtel), softened
2 cans (8 oz each) tomato sauce	½ cup fat-free (skim) milk
1 teaspoon dried basil leaves	1 small onion, chopped (⅓ cup)
½ teaspoon sugar	1 box (9 oz) frozen chopped spinach, cooked, well drained
½ teaspoon garlic powder	⅓ cup shredded reduced-fat Cheddar cheese
¼ teaspoon salt	
¼ teaspoon pepper	

1. Heat oven to 350°F. Spray 2-quart casserole with cooking spray. Cook noodles as directed on package, omitting salt and oil and using minimum cook time. Drain; set aside.

2. Meanwhile, in 12-inch skillet, cook beef over medium-high heat 5 to 7 minutes, stirring occasionally, until thoroughly cooked; drain. Stir in tomato sauce, basil, sugar, garlic powder, salt and pepper. Heat to boiling; reduce heat. Simmer uncovered 5 minutes.

3. In medium bowl, beat yogurt and cream cheese with electric mixer on medium speed until smooth. Stir in milk and onion. In casserole, layer half of the noodles (about 2 cups), half of the meat mixture (about 1½ cups), half of the cream cheese mixture (about 1 cup) and all of the spinach. Top with remaining meat mixture and noodles. Refrigerate remaining cream cheese mixture until needed.

4. Cover with lightly greased foil. Bake about 45 minutes or until thoroughly heated. Uncover; spread with remaining cream cheese mixture. Sprinkle with Cheddar cheese. Bake about 10 minutes longer or until cheese is melted. Let stand 10 minutes before serving.

1 Serving: Calories 400 (Calories from Fat 150); Total Fat 17g (Saturated Fat 8g; Trans Fat 0.5g); Cholesterol 100mg; Sodium 770mg; Total Carbohydrate 33g (Dietary Fiber 3g); Protein 28g **% Daily Value:** Vitamin A 90%; Vitamin C 8%; Calcium 25%; Iron 20% **Exchanges:** 1½ Starch, ½ Other Carbohydrate, 3½ Lean Meat, 1 Fat **Carbohydrate Choices:** 2

a little bit more

Make an easy Caesar salad to go with this delicious casserole. For each serving, toss 1 cup torn romaine lettuce with 1 tablespoon light Caesar dressing for an extra 60 calories.

moroccan spinach lasagna

Prep Time: 40 Minutes   **Start to Finish:** 1 Hour 35 Minutes   **Makes:** 12 servings

290 Calories

9 uncooked whole wheat lasagna noodles

2 tablespoons olive oil

1 can (15 oz) chickpeas (garbanzo beans), drained, rinsed

1 teaspoon ground cumin

¾ teaspoon paprika

¼ teaspoon ground red pepper (cayenne)

1 medium onion, chopped (½ cup)

2 cloves garlic, finely chopped

1 jar (25 oz) marinara sauce

1½ cups shredded carrots (2 medium)

1 container (15 oz) fat-free ricotta cheese

1 bag (1 lb) frozen cut leaf spinach, thawed, squeezed to drain

2 cups shredded mozzarella cheese (8 oz)

1. Heat oven to 350°F. Spray 13×9-inch (3-quart) glass baking dish with cooking spray. Cook and drain noodles as directed on package, omitting salt and oil and using minimum cook time. Drain; rinse with cold water to cool. Drain well; lay noodles flat.

2. Meanwhile, in 12-inch nonstick skillet, heat oil over medium heat. Cook chickpeas, cumin, paprika and red pepper in oil 5 minutes, stirring occasionally. Add onion and garlic; cook about 3 minutes, stirring occasionally, until vegetables are crisp-tender. Stir in marinara sauce and carrots. Heat to boiling; remove from heat.

3. In medium bowl, mix ricotta cheese and spinach. Spread about ½ cup marinara sauce mixture in baking dish. Top with 3 noodles, 1½ cups sauce mixture, half of the ricotta mixture and ¾ cup of the mozzarella cheese. Repeat layers once. Top with remaining noodles, sauce mixture and mozzarella cheese.

4. Cover; bake 35 minutes. Uncover dish; bake 10 to 15 minutes longer or until bubbly. Let stand 5 minutes before serving.

1 Serving: Calories 290 (Calories from Fat 80); Total Fat 9g (Saturated Fat 3g; Trans Fat 0g); Cholesterol 20mg; Sodium 560mg; Total Carbohydrate 35g (Dietary Fiber 5g); Protein 15g **% Daily Value:** Vitamin A 120%; Vitamin C 6%; Calcium 30%; Iron 15% **Exchanges:** 1 Starch, 1 Other Carbohydrate, 1 Vegetable, 1 Very Lean Meat, ½ Medium-Fat Meat, 1 Fat **Carbohydrate Choices:** 2

a little bit more

Round out this flavorful dish with a slice of baguette and a green salad with light balsamic vinaigrette dressing. A 1-inch slice of baguette and 1 cup salad greens with 1 tablespoon dressing will add 140 calories per serving.

slow cooker chipotle beef stew

Prep Time: 15 Minutes   **Start to Finish:** 8 Hours 15 Minutes   **Makes:** 6 servings (1⅓ cups each)

300 Calories

STEW

- 1   bag (12 oz) frozen whole kernel corn
- 1   lb boneless beef top sirloin, trimmed of fat, cut into 1-inch cubes
- 1   chipotle chile in adobo sauce (from 7-oz can), finely chopped
- 2   large onions, chopped (2 cups)
- 2   poblano chiles, seeded, chopped
- 3   cloves garlic, finely chopped
- 2   cans (14.5 oz each) diced tomatoes, undrained
- 1½ teaspoons ground cumin
- ½   teaspoon salt
- ¼   teaspoon cracked black pepper

TOPPINGS

- 1   avocado, pitted, peeled and cut into 12 wedges
- 12 baked tortilla chips, crushed
- 6   small sprigs cilantro, coarsely chopped
- 6   tablespoons reduced-fat sour cream

1. Spray 4- to 5-quart slow cooker with cooking spray. In small microwavable bowl, microwave corn uncovered on High 2 minutes or until thawed. In slow cooker, mix corn and remaining stew ingredients.

2. Cover; cook on Low heat setting 8 to 10 hours (or on High heat setting 4 to 5 hours).

3. Divide stew evenly among 6 bowls. Top with avocado, tortilla chips, cilantro and sour cream.

1 Serving: Calories 300 (Calories from Fat 80); Total Fat 9g (Saturated Fat 3g; Trans Fat 0g); Cholesterol 60mg; Sodium 590mg; Total Carbohydrate 29g (Dietary Fiber 5g); Protein 25g **% Daily Value:** Vitamin A 25%; Vitamin C 25%; Calcium 6%; Iron 20% **Exchanges:** 1½ Starch, 1 Vegetable, 2½ Lean Meat **Carbohydrate Choices:** 2

a little bit more

Chips and salsa are a crunchy and flavorful side to serve with this stew. One ounce of baked tortilla chips and 2 tablespoons salsa adds 130 calories per serving.

beef and sweet potato stew

Prep Time: 20 Minutes   **Start to Finish:** 7 Hours 20 Minutes   **Makes:** 4 servings (2 cups each)

430 Calories

1¼ lb lean beef stew meat, cut into 1-inch pieces
2 medium sweet potatoes, peeled, halved lengthwise and sliced ½ inch thick (3 cups)
1 medium onion, cut into wedges
1 can (14 oz) beef broth
1 teaspoon ground cumin
¼ teaspoon ground cinnamon
¼ teaspoon ground red pepper (cayenne)

⅛ teaspoon salt
4 cloves garlic, finely chopped
1 can (14.5 oz) no-salt-added diced tomatoes, undrained
½ cup dried apricots or plums, quartered
2 tablespoons chopped unsalted peanuts
   Sliced green onions, if desired

1. Spray 3½- to 4-quart slow cooker with cooking spray. In slow cooker, mix beef, sweet potatoes and onion. Stir in broth, cumin, cinnamon, red pepper, salt and garlic.

2. Cover; cook on Low heat setting 7 to 8 hours (or on High heat setting 3 hours 30 minutes to 4 hours).

3. Stir in tomatoes and apricots. Sprinkle individual servings with peanuts and green onions.

1 Serving: Calories 430 (Calories from Fat 160); Total Fat 17g (Saturated Fat 6g; Trans Fat 0.5g); Cholesterol 75mg; Sodium 550mg; Total Carbohydrate 37g (Dietary Fiber 5g); Protein 31g **% Daily Value:** Vitamin A 320%; Vitamin C 25%; Calcium 10%; Iron 20% **Exchanges:** 1½ Starch, 1 Other Carbohydrate, ½ Vegetable, 3½ Lean Meat, 1 Fat
Carbohydrate Choices: 2½

a little bit more

A slice of dark pumpernickel bread is a great addition to this stew. Not only does it round out the meal, but it can be used to soak up every bit of the delicious broth. One slice adds about 65 calories.

dijon steak and potato stew

Prep Time: 20 Minutes   **Start to Finish:** 45 Minutes   **Makes:** 4 servings

1	lb boneless beef sirloin, cut into [1/2]-inch pieces	¼	teaspoon dried thyme leaves
½	teaspoon peppered seasoned salt	4	unpeeled small red potatoes, cut into ½- to ¾-inch cubes (about 2 cups)
2	jars (12 oz each) home-style beef gravy	1½	cups frozen cut green beans
1	cup water	2	medium carrots, sliced (1 cup)
2	tablespoons Dijon mustard		

1. Sprinkle beef with peppered seasoned salt. In 4-quart Dutch oven or 12-inch nonstick skillet, cook beef over medium-high heat about 4 minutes, stirring frequently, until brown.

2. Stir in gravy, water, mustard and thyme until well blended. Stir in potatoes, green beans and carrots. Heat to boiling; reduce heat to medium-low.

3. Cover; cook 20 to 22 minutes, stirring occasionally, until potatoes and beans are tender.

1 Serving: Calories 300 (Calories from Fat 70); Total Fat 8g (Saturated Fat 3g, Trans Fat 0g); Cholesterol 65mg; Sodium 1370mg; Total Carbohydrate 28g (Dietary Fiber 5g, Sugars 3g); Protein 32g **% Daily Value:** Vitamin A 120%; Vitamin C 10%; Calcium 6%; Iron 30% **Exchanges:** 1 ½ Starch, 1 Vegetable, 3½ Very Lean Meat, 1 Fat
Carbohydrate Choices: 1½

whiskey-dijon barbecued pork chops with grilled veggies

Prep Time: 35 Minutes   **Start to Finish:** 35 Minutes   **Makes:** 4 servings

270 Calories

⅓ cup Dijon mustard
¼ cup packed brown sugar
¼ cup whiskey
2 tablespoons molasses
2 tablespoons cider vinegar
1 teaspoon red pepper sauce

1 large sweet onion, cut into ¼-inch-thick slices
2 medium tomatoes, cut in half
4 bone-in pork loin or rib chops, ½ inch thick (1 lb), trimmed of fat
Chopped fresh Italian (flat-leaf) parsley if desired

1. Spray grill rack with cooking spray. Heat gas or charcoal grill. In 1-quart saucepan, stir mustard, brown sugar, whiskey, molasses, vinegar and pepper sauce with whisk. Cook over medium-low heat 10 minutes, stirring occasionally, until slightly thickened. Remove from heat. Pour ¼ cup of the sauce into small bowl.

2. Generously brush cut sides of onion slices and tomato halves with 2 tablespoons of the sauce in bowl. Generously brush pork chops with half of the remaining sauce in pan. Place pork, onions and tomatoes, cut sides down, on grill over medium heat. Brush tops of onions and tomatoes with remaining 2 tablespoons sauce in bowl. Brush tops of pork chops with remaining sauce in pan.

3. Cover grill; cook 5 to 7 minutes, turning pork and onions once (do not turn tomatoes), until pork is no longer pink in center, onions are crisp-tender and tomatoes are tender. Discard any remaining sauce. Sprinkle with chopped fresh parsley if desired.

1 Serving: Calories 270 (Calories from Fat 70); Total Fat 8g (Saturated Fat 2.5g; Trans Fat 0g); Cholesterol 50mg; Sodium 570mg; Total Carbohydrate 29g (Dietary Fiber 2g); Protein 19g **% Daily Value:** Vitamin A 15%; Vitamin C 10%; Calcium 6%; Iron 10% **Exchanges:** 1½ Starch, ½ Other Carbohydrate, ½ Vegetable, ½ Very Lean Meat, 1½ Lean Meat, ½ Fat **Carbohydrate Choices:** 2

pork chops with raspberry-chipotle sauce and herbed rice

Prep Time: 25 Minutes **Start to Finish:** 25 Minutes **Makes:** 4 servings

380 Calories

4	bone-in pork rib chops, about ¾ inch thick
½	teaspoon garlic-pepper blend
1	package (8.8 oz) microwavable whole-grain brown rice
¼	teaspoon salt-free garlic-herb blend
½	teaspoon grated lemon peel
1	tablespoon chopped fresh cilantro
⅓	cup all-fruit raspberry spread
1	tablespoon water
1	tablespoon raspberry vinegar
1	large or 2 small chipotle chiles in adobo sauce (from 7-oz can), finely chopped

1. In 12-inch nonstick skillet, heat oil over medium-high heat. Sprinkle pork chops with garlic-pepper blend; add to skillet. Cook 8 to 10 minutes, turning once, until meat thermometer inserted in center reads 145°F. Transfer from skillet to serving platter; cover to keep warm. Reserve drippings in skillet.

2. Meanwhile, cook rice in microwave as directed on package. Stir in garlic-herb blend, lemon peel and cilantro; keep warm.

3. In small bowl, stir raspberry spread, water, vinegar and chile; add to skillet with drippings. Cook and stir over low heat until sauce is bubbly and slightly thickened. Serve pork chops with sauce and rice.

1 Serving: Calories 380 (Calories from Fat 110); Total Fat 12g (Saturated Fat 5g; Trans Fat 0g); Cholesterol 85mg; Sodium 100mg; Total Carbohydrate 35g (Dietary Fiber 1g); Protein 32g **% Daily Value:** Vitamin A 2%; Vitamin C 2%; Calcium 0%; Iron 8% **Exchanges:** 1½ Starch, 1 Other Carbohydrate, 3½ Lean Meat **Carbohydrate Choices:** 2

a little bit more

Green up your plate with green beans. A 1 cup serving of cooked fresh green beans adds 40 calories per serving.

marinated pork with summer corn salad

Prep Time: 40 Minutes   **Start to Finish:** 1 Hour 40 Minutes   **Makes:** 4 servings

250 Calories

1	lb boneless pork loin, trimmed of fat, cut into 1½-inch cubes	½	teaspoon salt
⅓	cup fresh lime juice	1	box (9 oz) frozen whole kernel corn
2	tablespoons honey	2	cups coarsely chopped fresh arugula or spinach
1	jalapeño chile, seeded, finely chopped	1	medium red bell pepper, chopped (1 cup)
¼	cup chopped fresh cilantro		

1. Place pork cubes in large resealable food-storage plastic bag. In small bowl, mix lime juice and honey; stir in chile, cilantro and salt. Pour ¼ cup of the lime juice mixture over pork. Seal bag; turn to coat. Refrigerate 1 hour, turning bag occasionally. Set remaining lime juice mixture aside.

2. Meanwhile, cook corn as directed on package; cool slightly. In medium bowl, toss corn, arugula and bell pepper with reserved lime juice mixture. Refrigerate until serving time, or set aside to serve at room temperature.

3. Heat gas or charcoal grill. Drain pork, discarding marinade. Thread pork cubes onto 8 (8-inch) metal or bamboo skewers,* leaving ¼-inch space between cubes. Place skewers on grill over medium heat. Cover grill; cook 18 to 20 minutes, turning occasionally, until pork is no longer pink. Serve pork with corn salad.

*If using bamboo skewers, soak in water at least 30 minutes before using to prevent burning.

1 Serving: Calories 250 (Calories from Fat 45); Total Fat 5g (Saturated Fat 1.5g; Trans Fat 0g); Cholesterol 50mg; Sodium 350mg; Total Carbohydrate 25g (Dietary Fiber 2g); Protein 24g **% Daily Value:** Vitamin A 35%; Vitamin C 50%; Calcium 4%; Iron 6% **Exchanges:** 1½ Starch, 1 Vegetable, 1½ Very Lean Meat, 1 Lean Meat **Carbohydrate Choices:** 1½

a little bit more

Nothing says summer like lemonade, yet an 8 ounce serving of lemonade can add 100 calories to your meal. Have an Arnold Palmer instead (half unsweetened iced tea and half lemonade) with this meal for only 55 added calories per 8 ounce glass.

pork mole-fajita quesadillas

Prep Time: 30 Minutes   **Start to Finish:** 30 Minutes   **Makes:** 4 servings

360 Calories

2 teaspoons canola oil	¼ teaspoon salt
½ lb boneless pork loin, trimmed of fat, cut into thin strips	¼ teaspoon ground cinnamon
1 medium green bell pepper, thinly sliced	¼ cup reduced-sodium chicken broth
1 medium red bell pepper, thinly sliced	2 tablespoons semisweet chocolate chips
1 medium onion, thinly sliced	Cooking spray
3 cloves garlic, finely chopped	4 fat-free flour tortillas (10 inch)
1 tablespoon chili powder	1 small tomato, chopped (½ cup)
1 teaspoon all-purpose flour	4 teaspoons chopped fresh cilantro
1 teaspoon ground cumin	½ cup shredded reduced-fat Monterey Jack cheese (2 oz)

1. In 12-inch nonstick skillet, heat 1 teaspoon of the oil over medium-high heat. Cook pork in oil 4 to 5 minutes, stirring frequently, until no longer pink. Remove from skillet; set aside.

2. In same skillet, heat remaining 1 teaspoon oil over medium heat. Cook bell peppers, onion and garlic in oil 3 to 5 minutes, stirring occasionally, until peppers are crisp-tender. Stir in chili powder, flour, cumin, salt and cinnamon; cook 30 seconds. Stir in broth; heat to boiling. Cook about 30 seconds, stirring constantly, until thickened and bubbly. Remove from heat; stir in chocolate chips until melted. Stir in pork.

3. Spray 1 side of each tortilla with cooking spray. On work surface, place tortillas, sprayed side down. Spoon pork mixture, tomato, cilantro and cheese evenly over half of each tortilla. Fold tortilla over filling, pressing gently.

4. Heat griddle over medium heat. Cook quesadillas 3 to 4 minutes, turning once, until tortillas begin to brown. Cut each into wedges, beginning from center of folded side.

1 Serving: Calories 360 (Calories from Fat 80); Total Fat 9g (Saturated Fat 3.5g; Trans Fat 0g); Cholesterol 35mg; Sodium 900mg; Total Carbohydrate 48g (Dietary Fiber 4g); Protein 21g **% Daily Value:** Vitamin A 40%; Vitamin C 60%; Calcium 20%; Iron 20% **Exchanges:** 3 Starch, 1 Vegetable, 1½ Lean Meat, ½ Fat **Carbohydrate Choices:** 3

cajun pork with couscous

Prep Time: 30 Minutes   **Start to Finish:** 30 Minutes   **Makes:** 4 servings

360 Calories

4	boneless pork loin chops, ¾ inch thick (4 oz each), trimmed of fat
½	teaspoon salt-free Cajun seasoning
1	medium red or orange bell pepper, or ½ of each, quartered, seeded
1	medium poblano chile, seeded, quartered

1	medium jalapeño chile, seeded, halved
	Cooking spray
1	cup reduced-sodium chicken broth
⅔	cup uncooked whole wheat couscous
½	cup sliced almonds, toasted*

1. Heat gas or charcoal grill. Sprinkle both sides of pork chops with Cajun seasoning. Spray bell peppers and chiles with cooking spray; set jalapeño halves aside.

2. Place pork chops, bell pepper and poblano quarters on grill over medium heat. Cover grill; cook 7 to 9 minutes, turning once, until meat thermometer inserted in center of pork reads 145°F and bell peppers are crisp-tender. Add jalapeño halves to grill for the last 2 to 3 minutes of cooking time.

3. Meanwhile, in 2-quart saucepan, heat broth to boiling. Stir in couscous; remove from heat. Cover; let stand 5 minutes. Slice bell pepper and poblano quarters into bite-size strips. Finely chop jalapeño. Stir peppers, chiles and almonds into couscous. Serve with pork chops.

*To toast almonds, cook in an ungreased skillet over medium heat for 5 to 7 minutes, stirring frequently, until almonds begin to brown, then stirring constantly until light brown.

1 Serving: Calories 360 (Calories from Fat 130); Total Fat 14g (Saturated Fat 3.5g; Trans Fat 0g); Cholesterol 70mg; Sodium 190mg; Total Carbohydrate 27g (Dietary Fiber 3g); Protein 31g **% Daily Value:** Vitamin A 20%; Vitamin C 35%; Calcium 4%; Iron 10% **Exchanges:** 2 Starch, 3½ Lean Meat, ½ Fat **Carbohydrate Choices:** 2

a little bit more

Sweet Potato Biscuits (below) add that "something extra" to this Southern-style meal. One biscuit spread with 2 teaspoons butter adds 200 calories.

Sweet Potato Biscuits Heat oven to 450°F. Stir together 2½ cups Original Bisquick® mix, ⅓ cup softened butter or margarine, 1 cup mashed cooked sweet potatoes and ½ cup milk until soft dough forms. Place dough on surface sprinkled with Bisquick mix; gently roll in Bisquick mix to coat. Shape into a ball; knead 3 or 4 times. Roll dough ½ inch thick. Cut with 2½-inch round cutter dipped in Bisquick mix. Place with edges touching on ungreased cookie sheet. Bake 10 to 12 minutes or until golden brown. Serve warm. Makes 16 to 18 biscuits.

teriyaki pork and mushroom lo mein

Prep Time: 45 Minutes   **Start to Finish:** 1 Hour 30 Minutes   **Makes:** 6 servings (1⅓ cups each)

310 Calories

¾ lb boneless pork loin, trimmed of fat

10 oz uncooked soba (buckwheat) noodles or whole wheat spaghetti

¼ cup oyster sauce

¼ cup reduced-sodium teriyaki sauce

¼ cup dry sherry, mirin (rice wine), sake or chicken broth

2 teaspoons canola oil

2 teaspoons sesame oil

1 tablespoon finely chopped gingerroot

1 medium red onion, halved lengthwise, thinly sliced (1 cup)

1 package (8 oz) sliced fresh mushrooms (about 3 cups)

1 bag (12 oz) frozen sugar snap peas, thawed

1. Freeze pork about 45 minutes or until partially frozen. Thinly slice pork across grain into bite-size strips; set aside.

2. Cook and drain noodles as directed on package. Rinse with cold water; drain well. Meanwhile, in small bowl, combine oyster sauce, teriyaki sauce and sherry; set aside.

3. In a wok or large nonstick skillet, heat canola oil and sesame oil over medium-high heat. Add ginger; cook and stir 15 seconds. Add onion; cook 2 minutes, stirring constantly. Add mushrooms; cook 2 minutes. Add sugar snap peas; cook 1 minute longer. Remove vegetables from wok; cover to keep warm.

4. Add pork to wok; cook about 3 minutes, stirring frequently, until no longer pink. Add noodles, vegetables and sauce. Using two spatulas or wooden spoons, lightly toss mixture 3 to 4 minutes or until thoroughly heated. Serve immediately.

1 Serving: Calories 310 (Calories from Fat 50); Total Fat 6g (Saturated Fat 1g; Trans Fat 0g); Cholesterol 25mg; Sodium 620mg; Total Carbohydrate 41g (Dietary Fiber 7g); Protein 21g **% Daily Value:** Vitamin A 15%; Vitamin C 10%; Calcium 4%; Iron 15% **Exchanges:** 2½ Starch, 1 Vegetable, 1½ Lean Meat **Carbohydrate Choices:** 3

a little bit more

Sliced fresh strawberries are a nice companion to the lo mein. A 1 cup serving of berries adds about 50 calories to your meal.

tex-mex pork and corn soup

Prep Time: 30 Minutes **Start to Finish:** 40 Minutes **Makes:** 5 servings

220 Calories

1	tablespoon olive oil
¾	lb pork tenderloin, trimmed of fat, cut into bite-size pieces
1	cup chopped red onion
4	cloves garlic, finely chopped
1	bag (12 oz) frozen whole kernel corn
3½	cups reduced-sodium chicken broth (from 32-oz carton)

1	cup chunky-style salsa
1	medium red or yellow bell pepper, or ½ of each, chopped (1 cup)
1	small tomato, chopped (½ cup)
¼	cup chopped fresh cilantro
	Reduced-fat sour cream, if desired

1. In 3-quart saucepan, heat oil over medium-high heat. Cook pork in oil 4 to 5 minutes, stirring frequently, until no longer pink. Remove pork from pan; cover to keep warm.

2. Add onion and garlic to saucepan. Cook 3 to 4 minutes, stirring frequently, until onion is tender. Add corn; cook 4 minutes longer. Stir in broth, salsa and bell pepper. Heat to boiling; reduce heat. Simmer uncovered 10 minutes.

3. Return pork to soup; heat through. Remove from heat; stir in tomato and cilantro. Top individual servings with sour cream.

1 Serving: Calories 220 (Calories from Fat 50); Total Fat 6g (Saturated Fat 1.5g; Trans Fat 0g); Cholesterol 30mg; Sodium 740mg; Total Carbohydrate 24g (Dietary Fiber 4g); Protein 19g **% Daily Value:** Vitamin A 30%; Vitamin C 40%; Calcium 4%; Iron 6% **Exchanges:** 1½ Starch, 1 Vegetable, 1½ Lean Meat **Carbohydrate Choices:** 1½

almond-crusted cod

250 Calories

2 tablespoons all-purpose flour	½ teaspoon chopped fresh or
1 egg white	¼ teaspoon dried thyme leaves
1 tablespoon fat-free (skim) milk	½ lb cod fillets, cut into
2 tablespoons plain bread crumbs	2 serving pieces
2 tablespoons finely chopped almonds	2 teaspoons canola oil

1. Heat oven to 450°F. Lightly spray 9-inch square pan with cooking spray.

2. Place flour in shallow dish. In another shallow dish, beat egg white and milk. In third shallow dish, mix bread crumbs, almonds and thyme. Coat both sides of fillets with flour. Dip in egg mixture, then coat with crumb mixture. Place fish in pan. Drizzle with oil.

3. Bake uncovered until fish flakes with fork (allow 4 to 6 minutes per ½-inch thickness of fish).

1 Serving: Calories 250 (Calories from Fat 90); Total Fat 10g (Saturated Fat 1g; Trans Fat 0g); Cholesterol 60mg; Sodium 170mg; Total Carbohydrate 13g (Dietary Fiber 1g); Protein 26g **% Daily Value:** Vitamin A 0%; Vitamin C 0%; Calcium 6%; Iron 8% **Exchanges:** 1 Starch, 3 Lean Meat **Carbohydrate Choices:** 1

a little bit more

For even more almond flavor and crunch, top each piece of fish with 1 tablespoon sliced almonds before baking. It'll add texture and 35 calories per serving.

tilapia-crab cakes with roasted pepper aioli

Prep Time: 30 Minutes **Start to Finish:** 50 Minutes **Makes:** 4 servings

170 Calories

TILAPIA-CRAB CAKES

1 teaspoon olive oil
1 stalk celery, finely chopped (¼ cup)
4 medium green onions, finely chopped (¼ cup)
1 clove garlic, finely chopped
1 small jalapeño chile, seeded, finely chopped
¼ cup chopped drained roasted red bell peppers (from 7-oz jar)
1 tablespoon chopped fresh Italian (flat-leaf) parsley
¼ teaspoon salt
½ lb tilapia fillets, cut into pieces

1 package (6 oz) refrigerated fresh lump crabmeat, drained, rinsed (1 cup)
½ cup panko crispy bread crumbs
¼ cup fat-free egg product
Cooking spray

AIOLI

¼ cup fat-free mayonnaise
2 tablespoons finely chopped drained roasted red bell peppers (from 7-oz jar)
¼ teaspoon grated lemon peel
1½ teaspoons fresh lemon juice
1 clove garlic, finely chopped
Mixed greens, if desired

1. Heat oven to 400°F. Spray large cookie sheet with cooking spray.

2. In 10-inch skillet, heat oil over medium-high heat. Cook celery, onions, 1 clove garlic and the chile 3 minutes, stirring frequently, until celery is just tender. Remove from heat. Stir in ¼ cup roasted peppers, the parsley and salt. Spoon into medium bowl.

3. In food processor, place tilapia pieces. Cover; process with on-and-off pulses until coarsely chopped. Place in bowl with celery mixture. Add crabmeat, bread crumbs and egg product; stir gently until combined. Shape mixture by ⅓ cupfuls into 8 patties, about ½ inch thick. Place on cookie sheet. Spray tops of patties with cooking spray.

4. Bake 18 to 20 minutes, turning once, until golden brown.

5. Meanwhile, in small bowl, mix all aioli ingredients. Serve tilapia-crab cakes on mixed greens with aioli.

1 Serving: Calories 170 (Calories from Fat 45); Total Fat 5g (Saturated Fat 0.5g; Trans Fat 0g); Cholesterol 60mg; Sodium 550mg; Total Carbohydrate 15g (Dietary Fiber 1g); Protein 16g **% Daily Value:** Vitamin A 20%; Vitamin C 25%; Calcium 6%; Iron 6% **Exchanges:** 1 Starch, ½ Very Lean Meat, 1½ Lean Meat **Carbohydrate Choices:** 1

a little bit more

Prefer the taste of real mayonnaise? For an additional 50 calories per serving, substitute real mayonnaise for the fat-free mayonnaise in the aioli.

cobia with lemon-caper sauce

Prep Time: 25 Minutes   **Start to Finish:** 25 Minutes   **Makes:** 4 servings

240 Calories

⅓   cup all-purpose flour
¼   teaspoon salt
¼   teaspoon pepper
1¼   lb cobia or sea bass fillets, cut into 4 serving pieces
2   tablespoons olive oil
⅓   cup dry white wine

½   cup reduced-sodium chicken broth
2   tablespoons fresh lemon juice
1   tablespoon capers, rinsed, drained
1   tablespoon chopped fresh Italian (flat-leaf) parsley

1. In shallow dish, mix flour, salt and pepper. Coat fish pieces in flour mixture (reserve remaining flour mixture). In 12-inch nonstick skillet, heat oil over medium-high heat. Cook fish in oil 8 to 10 minutes, turning once, until fish flakes easily with fork. Transfer fish from skillet to serving platter with slotted spatula (reserve drippings in skillet); cover to keep warm.

2. Heat reserved drippings in skillet over medium heat. Stir in 1 tablespoon reserved flour mixture; cook and stir 30 seconds. Stir in wine: cook about 30 seconds or until thickened and slightly reduced. Stir in broth and lemon juice; cook 1 to 2 minutes, stirring constantly, until sauce is smooth and slightly thickened. Stir in capers.

3. Serve sauce over fish; sprinkle with parsley.

1 Serving: Calories 240 (Calories from Fat 80); Total Fat 9g (Saturated Fat 1.5g; Trans Fat 0g); Cholesterol 75mg; Sodium 400mg; Total Carbohydrate 9g (Dietary Fiber 0g); Protein 28g **% Daily Value:** Vitamin A 2%; Vitamin C 4%; Calcium 2%; Iron 6% **Exchanges:** ½ Starch, 1 Very Lean Meat, 2½ Lean Meat **Carbohydrate Choices:** ½

a little bit more

This fish would be delicious served with a rice blend. Look for one with wild and whole-grain brown rice that's low in sodium. Alternatively, substitute dry white wine or reduced-sodium chicken broth for half of the liquid and omit the butter and salt. A ½ cup serving of the rice adds about 100 calories.

seared tilapia with lemon-tarragon sauce and spinach orzo

Prep Time: 35 Minutes   **Start to Finish:** 35 Minutes   **Makes:** 6 servings

270 Calories

SPINACH ORZO

- 1⅓ cups uncooked whole-grain orzo or rosamarina pasta (8 oz)
- 1 bag (6 oz) fresh baby spinach leaves
- 1 tablespoon olive oil
- 2 teaspoons grated lemon or orange peel
- ¼ teaspoon salt

TILAPIA AND SAUCE

- 1½ lb tilapia or other lean whitefish fillets, cut into 4 serving pieces
- ½ teaspoon seasoned salt
- 1 tablespoon olive oil
- ¼ cup reduced-sodium chicken broth
- 1 tablespoon fresh lemon juice
- 1 teaspoon Dijon mustard
- 1 teaspoon chopped fresh or ¼ teaspoon dried tarragon leaves
  Paprika, if desired

1. Cook and drain orzo as directed on package. Return to saucepan; immediately toss orzo with spinach, 1 tablespoon oil, the lemon peel and salt. Cover to keep warm.

2. Meanwhile, sprinkle both sides of fish with seasoned salt. In 12-inch skillet, heat 1 tablespoon oil over medium heat. Cook fish in oil 4 minutes, carefully turning once, until fish flakes easily with fork. Transfer fish to serving platter; cover to keep warm.

3. Add broth and lemon juice to skillet. Using whisk, scrape up any crusty bits in skillet. Stir in mustard and tarragon; heat through.

4. To serve, place 1 piece of fish on each of 4 plates; top with 1 tablespoon lemon-tarragon sauce. Serve each with ⅔ cup spinach orzo.

1 Serving: Calories 270 (Calories from Fat 60); Total Fat 7g (Saturated Fat 1g; Trans Fat 0g); Cholesterol 60mg; Sodium 370mg; Total Carbohydrate 26g (Dietary Fiber 2g); Protein 27g **% Daily Value:** Vitamin A 50%; Vitamin C 8%; Calcium 6%; Iron 10% **Exchanges:** 1½ Starch, ½ Vegetable, 1 Very Lean Meat, 2 Lean Meat **Carbohydrate Choices:** 2

a little bit more

Brussels sprouts are a great accompaniment for this tilapia dish. An excellent source of vitamin C, 1 cup cooked Brussels sprouts add only 65 calories per serving, to fill you up without filling you out.

fish with tomato and cannellini relish

Prep Time: 30 Minutes   **Start to Finish:** 30 Minutes   **Makes:** 4 servings

350 Calories

1   lb mild-flavored, medium to medium-firm fish fillets (catfish, flounder or cod), cut into 4 serving pieces
½   teaspoon salt
⅛   teaspoon pepper
3   tablespoons fresh lemon juice
4   medium plum (Roma) tomatoes, cut lengthwise in half
4   teaspoons olive oil

1   can (19 oz) cannellini beans, drained, rinsed
1   clove garlic, finely chopped
1   teaspoon chopped fresh or ¼ teaspoon dried rosemary leaves, crushed
Lemon wedges
Fresh rosemary sprigs, if desired

1. Sprinkle fish with ¼ teaspoon of the salt and the pepper; drizzle with 1 tablespoon of the lemon juice. Set aside.

2. Heat nonstick or well-seasoned grill pan or skillet over medium heat. Brush tomatoes lightly with 1 teaspoon of the oil. Add tomato halves, cut sides down, to grill pan. Cook 6 to 8 minutes, turning once, until very tender. Remove tomatoes from pan; set aside to cool slightly.

3. Place fish fillets on grill pan. Cook 4 to 6 minutes per ½-inch thickness of fish, turning once, until fish flakes easily with fork.

4. Coarsely chop grilled tomatoes. In medium bowl, gently toss tomatoes, beans, garlic, chopped rosemary, and remaining 2 tablespoons lemon juice, 3 teaspoons oil and ¼ teaspoon salt.

5. To serve, place ½ cup tomato-bean relish on each of 4 plates. Place fish on relish. Serve with lemon and garnish with rosemary sprigs.

1 Serving: Calories 350 (Calories from Fat 60); Total Fat 7g (Saturated Fat 1g; Trans Fat 0g); Cholesterol 60mg; Sodium 400mg; Total Carbohydrate 38g (Dietary Fiber 9g); Protein 35g **% Daily Value:** Vitamin A 10%; Vitamin C 15%; Calcium 15%; Iron 30% **Exchanges:** 2 Starch, 1 Vegetable, 2 Very Lean Meat, 2 Lean Meat **Carbohydrate Choices:** 2½

a little bit more

Honeydew melon is a nice contrast in flavor, color and texture for this fish dish. A 1 cup serving of cubed melon adds 60 calories.

grilled fish with strawberry-poblano relish

Prep Time: 40 Minutes   **Start to Finish:** 40 Minutes   **Makes:** 4 servings

120 Calories

1	small lime
¼	teaspoon salt
¼	teaspoon ground red pepper (cayenne)
4	sea bass or halibut steaks, 1 inch thick (4 oz each)
1	cup chopped fresh strawberries
¼	cup finely chopped seeded poblano chile
2	tablespoons chopped fresh cilantro
½	teaspoon cumin seed, toasted*
⅛	teaspoon salt

1. Heat gas or charcoal grill. Grate peel of lime. Section and chop lime; set aside. In small bowl, mix grated lime peel, ¼ teaspoon salt and the red pepper. Rub mixture evenly over both sides of each fish steak.

2. Carefully brush oil on grill rack. Place fish on grill over medium heat. Cover grill; cook 14 to 18 minutes, gently turning once, until fish flakes easily with fork.

3. Meanwhile, in medium bowl, mix reserved chopped lime, the strawberries, chile, cilantro, cumin seed and ⅛ teaspoon salt. Serve relish with grilled fish.

*To toast cumin seed, heat in a small skillet over medium heat, shaking skillet occasionally, until fragrant.

1 Serving: Calories 120 (Calories from Fat 15); Total Fat 1.5g (Saturated Fat 0g; Trans Fat 0g); Cholesterol 60mg; Sodium 320mg; Total Carbohydrate 5g (Dietary Fiber 1g); Protein 22g **% Daily Value:** Vitamin A 4%; Vitamin C 25%; Calcium 4%; Iron 4% **Exchanges:** ½ Fruit, 3 Very Lean Meat **Carbohydrate Choices:** ½

a little bit more

Make it Fish Taco Night! Place each piece of grilled fish on one side of an 8-inch whole wheat tortilla for 130 calories per serving. Top with relish and fold other side of tortilla over relish.

ginger-teriyaki grilled salmon with honey-mango salsa

Prep Time: 30 Minutes   **Start to Finish:** 1 Hour 45 Minutes   **Makes:** 4 servings

310 Calories

HONEY-MANGO SALSA
1	teaspoon grated lime peel
2	tablespoons fresh lime juice
1	tablespoon honey
	Dash red pepper sauce
2	ripe medium mangoes, seed removed, peeled and diced (1 cup)
2	tablespoons finely chopped red onion

SALMON
3	tablespoons teriyaki baste and glaze (from 12-oz bottle)
1	tablespoon grated gingerroot
1	lb salmon fillet, cut into 4 serving pieces

1. In small bowl, mix lime peel, lime juice, honey and pepper sauce. Add mangoes and onion; toss. Cover; refrigerate 1 hour.

2. Heat gas or charcoal grill. In shallow glass or plastic dish, mix teriyaki glaze and gingerroot. Place salmon, skin sides up, in marinade. Let stand 15 minutes.

3. Remove salmon from marinade; discard marinade. Carefully brush oil on grill rack. Place salmon, skin sides up, on grill over medium heat. Cover grill; cook 2 minutes. Turn salmon. Cover grill; cook 5 to 10 minutes longer or until fish flakes easily with fork. Serve with salsa.

1 Serving: Calories 310 (Calories from Fat 60); Total Fat 7g (Saturated Fat 2g; Trans Fat 0g); Cholesterol 75mg; Sodium 380mg; Total Carbohydrate 35g (Dietary Fiber 3g); Protein 26g **% Daily Value:** Vitamin A 40%; Vitamin C 60%; Calcium 6%; Iron 8% **Exchanges:** ½ Fruit, 2 Other Carbohydrate, 1½ Very Lean Meat, 2 Lean Meat **Carbohydrate Choices:** 2

mediterranean salmon pasta

Prep Time: 30 Minutes   **Start to Finish:** 30 Minutes   **Makes:** 6 servings

250 Calories

2 cups uncooked whole-grain penne or rotini pasta (6 oz)

2 cloves garlic, finely chopped

4 large plum (Roma) tomatoes, chopped

8 medium green onions, sliced (½ cup)

2 cans (6 oz each) water-packed chunk-style boneless skinless salmon, drained

3 tablespoons chopped fresh basil

½ teaspoon pepper

⅛ teaspoon salt

2 teaspoons olive oil

½ cup crumbled reduced-fat feta cheese (2 oz)

1. In 4-quart Dutch oven, cook pasta as directed on package, omitting salt and oil. Drain and return to Dutch oven; cover to keep warm.

2. Lightly spray large skillet with cooking spray; heat over medium-high heat. Add garlic; cook and stir 15 seconds. Add tomatoes and onions; cook just until tender. Add salmon, basil, pepper and salt; cook, stirring occasionally, until thoroughly heated.

3. Add oil to drained pasta; toss to mix. Add salmon mixture and cheese; toss gently. Serve immediately.

1 Serving: Calories 250 (Calories from Fat 60); Total Fat 6g (Saturated Fat 1.5g; Trans Fat 0g); Cholesterol 50mg; Sodium 420mg; Total Carbohydrate 28g (Dietary Fiber 2g); Protein 20g **% Daily Value:** Vitamin A 10%; Vitamin C 6%; Calcium 20%; Iron 10% **Exchanges:** 2 Starch, 2 Lean Meat **Carbohydrate Choices:** 2

a little bit more

Fresh raspberries on the side make a "berry" delicious addition to this meal. A 1 cup serving will add 65 calories.

salmon and vegetable foil-pack dinners

Prep Time: 30 Minutes **Start to Finish:** 1 Hour **Makes:** 4 Servings

350 Calories

2 cups thinly sliced fresh carrots	¼ teaspoon salt
2 cups sliced fresh mushrooms	¼ teaspoon pepper
4 medium green onions, sliced (¼ cup)	1 lb salmon fillet (about ¾ inch thick), skin removed, cut into 4 serving pieces
1 tablespoon chopped fresh or 1 teaspoon dried oregano leaves	4 teaspoons olive oil
4 cloves garlic, thinly sliced	2 medium oranges, thinly sliced
2 teaspoons grated orange peel	4 sprigs fresh oregano, if desired

1. Heat oven to 350°F. Cut 4 (18×12-inch) sheets of heavy-duty foil.

2. In small saucepan, place carrots and just enough water to cover; heat to boiling. Cook 2 minutes; drain. In large bowl, gently toss carrots, mushrooms, onions, chopped oregano, garlic, orange peel and ⅛ teaspoon each of the salt and pepper.

3. Divide vegetables among 4 foil sheets, placing vegetables in center of foil. Place 1 piece of salmon on top of each portion of vegetables. Drizzle 1 teaspoon oil over each piece of salmon. Sprinkle evenly with remaining ⅛ teaspoon each salt and pepper; top with orange slices and oregano sprigs. Bring up 2 sides of foil over fish and vegetables so edges meet. Seal edges, making tight ½-inch fold; fold again, allowing space for heat circulation and expansion. Fold other sides to seal.

4. Place packets on cookie sheet. Bake 30 minutes or until carrots are tender and fish flakes easily with fork. To serve, cut large X across top of each packet; carefully peel back foil to allow steam to escape.

1 Serving: Calories 350 (Calories from Fat 180); Total Fat 20g (Saturated Fat 4g; Trans Fat 0g); Cholesterol 60mg; Sodium 260mg; Total Carbohydrate 17g (Dietary Fiber 4g); Protein 26g **% Daily Value:** Vitamin A 210%; Vitamin C 80%; Calcium 8%; Iron 6% **Exchanges:** ½ Fruit, ½ Other Carbohydrate, 1 Vegetable, 3½ Lean Meat, 2 Fat **Carbohydrate Choices:** 1

a little bit more

A slice of warm Garlic Bread (below) goes great with this meal, adding 90 calories.

Garlic Bread Heat oven to 400°F. Cut 1 loaf (1 lb) French bread into 18 (1-inch) slices. Mix 1 finely chopped clove garlic (or ¼ teaspoon garlic powder) and ⅓ cup softened butter; spread over 1 side of each bread slice. Reassemble loaf; wrap tightly in heavy-duty foil. Bake 15 to 20 minutes or until hot.

citrus-glazed salmon

Prep Time: 10 Minutes   **Start to Finish:** 30 Minutes   **Makes:** 4 servings

320 Calories

1¼ lb salmon fillet, cut into 4 serving pieces	4 cloves garlic, finely chopped
2 medium limes	2 medium green onions, sliced (2 tablespoons)
1 small orange	1 lime slice, cut into 4 wedges
⅓ cup agave syrup	1 orange slice, cut into 4 wedges
½ teaspoon salt	Hot cooked orzo or rosamarina, if desired
1 teaspoon pepper	

1. Heat oven to 400°F. Line 15×10×1-inch pan with cooking parchment paper or foil. Place salmon fillets, skin sides down, in pan.

2. Grate lime peel into small bowl. Squeeze enough juice to equal 2 tablespoons; add to peel in bowl. Grate orange peel into bowl. Squeeze enough juice to equal 2 tablespoons; add to peel mixture. Stir in agave syrup, salt, pepper and garlic. Remove ¼ cup citrus mixture; set remaining citrus mixture aside. Brush tops and sides of salmon with ¼ cup citrus mixture.

3. Bake 13 to 17 minutes or until fish flakes easily with fork.

4. Lift salmon pieces from skin with metal spatula onto serving plates. Sprinkle with onions. Top with lime and orange wedges. Drizzle with reserved citrus mixture. Serve over pasta.

1 Serving: Calories 320 (Calories from Fat 80); Total Fat 9g (Saturated Fat 1.5g; Trans Fat 0g); Cholesterol 80mg; Sodium 360mg; Total Carbohydrate 30g (Dietary Fiber 3g); Protein 29g **% Daily Value:** Vitamin A 4%; Vitamin C 25%; Calcium 4%; Iron 10% **Exchanges:** ½ Fruit, 1½ Other Carbohydrate, 2 Very Lean Meat, 2 Lean Meat, ½ Fat **Carbohydrate Choices:** 2

a little bit more

Serving one of these salmon fillets over ¾ cup hot cooked orzo pasta adds an extra 140 calories per serving.

spicy apricot-glazed salmon

Prep Time: 40 Minutes   **Start to Finish:** 40 Minutes   **Makes:** 4 servings

280 Calories

1½ cups apricot nectar	2 cloves garlic, finely chopped
⅓ cup chopped dried apricots	¼ teaspoon ground cinnamon
2 tablespoons honey	⅛ teaspoon ground red pepper (cayenne)
2 tablespoons reduced-sodium soy sauce	1 lb salmon fillet (1 inch thick), skin removed
1 tablespoon grated gingerroot	

1. In 2-quart saucepan, stir together all ingredients except salmon. Heat to boiling; reduce heat. Simmer uncovered about 20 minutes, stirring occasionally, until mixture is thickened and reduced by about half. Remove ¼ cup glaze for basting; set remaining glaze aside for serving.

2. Set oven control to broil. Spray broiler pan with cooking spray. Place salmon on broiler pan, tucking under any thin edges.

3. Broil about 4 inches from heat 8 to 12 minutes, gently turning once, until fish flakes easily with fork. Brush occasionally with ¼ cup glaze during the last 4 minutes of cooking time. Cut salmon into 4 portions; serve with reserved glaze.

1 Serving: Calories 280 (Calories from Fat 60); Total Fat 7g (Saturated Fat 2g; Trans Fat 0g); Cholesterol 75mg; Sodium 340mg; Total Carbohydrate 31g (Dietary Fiber 1g); Protein 25g **% Daily Value:** Vitamin A 35%; Vitamin C 2%; Calcium 4%; Iron 10% **Exchanges:** 2 Other Carbohydrate, 3½ Very Lean Meat, 1 Fat **Carbohydrate Choices:** 2

a little bit less
Cut the fish into 6 pieces to reduce the dish to 190 calories per serving.

orange and dill pan-seared tuna

Prep Time: 20 Minutes   **Cook:** 20 Minutes   **Makes:** 4 servings

4	tuna or swordfish steaks, ¾ inch thick (4 oz each)	1	tablespoon chopped fresh or ¼ teaspoon dried dill weed
½	teaspoon peppered seasoned salt	1	tablespoon butter or margarine
1	small red onion, thinly sliced (½ cup)	1	teaspoon grated orange peel, if desired
¾	cup orange juice		

1. Spray 10-inch skillet with cooking spray; heat over medium-high heat. Sprinkle both sides of fish with peppered seasoned salt. Add fish to skillet; reduce heat to medium-low. Cover; cook 6 to 8 minutes, turning once, until fish flakes easily with fork and tuna is slightly pink in center. Remove fish from skillet; cover to keep warm.

2. Add onion to skillet. Cook over medium-high heat 2 minutes, stirring occasionally. Stir in orange juice; cook 2 minutes. Stir in dill weed, butter and orange peel. Cook 1 to 2 minutes or until slightly thickened. Serve sauce over fish.

1 Serving: Calories 200 (Calories from Fat 80); Total Fat 9g (Saturated Fat 3.5g; Trans Fat 0g); Cholesterol 75mg; Sodium 260mg; Total Carbohydrate 7g (Dietary Fiber 0g); Protein 22g **% Daily Value:** Vitamin A 4%; Vitamin C 15%; Calcium 2%; Iron 4% **Exchanges:** ½ Other Carbohydrate, 3 Very Lean Meat, 1½ Fat **Carbohydrate Choices:** ½

a little bit more

Balance this dish with the addition of fresh asparagus and lightly buttered new potatoes. Toss ½ cup asparagus and ½ cup new potatoes with 1 teaspoon butter to add 175 calories per serving.

gremolata-topped sea bass

Prep Time: 5 Minutes   **Start to Finish:** 25 Minutes   **Makes:** 4 servings

130 Calories

¼ cup Italian-style dry bread crumbs

¼ cup chopped fresh Italian (flat-leaf) parsley

Grated peel of 1 lemon (1½ to 3 teaspoons)

1 tablespoon butter or margarine, melted

1 lb sea bass, mahi mahi or other medium-firm fish fillets, cut into 4 serving pieces

¼ teaspoon seasoned salt

1 tablespoon fresh lemon juice

1. Heat oven to 425°F. Line 13×9-inch pan with foil; spray foil with cooking spray. In small bowl, mix bread crumbs, parsley, lemon peel and butter.

2. Place fish in pan. Sprinkle with seasoned salt. Drizzle with lemon juice. Spoon crumb mixture over each piece; press lightly.

3. Bake uncovered 15 to 20 minutes or until fish flakes easily with fork.

1 Serving: Calories 130 (Calories from Fat 50); Total Fat 5g (Saturated Fat 2.5g; Trans Fat 0g); Cholesterol 55mg; Sodium 320mg; Total Carbohydrate 6g (Dietary Fiber 0g); Protein 14g **% Daily Value:** Vitamin A 8%; Vitamin C 6%; Calcium 4%; Iron 4% **Exchanges:** ½ Other Carbohydrate, 2 Very Lean Meat, 1 Fat **Carbohydrate Choices:** ½

tuna and rigatoni bake

Prep Time: 30 Minutes   **Start to Finish:** 55 Minutes   **Makes:** 5 servings (1 cup each)

330
Calories

2	cups uncooked rigatoni or penne pasta (6 oz)
1	tablespoon olive oil
1	cup coarsely chopped celery
1	small onion, chopped (⅓ cup)
2	cloves garlic, finely chopped
¼	cup all-purpose flour
2	tablespoons Dijon mustard
1	tablespoon chopped fresh or 1 teaspoon dried dill weed
1	teaspoon grated lemon peel

¼	teaspoon pepper
2	cups reduced-sodium chicken broth (from 32-oz carton)
2	cans (5 oz each) chunk light tuna in water, drained
½	cup finely crushed herb-seasoned croutons
2	tablespoons butter, melted
1	small lemon, thinly sliced
1	tablespoon capers, if desired
	Fresh dill weed sprigs, if desired

1. Heat oven to 375°F. Spray 1½-quart casserole with cooking spray. Cook pasta as directed on package, omitting salt and oil and using minimum cook time; drain.

2. Meanwhile, in 3-quart saucepan, heat oil over medium heat. Cook celery, onion and garlic in oil, stirring occasionally, until tender. Stir in flour, mustard, dill, lemon peel and pepper. Add broth all at once. Cook until thickened and bubbly, stirring with whisk to remove any lumps. Stir in tuna and pasta. Spoon into casserole.

3. In small bowl, toss croutons and melted butter. Sprinkle over casserole.

4. Cover; bake 15 minutes. Uncover; top with lemon slices. Bake 5 minutes longer or until thoroughly heated. Let stand 5 minutes before serving. Sprinkle with capers and garnish with dill weed sprigs.

1 Serving: Calories 330 (Calories from Fat 90); Total Fat 10g (Saturated Fat 4g; Trans Fat 0g); Cholesterol 25mg; Sodium 630mg; Total Carbohydrate 41g (Dietary Fiber 3g); Protein 20g **% Daily Value:** Vitamin A 6%; Vitamin C 6%; Calcium 4%; Iron 15% **Exchanges:** 1½ Starch, 1 Other Carbohydrate, ½ Vegetable, 2 Very Lean Meat, 1½ Fat **Carbohydrate Choices:** 3

a little bit less
Omit the croutons and butter to reduce the calories to 270 per serving.

lemon shrimp fettuccine

Prep Time: 20 Minutes   **Start to Finish:** 20 Minutes   **Makes:** 4 servings

370 Calories

8 oz uncooked whole-grain or spinach fettuccine

2 teaspoons olive oil

4 cloves garlic, finely chopped

1 lb uncooked medium shrimp, peeled (tails left on, if desired), deveined

1 cup reduced-sodium chicken broth

1 cup frozen sweet peas (from 12-oz bag), thawed

2 medium plum (Roma) tomatoes, finely chopped

1 teaspoon grated lemon peel

½ teaspoon ground nutmeg

¼ teaspoon salt

2 teaspoons chopped fresh Italian (flat-leaf) parsley

4 slices whole-grain baguette French bread, if desired

1. Cook fettuccine as directed on package, omitting salt and oil. Drain and return to pan; cover to keep warm.

2. Meanwhile, in 12-inch skillet, heat oil over medium heat. Add garlic; cook and stir 30 seconds. Add shrimp, broth and peas. Cook 3 to 4 minutes, stirring constantly, until shrimp are pink and peas are hot. Stir in tomatoes, lemon peel, nutmeg and salt.

3. Add shrimp mixture to fettuccine in saucepan; toss and heat through. Sprinkle with parsley. Serve with baguette slices.

1 Serving: Calories 370 (Calories from Fat 45); Total Fat 5g (Saturated Fat 0.5g; Trans Fat 0g); Cholesterol 175mg; Sodium 1100mg; Total Carbohydrate 51g (Dietary Fiber 6g); Protein 30g **% Daily Value:** Vitamin A 25%; Vitamin C 8%; Calcium 10%; Iron 15% **Exchanges:** 2½ Starch, ½ Other Carbohydrate, 1 Vegetable, 3 Very Lean Meat, ½ Fat **Carbohydrate Choices:** 3½

a little bit more

Top each serving with 1 tablespoon grated Parmesan cheese for an additional 20 calories.

cajun shrimp with mango-edamame salsa

Prep Time: 30 Minutes   **Start to Finish:** 30 Minutes   **Makes:** 4 servings

310 Calories

1   cup frozen shelled edamame (from 10- to 12-oz bag)
2   mangoes, seed removed, peeled and chopped
1   red bell pepper, chopped
8   medium green onions, finely chopped (½ cup)
¼   cup chopped fresh cilantro

2   tablespoons fresh lime juice
1½ teaspoons canola oil
¼   teaspoon salt
1   lb uncooked large shrimp, peeled (tails left on, if desired), deveined
2   teaspoons salt-free Cajun seasoning
1   tablespoon canola oil

1. Cook edamame as directed on bag; cool slightly. In medium bowl, gently toss edamame, mangoes, bell pepper, onions, cilantro, lime juice, 1½ teaspoons oil and the salt. Cover; refrigerate until serving time or up to 2 hours.

2. In large bowl, toss shrimp with Cajun seasoning. In 12-inch skillet, heat 1 tablespoon oil over medium-high heat. Add shrimp; cook about 5 minutes, stirring frequently, until shrimp are pink. Serve shrimp with mango-edamame salsa.

1 Serving: Calories 310 (Calories from Fat 80); Total Fat 9g (Saturated Fat 1g; Trans Fat 0g); Cholesterol 175mg; Sodium 940mg; Total Carbohydrate 33g (Dietary Fiber 4g); Protein 24g **% Daily Value:** Vitamin A 60%; Vitamin C 90%; Calcium 15%; Iron 8% **Exchanges:** ½ Starch, 1 Fruit, ½ Other Carbohydrate, 1 Vegetable, 3 Very Lean Meat, 1½ Fat **Carbohydrate Choices:** 2

thai shrimp and quinoa curry

Prep Time: 20 Minutes   **Start to Finish:** 45 Minutes   **Makes:** 4 Servings

330 Calories

1½ cups water	1 lb uncooked large shrimp, peeled (tails left on, if desired), deveined
1 cup uncooked quinoa, rinsed, well drained	2 cups frozen sugar snap peas (from 12-oz bag), thawed, halved lengthwise
1 teaspoon olive oil	¼ cup orange juice
1 large onion, chopped (1 cup)	3 tablespoons unsweetened light coconut milk (not cream of coconut)
1 tablespoon grated gingerroot	
½ teaspoon curry powder	¼ teaspoon salt
½ teaspoon ground cumin	½ cup chopped fresh cilantro
¼ teaspoon ground red pepper (cayenne)	

1. In 2-quart saucepan, heat water to boiling; add quinoa. Return to boiling; reduce heat. Cover; cook 15 minutes. When all of the water is absorbed, remove quinoa from heat and let stand 5 minutes.

2. Meanwhile, in 12-inch nonstick skillet, heat oil over medium heat. Cook onion in oil 3 to 5 minutes, stirring frequently, until tender. Add gingerroot, curry powder, cumin and red pepper; cook 1 minute, stirring constantly.

3. Add shrimp and peas to skillet, stirring to coat with spices. Cook about 3 minutes, stirring frequently, until shrimp are pink and peas are hot. Stir in orange juice, coconut milk and salt; heat through.

4. Serve shrimp mixture with quinoa. Sprinkle with cilantro.

1 Serving: Calories 330 (Calories from Fat 50); Total Fat 6g (Saturated Fat 1.5g; Trans Fat 0g); Cholesterol 175mg; Sodium 950mg; Total Carbohydrate 41g (Dietary Fiber 6g); Protein 27g **% Daily Value:** Vitamin A 25%; Vitamin C 20%; Calcium 15%; Iron 25% **Exchanges:** 1 Starch, 1 Other Carbohydrate, 1½ Vegetable, 3 Very Lean Meat, 1 Fat **Carbohydrate Choices:** 3

a little bit more

Orange segments or wedges are a natural companion to this citrus-infused Thai dish. One medium orange adds vitamin C, fiber and 75 calories.

grilled vegetables and ravioli

Prep Time: 25 Minutes   **Start to Finish:** 25 Minutes   **Makes:** 4 servings

290
Calories

2 tablespoons olive oil	1 package (9 oz) refrigerated reduced-fat cheese-filled ravioli
1 teaspoon garlic-pepper blend	1 tablespoon chopped fresh or 1 teaspoon dried basil leaves
¼ teaspoon salt	
2 small zucchini, cut lengthwise in half	1 teaspoon chopped fresh or ¼ teaspoon dried thyme leaves
2 medium bell peppers (any color), cut lengthwise in half, seeded	¼ cup shredded Parmesan cheese (1 oz)
1 small red onion, quartered	

1. Heat gas or charcoal grill. In small bowl, mix 1 tablespoon of the oil, the garlic-pepper blend and salt. Brush on cut sides of zucchini, bell peppers and onion.

2. Carefully brush oil on grill rack. Place vegetables, cut sides down, on grill over medium heat. Cover grill; cook 10 to 12 minutes, turning once and brushing occasionally with oil mixture, or until each kind of vegetable is tender, removing from grill when done.

3. Meanwhile, cook ravioli as directed on package. Drain and return to saucepan; cover to keep warm.

4. Cut zucchini crosswise into ¼-inch slices. Cut bell peppers into slices. Separate onion into pieces. Add vegetables to ravioli in saucepan. Add remaining 1 tablespoon oil, the basil and thyme; toss and heat through. Sprinkle each serving with 1 tablespoon cheese.

1 Serving: Calories 290 (Calories from Fat 110); Total Fat 12g (Saturated Fat 3.5g; Trans Fat 0g); Cholesterol 35mg; Sodium 560mg; Total Carbohydrate 33g (Dietary Fiber 3g); Protein 12g **% Daily Value:** Vitamin A 45%; Vitamin C 70%; Calcium 15%; Iron 280% **Exchanges:** 1½ Starch, 2 Vegetable, ½ Lean Meat, 2 Fat **Carbohydrate Choices:** 2

a little bit more

Crisp breadsticks add a nice textural contrast to this dish. Two packaged thin breadsticks add 80 calories per serving.

grilled marinated tofu gyros

Prep Time: 30 Minutes   **Start to Finish:** 1 Hour   **Makes:** 4 servings

370 Calories

YOGURT-CUCUMBER SAUCE

1	container (6 oz) fat-free Greek plain yogurt
¼	cup chopped cucumber
2	teaspoons fresh lemon juice

GYROS

⅓	cup fresh lemon juice
2	tablespoons olive oil
1	teaspoon dried oregano leaves
½	teaspoon salt-free garlic-pepper blend
1	package (12 oz) extra-firm tofu, drained, rinsed and patted dry
1	red bell pepper, cut into thin strips
1	medium red onion, cut into ¼-inch strips (about 2 cups)
4	whole wheat pita (pocket) breads (6 inch), cut in half to form pockets
	Cooking spray
½	cup shredded romaine lettuce

1. In small bowl, mix all sauce ingredients; refrigerate until serving time.

2. In shallow glass dish, mix ⅓ cup lemon juice, the oil, oregano and garlic-pepper blend with whisk. Reserve 2 tablespoons marinade; set aside. Cut tofu crosswise into 8 (½-inch) slices. Add to marinade in dish and turn to coat. Cover; refrigerate at least 30 minutes but no longer than 8 hours.

3. Heat gas or charcoal grill. Remove tofu from marinade, reserving marinade; set aside. Cut 18×18-inch sheet of heavy-duty foil; fold or roll up edges of foil. Spray foil with cooking spray. Place bell pepper and onion on foil; drizzle with reserved 2 tablespoons marinade. Place on grill over medium-high heat. Cover grill; cook 5 to 6 minutes, turning occasionally, until tender. Place tofu on grill next to vegetables. Cook 4 to 6 minutes, turning once and basting occasionally with reserved tofu marinade, until lightly browned. Remove vegetables and tofu from grill to plate; cover to keep warm.

4. Spray both sides of pita pockets with cooking spray. Place on grill over medium-high heat. Cover grill; cook 2 minutes, turning once, until toasted.

5. For each sandwich, place 1 tofu slice in each pita pocket. Tuck grilled vegetables on one side of tofu and lettuce on other side. Serve with sauce.

1 Serving: Calories 370 (Calories from Fat 130); Total Fat 14g (Saturated Fat 1.5g; Trans Fat 0g); Cholesterol 0mg; Sodium 320mg; Total Carbohydrate 41g (Dietary Fiber 6g); Protein 18g **% Daily Value:** Vitamin A 35%; Vitamin C 40%; Calcium 25%; Iron 20% **Exchanges:** 2 Starch, ½ Other Carbohydrate, 1 Vegetable, 1½ Very Lean Meat, 2½ Fat **Carbohydrate Choices:** 3

a little bit more

Add 2 tablespoons crumbled feta cheese to each pita half for an additional 50 calories per serving.

whole wheat lasagna wheels

Prep Time: 50 Minutes   **Start to Finish:** 1 Hour 20 Minutes   **Makes:** 4 servings

430 Calories

8	uncooked whole wheat lasagna noodles
3	cups sliced fresh cremini mushrooms
2	small zucchini, unpeeled, halved lengthwise and sliced
½	teaspoon pepper
1	cup part-skim ricotta cheese

½	cup shredded part-skim mozzarella cheese (2 oz)
¼	cup grated Parmesan cheese
½	cup fresh basil leaves, chopped
1½	cups tomato pasta sauce (from 24-oz jar)

1. Heat oven to 350°F. Spray 13×9-inch (3-quart) glass baking dish with cooking spray. Cook noodles as directed on package, omitting salt and oil and using minimum cook time. Drain; rinse with cold water to cool. Drain well; lay noodles flat.

2. Meanwhile, spray 10-inch skillet with cooking spray; heat over medium-high heat. Add mushrooms and zucchini; sprinkle with pepper. Cook 5 to 8 minutes, stirring frequently, until vegetables are very tender. Remove from heat. Drain; return to skillet. Stir in ricotta cheese, mozzarella cheese, Parmesan cheese and basil until well blended.

3. In baking dish, spread ½ cup pasta sauce. Spoon ⅓ cup vegetable mixture on center of each cooked noodle; spread to ends. Carefully roll up from short end, forming wheel. Place wheels, seam side down, on sauce in dish. Spoon remaining 1 cup sauce evenly over tops of wheels.

4. Cover; bake 30 minutes or until sauce is bubbly. Spoon sauce from baking dish over top of each wheel when serving.

1 Serving: Calories 430 (Calories from Fat 120); Total Fat 14g (Saturated Fat 6g; Trans Fat 0g); Cholesterol 30mg; Sodium 750mg; Total Carbohydrate 55g (Dietary Fiber 5g); Protein 22g **% Daily Value:** Vitamin A 25%; Vitamin C 15%; Calcium 40%; Iron 20% **Exchanges:** 2½ Starch, 3½ Vegetable, 1 Lean Meat, 2 Fat **Carbohydrate Choices:** 3½

broccoli raab and ravioli

Prep Time: 15 Minutes   **Start to Finish:** 25 Minutes   **Makes:** 4 servings (1½ cups each)

240 Calories

1 tablespoon olive oil
⅓ cup sliced leek (1 medium)
3 cloves garlic, finely chopped
1 can (14 oz) reduced-sodium beef broth
¾ cup water
¼ teaspoon crushed red pepper flakes, if desired
5 cups coarsely chopped broccoli raab leaves

1 can (14.5 oz) stewed tomatoes, undrained
1 package (9 oz) refrigerated reduced-fat cheese-filled ravioli
1 tablespoon chopped fresh or 1 teaspoon dried rosemary leaves, crushed
Grated Asiago or Parmesan cheese, if desired

1. In 3-quart saucepan, heat oil over medium heat. Cook leek and garlic in oil 5 minutes. Add broth, water and pepper flakes. Heat to boiling.

2. Stir in broccoli raab, tomatoes, ravioli and rosemary. Return to boiling; reduce heat. Cover; simmer 7 to 8 minutes or until broccoli raab and ravioli are tender. Sprinkle individual servings with cheese.

1 Serving: Calories 240 (Calories from Fat 60); Total Fat 7g (Saturated Fat 2g; Trans Fat 0g); Cholesterol 30mg; Sodium 650mg; Total Carbohydrate 33g (Dietary Fiber 3g); Protein 12g **% Daily Value:** Vitamin A 40%; Vitamin C 20%; Calcium 15%; Iron 290% **Exchanges:** 1½ Starch, 2 Vegetable, ½ Lean Meat, 1 Fat **Carbohydrate Choices:** 2

a little bit more

Pair this dish with pears! A juicy, ripe pear makes a great addition to this meal. Served whole or sliced, a medium pear adds 100 calories per serving.

three-cheese manicotti

Prep Time: 30 Minutes   **Start to Finish:** 1 Hour 25 Minutes   **Makes:** 4 servings

410 Calories

8 uncooked manicotti pasta shells
1 cup chopped fresh mushrooms
¾ cup shredded carrots (from 10-oz bag)
3 to 4 cloves garlic, finely chopped
1 cup part-skim ricotta cheese or reduced-fat cottage cheese
¾ cup shredded reduced-fat mozzarella cheese (3 oz)

2 eggs, slightly beaten
¼ cup grated Parmesan cheese
2 teaspoons Italian seasoning
1 can (14.5 oz) no-salt-added diced tomatoes, undrained
1 cup chopped drained roasted red bell peppers (from 7-oz jar)

1. Heat oven to 350°F. Cook pasta shells as directed on package, omitting salt and oil and using minimum cook time; drain. Rinse with cold water and drain; set aside.

2. Meanwhile, spray large skillet with cooking spray; heat over medium heat. Add mushrooms, carrots and garlic. Cook 3 to 5 minutes, stirring occasionally, just until vegetables are tender. Remove from heat; cool slightly. Stir in ricotta cheese, ½ cup of the mozzarella cheese, the eggs, Parmesan cheese and Italian seasoning. Spoon filling into pasta shells.

3. Place tomatoes in blender or food processor. Cover; blend on high speed until smooth. Stir in roasted peppers. Spread about ⅓ cup of the tomato-pepper sauce into ungreased 11×7-inch (2-quart) glass baking dish or 4 (12- to 16-oz) individual baking dishes. Place all stuffed shells in baking dish, overlapping slightly if necessary, or place 2 shells in each individual baking dish. Pour remaining sauce over stuffed shells.

4. Cover; bake 35 to 40 minutes for large baking dish, 20 to 25 minutes for individual baking dishes, or until thoroughly heated. Uncover; sprinkle evenly with remaining ¼ cup mozzarella cheese. Bake 5 minutes longer or until cheese is melted. Let stand 10 minutes before serving.

1 Serving: Calories 410 (Calories from Fat 140); Total Fat 15g (Saturated Fat 8g; Trans Fat 0g); Cholesterol 130mg; Sodium 480mg; Total Carbohydrate 43g (Dietary Fiber 4g); Protein 25g **% Daily Value:** Vitamin A 110%; Vitamin C 60%; Calcium 45%; Iron 15% **Exchanges:** 2 Starch, 2½ Vegetable, 1½ Lean Meat, ½ Medium-Fat Meat, 1½ Fat **Carbohydrate Choices:** 3

a little bit more

Serve the manicotti with an easy green side salad. One cup mixed greens tossed with 1 tablespoon reduced-calorie Italian dressing will add 30 calories per serving.

creamy ricotta-artichoke lasagna

Prep Time: 45 Minutes   **Start to Finish:** 1 Hour 40 Minutes   **Makes:** 8 servings

330 Calories

9 uncooked whole wheat lasagna noodles
1 tablespoon olive oil
2 boxes (9 oz each) frozen artichoke hearts, thawed, well drained
¼ cup pine nuts
4 cloves garlic, finely chopped
1 container (15 oz) reduced-fat ricotta cheese
1½ cups shredded reduced-fat Italian cheese blend or part-skim mozzarella cheese (6 oz)

1 cup chopped fresh or 2 tablespoons dried basil leaves
1 egg
¼ teaspoon salt
1 cup reduced-sodium chicken broth
¼ cup all-purpose flour
2 cups fat-free (skim) milk
Chopped fresh tomato, if desired
Chopped fresh Italian (flat-leaf) parsley, if desired

1. Heat oven to 350°F. Cook noodles as directed on package, omitting salt and oil and using minimum cook time. Drain; rinse with cold water to cool. Drain well; lay noodles flat.

2. Meanwhile, in 12-inch skillet, heat oil over medium heat. Add artichokes, pine nuts and garlic; cook about 5 minutes, stirring frequently, until lightly browned. Transfer to large bowl. Stir in ricotta cheese, ½ cup of the Italian cheese blend, ½ cup of the fresh basil (or 1 tablespoon of the dried basil), the egg and salt. Set aside.

3. In 2-quart saucepan, stir broth and flour with whisk until smooth. Stir in milk. Cook and stir over medium heat until sauce is slightly thickened and bubbly. Remove from heat. Stir in the remaining ½ cup fresh basil (or 1 tablespoon dried basil).

4. Pour 1 cup of the sauce into ungreased 13×9-inch (3-quart) glass baking dish. Top with 3 noodles. Carefully spread one-third of the ricotta mixture (about 1⅓ cups) evenly over noodles. Top with one-third of the remaining sauce (about ⅔ cup). Sprinkle with ⅓ cup of the remaining Italian cheese blend. Repeat layers twice more, beginning with noodles and ending with Italian cheese.

5. Bake uncovered about 40 minutes or until thoroughly heated and top is lightly browned. Let stand 15 minutes before serving. Garnish with tomato and parsley.

1 Serving: Calories 330 (Calories from Fat 120); Total Fat 14g (Saturated Fat 6g; Trans Fat 0g); Cholesterol 50mg; Sodium 440mg; Total Carbohydrate 32g (Dietary Fiber 6g); Protein 21g **% Daily Value:** Vitamin A 15%; Vitamin C 4%; Calcium 60%; Iron 10% **Exchanges:** 1½ Starch, ½ Skim Milk, 1 Vegetable, 1½ Lean Meat, 1½ Fat **Carbohydrate Choices:** 2

a little bit more

Go for the garnish! Sprinkling 1 cup chopped tomato and 2 tablespoons chopped parsley on top of each serving adds only 25 calories per serving.

ravioli skillet

Prep Time: 20 Minutes   **Start to Finish:** 20 Minutes   **Makes:** 4 servings (1⅔ cups each)

330 Calories

1	can (14.5 oz) diced tomatoes, undrained
½	teaspoon Italian seasoning
½	cup water
2	medium zucchini or yellow summer squash, or 1 of each, halved lengthwise, cut into ½-inch-thick slices
1	package (9 oz) refrigerated reduced-fat cheese-filled ravioli

⅛	teaspoon pepper
1	can (15 oz) cannellini beans, drained, rinsed
2	tablespoons chopped fresh basil or Italian (flat-leaf) parsley
2	tablespoons finely shredded or grated Parmesan cheese

1. In very large skillet, heat tomatoes, Italian seasoning and water to boiling. Add squash, ravioli and pepper. Return to boiling; reduce heat. Cover; boil gently 6 to 7 minutes, stirring once or twice, until ravioli is tender.

2. Stir beans into ravioli mixture; heat through. Sprinkle individual servings with basil and cheese.

1 Serving: Calories 330 (Calories from Fat 40); Total Fat 4.5g (Saturated Fat 2g; Trans Fat 0g); Cholesterol 30mg; Sodium 830mg; Total Carbohydrate 54g (Dietary Fiber 8g); Protein 19g **% Daily Value:** Vitamin A 20%; Vitamin C 30%; Calcium 20%; Iron 300% **Exchanges:** 1½ Starch, 1½ Other Carbohydrate, 2 Vegetable, ½ Very Lean Meat, 1 Lean Meat **Carbohydrate Choices:** 3½

tomato-basil pasta primavera

Prep Time: 35 Minutes **Start to Finish:** 35 Minutes **Makes:** 6 servings (1⅓ cups each)

280 Calories

2⅓ cups whole-grain penne or mostaccioli pasta (8 oz)

2 cups frozen sugar snap peas (from 12-oz bag)

1 cup assorted fresh vegetables (such as red bell pepper strips, julienne carrots and 2-inch pieces fresh asparagus)

1 cup sliced zucchini or yellow summer squash

1 cup halved cherry tomatoes

½ cup reduced-sodium chicken broth

3 tablespoons all-purpose flour

¼ teaspoon salt

1¼ cups low-fat (1%) milk

¼ cup dry sherry or additional reduced-sodium chicken broth

¾ cup finely shredded Parmesan or Asiago cheese (3 oz)

½ cup lightly packed fresh basil leaves, coarsely chopped

4 teaspoons chopped fresh thyme or oregano leaves

Sliced green onions, if desired

1. In 4-quart Dutch oven, cook pasta as directed on package, omitting salt and oil, and adding frozen sugar snap peas and 1 cup assorted vegetables during last 2 minutes of cooking time. Drain and return to Dutch oven. Add squash and tomatoes; cover to keep warm.

2. In 2-quart saucepan, stir broth, flour and salt with whisk until smooth. Stir in milk and sherry. Cook and stir until thickened and bubbly; cook and stir 2 minutes longer. Remove from heat; stir in cheese, basil and thyme.

3. Add herb sauce to pasta and vegetables in Dutch oven; toss gently to coat. Garnish individual servings with onions.

1 Serving: Calories 280 (Calories from Fat 45); Total Fat 5g (Saturated Fat 3g; Trans Fat 0g); Cholesterol 10mg; Sodium 410mg; Total Carbohydrate 41g (Dietary Fiber 5g); Protein 15g **% Daily Value:** Vitamin A 60%; Vitamin C 25%; Calcium 30%; Iron 15% **Exchanges:** 2½ Starch, 1 Vegetable, 1 Lean Meat **Carbohydrate Choices:** 3

a little bit more

Got to have "meat"? Add 2 cups cut-up cooked chicken breast with the cheese to add 150 calories per serving.

winter veggie pasta

Prep Time: 25 Minutes Start to Finish: 25 Minutes Makes: 6 servings

290 Calories

8   oz uncooked whole wheat spaghetti

3   cups frozen broccoli florets (from 12-oz bag)

1   can (14.5 oz) no-salt-added diced tomatoes, drained

1   can (15 oz) cannellini beans, drained, rinsed

2   tablespoons no-salt-added tomato paste

2   cloves garlic, finely chopped

¼   teaspoon salt

¼   teaspoon pepper

2   tablespoons chopped fresh Italian (flat-leaf) parsley

¼   cup grated Parmesan cheese

1. In 4-quart Dutch oven, cook spaghetti as directed on package, omitting salt and oil, and adding broccoli during last 3 minutes of cooking time. Drain and return to Dutch oven.

2. Stir in tomatoes, beans, tomato paste, garlic, salt and pepper; cook over medium-low heat until thoroughly heated. Stir in parsley. Sprinkle each serving with 2 teaspoons cheese.

1 Serving: Calories 290 (Calories from Fat 20); Total Fat 2g (Saturated Fat 1g; Trans Fat 0g); Cholesterol 0mg; Sodium 360mg; Total Carbohydrate 51g (Dietary Fiber 9g); Protein 15g **% Daily Value:** Vitamin A 25%; Vitamin C 30%; Calcium 15%; Iron 20% **Exchanges:** 3 Starch, 1 Vegetable, ½ Very Lean Meat **Carbohydrate Choices:** 3½

asparagus linguine

330 Calories

8	oz uncooked multigrain linguine
1	tablespoon olive oil
4	cloves garlic, finely chopped
¼	teaspoon freshly ground black pepper
1	lb fresh asparagus spears, trimmed, cut diagonally into 1½-inch pieces
1	package (8 oz) fresh whole mushrooms, cut in half
¼	cup dry white wine
¼	teaspoon salt
2	tablespoons butter
¼	cup shredded fresh basil leaves
¼	teaspoon crushed red pepper flakes

1. Cook linguine as directed on package, omitting salt and oil. Drain and return to saucepan; cover to keep warm.

2. Meanwhile, in large skillet, heat oil over medium heat. Add garlic and pepper; cook and stir 30 seconds. Add asparagus, mushrooms, wine and salt. Heat to boiling; reduce heat. Cook uncovered 4 minutes, stirring occasionally, until asparagus is crisp-tender. Remove from heat; stir in butter.

3. Add linguine to skillet; toss gently to combine with vegetables. Sprinkle with basil and pepper flakes.

1 Serving: Calories 330 (Calories from Fat 90); Total Fat 10g (Saturated Fat 4.5g; Trans Fat 0g); Cholesterol 15mg; Sodium 210mg; Total Carbohydrate 48g (Dietary Fiber 6g); Protein 12g **% Daily Value:** Vitamin A 15%; Vitamin C 4%; Calcium 6%; Iron 20% **Exchanges:** 2 Starch, ½ Other Carbohydrate, 2 Vegetable, 2 Fat **Carbohydrate Choices:** 3

a little bit more

For a special touch, enjoy a glass of Chardonnay with this linguine dish. A 5 ounce glass will add about 125 calories per serving.

brown rice-stuffed butternut squash

Prep Time: 30 Minutes   **Start to Finish:** 1 Hour 10 Minutes   **Makes:** 4 servings

360 Calories

2	small butternut squash (about 2 lb each)
4	teaspoons olive oil
¼	teaspoon salt
½	teaspoon freshly ground black pepper
⅓	cup uncooked brown basmati rice
1¼	cups reduced-sodium chicken broth
1	sprig fresh thyme
1	dried bay leaf
2	links (3 oz each) sweet Italian turkey sausage, casings removed
1	small onion, chopped (⅓ cup)
1	cup sliced fresh cremini mushrooms
1	cup fresh baby spinach leaves
1	teaspoon chopped fresh or ¼ teaspoon dried sage leaves

1. Heat oven to 375°F. Cut each squash lengthwise in half; remove seeds and fibers. Drizzle cut sides with 3 teaspoons of the oil; sprinkle with salt and pepper. On cookie sheet, place squash, cut sides down. Bake 35 to 40 minutes until squash is tender at thickest portion when pierced with fork.

2. Meanwhile, in 1-quart saucepan, heat remaining 1 teaspoon oil over medium heat. Add rice to oil, stirring well to coat. Stir in broth, thyme and bay leaf. Heat to boiling; reduce heat. Cover; simmer 30 to 35 minutes until liquid is absorbed and rice is tender. Remove from heat; discard thyme sprig and bay leaf.

3. In 10-inch nonstick skillet, cook sausage and onion over medium-high heat 8 to 10 minutes, stirring frequently, until sausage is thoroughly cooked. Add mushrooms; cook 4 minutes or until tender. Stir in cooked rice, spinach and sage; cook about 3 minutes or until spinach is wilted and mixture is hot.

4. When squash is cool enough to handle, cut off long ends to within ½ inch edge of cavities (peel and refrigerate ends for later use). Divide sausage-rice mixture between squash halves, pressing down on filling so it forms a slight mound.

1 Serving: Calories 360 (Calories from Fat 80); Total Fat 9g (Saturated Fat 1.5g; Trans Fat 0g); Cholesterol 20mg; Sodium 610mg; Total Carbohydrate 58g (Dietary Fiber 13g); Protein 13g **% Daily Value:** Vitamin A 890%; Vitamin C 50%; Calcium 20%; Iron 20% **Exchanges:** ½ Starch, 2 Other Carbohydrate, 4 Vegetable, ½ Lean Meat, 1½ Fat **Carbohydrate Choices:** 4

a little bit more

One clementine (a small, flavorful member of the mandarin orange family) adds 25 calories served with this dish. Simple to peel, one of these little citrus fruits is easy portion control!

african squash and chickpea stew

Prep Time: 45 Minutes   **Start to Finish:** 45 Minutes   **Makes:** 4 servings (about 1¾ cups each)

340 Calories

4 teaspoons olive oil	2 cups vegetable broth (from 32-oz carton)
2 large onions, chopped (2 cups)	1 can (14.5 oz) no-salt-added diced tomatoes, undrained
1 teaspoon ground coriander	1 can (15 oz) chickpeas (garbanzo beans), drained, rinsed
1½ teaspoons ground cumin	1½ cups okra, thinly sliced
½ teaspoon ground cinnamon	½ cup fresh cilantro leaves, chopped
½ teaspoon ground turmeric	⅓ cup raw unsalted hulled pumpkin seeds (pepitas), toasted*
¼ teaspoon salt	
¼ teaspoon ground red pepper (cayenne)	
2 cups cubed (1 inch) seeded peeled butternut squash	

1. In 5-quart Dutch oven, heat 3 teaspoons of the oil over medium heat. Cook onions in oil 10 minutes, stirring occasionally, until golden brown. Add all spices; stir until onion is well coated. Cook about 3 minutes longer, stirring frequently, until glazed and deep golden brown.

2. Stir in squash; coat well with seasoned mixture. Stir in broth, tomatoes and chickpeas. Heat to boiling; reduce heat. Cover; simmer about 15 minutes or until squash is tender.

3. Meanwhile, in 8-inch skillet, heat remaining 1 teaspoon oil over medium-high heat. Cook okra in oil 3 to 5 minutes, stirring frequently, until tender and edges are golden brown. Stir okra into stew.

4. Divide stew evenly among 4 bowls. Top each serving with 2 tablespoons cilantro and about 1 tablespoon pumpkin seeds.

*Pumpkin seeds are commonly found in the natural food aisle at the grocery store. To toast pumpkin seeds, sprinkle in ungreased heavy skillet. Heat over medium heat 3 to 5 minutes, stirring occasionally, until light brown. (Watch carefully; they can burn quickly.)

1 Serving: Calories 340 (Calories from Fat 110); Total Fat 12g (Saturated Fat 1.5g; Trans Fat 0g); Cholesterol 0mg; Sodium 750mg; Total Carbohydrate 47g (Dietary Fiber 11g); Protein 13g **% Daily Value:** Vitamin A 160%; Vitamin C 30%; Calcium 15%; Iron 30% **Exchanges:** 2½ Starch, 2½ Vegetable, 2 Fat **Carbohydrate Choices:** 3

chipotle four-bean chili with lime

Prep Time: 15 Minutes   **Start to Finish:** 6 Hours 15 Minutes   **Makes:** 6 servings

350 Calories

1   medium onion, finely chopped (½ cup)

2   cans (14.5 oz each) diced tomatoes, undrained

1   can (15.5 oz) red beans, drained, rinsed

1   can (15 oz) black beans, drained, rinsed

1   can (15 oz) chickpeas or garbanzo beans, drained, rinsed

1   can (15 oz) pinto beans, drained, rinsed

1   chipotle chile in adobo sauce (from 7-oz can), finely chopped

1   tablespoon dried minced garlic

2   teaspoons ground cumin

2   teaspoons chili powder

2   teaspoons packed brown sugar

¼   teaspoon salt

2   tablespoons fresh lime juice

1. Spray 5- to 6-quart slow cooker with cooking spray. In slow cooker, mix all ingredients except lime juice.

2. Cover; cook on Low heat setting 6 to 8 hours (or on High heat setting 2 to 3 hours). Just before serving, stir in lime juice.

1 Serving: Calories 350 (Calories from Fat 25); Total Fat 2.5g (Saturated Fat 0g; Trans Fat 0g); Cholesterol 0mg; Sodium 970mg; Total Carbohydrate 62g (Dietary Fiber 16g); Protein 19g **% Daily Value:** Vitamin A 25%; Vitamin C 25%; Calcium 15%; Iron 35% **Exchanges:** 1 Starch, 2½ Other Carbohydrate, 1½ Vegetable, 1½ Very Lean Meat, ½ Lean Meat **Carbohydrate Choices:** 4

Chapter 4
Snacks & Desserts

mai tai chicken skewers

Prep Time: 40 Minutes **Start to Finish:** 40 Minutes **Makes:** 10 servings

110 Calories

10 bamboo skewers (6 inch)	½ teaspoon grated lime peel
2 large boneless skinless chicken breasts (about 10 oz)	1 tablespoon fresh lime juice
7 green onions	½ teaspoon almond extract
⅓ cup light corn syrup	10 chunks (1½ inch) fresh pineapple (about 1½ cups)
1 tablespoon dark rum	10 maraschino cherries with stems
1 tablespoon fresh lemon juice	⅓ cup flaked coconut, toasted

1. Soak skewers in water at least 30 minutes to prevent burning. Spray grill rack with cooking spray. Heat gas or charcoal grill.

2. Cut each chicken breast in half lengthwise, then cut crosswise to make 10 (about 1-inch) pieces. Cut onions into 20 (about 2-inch) pieces. In small bowl, mix corn syrup, rum, lemon juice, lime peel, lime juice and almond extract. Reserve 3 tablespoons.

3. On each skewer, alternately thread 2 chicken pieces, 2 onion pieces and 1 pineapple chunk. Brush kabobs with about half of the remaining sauce.

4. Place kabobs on grill over medium heat. Cover grill; cook 7 to 10 minutes, turning and brushing with remaining sauce after 5 minutes, or until chicken is no longer pink in center. Place kabobs on serving platter. Thread end of each skewer with cherry. Spoon reserved 3 tablespoons sauce evenly over kabobs; sprinkle with coconut.

*To toast coconut, sprinkle in ungreased heavy skillet. Cook over medium-low heat 6 to 14 minutes, stirring frequently until browning begins, then stirring constantly until golden brown.

1 Serving: Calories 110 (Calories from Fat 20); Total Fat 2g (Saturated Fat 1g; Trans Fat 0g); Cholesterol 20mg; Sodium 30mg; Total Carbohydrate 15g (Dietary Fiber 0g); Protein 6g **% Daily Value:** Vitamin A 0%; Vitamin C 10%; Calcium 0%; Iron 2% **Exchanges:** 1 Other Carbohydrate, 1 Very Lean Meat, ½ Fat **Carbohydrate Choices:** 1

spicy chipotle, lime and ginger shrimp

Prep Time: 25 Minutes   **Start to Finish:** 45 Minutes   **Makes:** 8 servings

MARINADE

⅓ cup packed brown sugar
2 tablespoons water
2 tablespoons grated gingerroot
3 cloves garlic, finely chopped
1 teaspoon chopped chipotle chile in adobo sauce (from 7-oz can)
2 tablespoons adobo sauce (from can of chipotle chiles)
1 teaspoon grated lime peel
2 tablespoons fresh lime juice
¼ teaspoon salt

SHRIMP

1 lb uncooked large shrimp (21 to 30 count), peeled (with tail shells left on), deveined
¼ teaspoon salt
¼ cup chopped fresh cilantro

1. In 1-quart saucepan, stir brown sugar and water. Cook over medium heat 2 minutes, stirring occasionally, until sugar is dissolved. Remove from heat. Stir in remaining marinade ingredients. Reserve 2 tablespoons marinade in medium bowl.

2. Pat shrimp dry; place in another medium bowl. Add remaining marinade and stir to coat. Let stand at room temperature to marinate 20 minutes, stirring occasionally.

3. Heat gas or charcoal grill. Spray grill basket (grill "wok") with cooking spray. Spoon shrimp into basket. Place basket on grill over medium-high heat. Cover grill; cook 4 to 5 minutes, stirring once, or until shrimp are pink. Transfer shrimp to medium bowl with reserved marinade. Sprinkle with ¼ teaspoon salt and the cilantro; toss to thoroughly combine.

1 Serving: Calories 70 (Calories from Fat 5); Total Fat 0.5g (Saturated Fat 0g; Trans Fat 0g); Cholesterol 60mg; Sodium 430mg; Total Carbohydrate 11g (Dietary Fiber 0g); Protein 6g **% Daily Value:** Vitamin A 2%; Vitamin C 0%; Calcium 4%; Iron 0% **Exchanges:** ½ Other Carbohydrate, 1 Very Lean Meat **Carbohydrate Choices:** 1

a little bit more

Turn this into a hearty main dish that serves 6 by tossing the cooked shrimp with 6 cups cooked whole grain pasta for a total of about 240 calories per serving.

spicy orange crunchy shrimp

Prep Time: 30 Minutes   **Start to Finish:** 1 Hour 15 Minutes   **Makes:** 4 servings

200 Calories

8 to 10 bamboo skewers (6 inch)	1 to 2 teaspoons red pepper sauce
1 lb uncooked extra-large (16 to 20 count) shrimp	1½ cups Wheaties® cereal, finely crushed
½ cup buttermilk	2 tablespoons sesame seed
1 tablespoon reduced-sodium soy sauce	1½ teaspoons grated orange peel
	¼ teaspoon salt

1. Soak skewers in water at least 30 minutes to prevent burning. Peel shrimp (if shrimp are frozen, do not thaw; peel in cold water). Make a shallow cut lengthwise down back of each shrimp; wash out vein.

2. Place shrimp in resealable food-storage plastic bag. In small bowl, mix buttermilk, soy sauce and pepper sauce. Pour over shrimp; seal bag. Refrigerate 30 minutes or up to 2 hours, turning bag occasionally.

3. Heat oven to 425°F. Line cookie sheet with cooking parchment paper or foil. In shallow bowl, mix cereal, sesame seed, orange peel and salt. Drain shrimp; discard marinade. Coat shrimp with cereal mixture, pressing to make it stick. On each skewer, thread 2 shrimp. Place shrimp on cookie sheet; press any remaining coating onto shrimp.

4. Bake 10 to 12 minutes or until shrimp are pink and coating is golden brown. Serve immediately.

1 Serving: Calories 200 (Calories from Fat 45); Total Fat 5g (Saturated Fat 1g; Trans Fat 0g); Cholesterol 175mg; Sodium 1230mg; Total Carbohydrate 15g (Dietary Fiber 2g); Protein 22g **% Daily Value:** Vitamin A 10%; Vitamin C 4%; Calcium 15%; Iron 25% **Exchanges:** 1 Starch, 2½ Very Lean Meat, ½ Fat **Carbohydrate Choices:** 1

a little bit more

Get an extra kick of orange flavor by serving this shrimp with Orange Sauce (below). Two tablespoons sauce adds about 100 calories per serving.

Orange Sauce   In small bowl, mix together ½ cup orange marmalade, 1 teaspoon cider vinegar and ¼ teaspoon crushed red pepper flakes until blended.

spicy bacon-jalapeño poppers

Prep Time: 20 Minutes   **Start to Finish:** 50 Minutes   **Makes:** 8 servings

40 Calories

8 medium (about 3 inch) jalapeño chiles, halved lengthwise, seeded

½ cup fat-free cream cheese spread (from 8-oz container)

¼ cup shredded pepper Jack cheese (1 oz)

2 medium green onions, finely chopped (2 tablespoons)

1 tablespoon cooked real bacon pieces or bits (from 3-oz jar)

½ teaspoon salt

1 tablespoon chopped fresh cilantro

1. Heat oven to 350°F. Spray cookie sheet with cooking spray. Place chile halves, cut sides up, on cookie sheet.

2. In small bowl, mix cream cheese spread, pepper Jack cheese, onions, bacon and salt. Divide mixture evenly among chile halves, spreading filling out level with sides of each chile.

3. Bake 30 minutes or until tops are light golden brown and chiles are tender. Sprinkle with cilantro. Serve warm.

1 Serving: Calories 40 (Calories from Fat 15); Total Fat 1.5g (Saturated Fat 1g; Trans Fat 0g); Cholesterol 5mg; Sodium 310mg; Total Carbohydrate 2g (Dietary Fiber 0g); Protein 3g **% Daily Value:** Vitamin A 8%; Vitamin C 15%; Calcium 8%; Iron 0% **Exchanges:** ½ Lean Meat **Carbohydrate Choices:** 0

tomato-basil bruschetta

Prep Time: 15 Minutes **Start to Finish:** 15 Minutes **Makes:** 16 appetizers

50 Calories

16 slices (½ inch thick) baguette French bread (8 oz)

1 can (14.5 oz) diced tomatoes, drained

2 tablespoons chopped fresh basil leaves

1 tablespoon extra-virgin olive oil

1 clove garlic, finely chopped

1. Heat oven to 375°F. Place bread slices on ungreased cookie sheet. Bake about 10 minutes or until golden.

2. Meanwhile, in medium bowl, mix remaining ingredients. Spoon tomato mixture onto toasted bread slices. Serve immediately.

1 Appetizer: Calories 50 (Calories from Fat 10); Total Fat 1g (Saturated Fat 0g; Trans Fat 0g); Cholesterol 0mg; Sodium 130mg; Total Carbohydrate 9g (Dietary Fiber 0g); Protein 2g **% Daily Value:** Vitamin A 4%; Vitamin C 4%; Calcium 0%; Iron 4% **Exchanges:** ½ Starch **Carbohydrate Choices:** ½

a little bit more

Top each appetizer with 1 cooked medium shrimp (31 to 35 shrimp per pound) for an added 5 calories.

strawberry-honey bruschetta

Prep Time: 20 Minutes   **Start to Finish:** 20 Minutes   **Makes:** 16 appetizers

16 slices (½ inch thick) baguette French bread (8 oz)	2 tablespoons packed brown sugar
1 container (6 oz) fat-free Greek plain yogurt	¼ teaspoon ground cinnamon
	16 fresh strawberries, sliced
	¼ cup honey

1. Heat oven to 375°F. Place bread slices on ungreased cookie sheet. Bake about 10 minutes or until golden. Set oven control to broil.

2. In small bowl, mix yogurt, brown sugar and cinnamon. Spread yogurt mixture on 1 side of each toasted bread slice.

3. Broil with tops 4 inches from heat about 1 minute or until mixture is hot. Arrange strawberry slices on top; lightly drizzle with honey. Serve immediately.

1 Appetizer: Calories 80 (Calories from Fat 0); Total Fat 0g (Saturated Fat 0g; Trans Fat 0g); Cholesterol 0mg; Sodium 80mg; Total Carbohydrate 16g (Dietary Fiber 0g); Protein 2g **% Daily Value:** Vitamin A 0%; Vitamin C 6%; Calcium 4%; Iron 4% **Exchanges:** ½ Starch, ½ Other Carbohydrate **Carbohydrate Choices:** 1

roasted pepper roll-ups

Prep Time: 30 Minutes   Start to Finish: 2 Hours 30 Minutes   Makes: 24 servings

60
Calories

4   oz (half of 8-oz package) fat-free cream cheese, softened
1   cup crumbled chèvre (goat) cheese (4 oz)
1   tablespoon fat-free (skim) milk
2   cloves garlic, finely chopped
¼   teaspoon freshly ground pepper

½   cup finely chopped drained roasted red bell peppers (from 7-oz jar)
¼   cup chopped fresh basil leaves
8   whole wheat flour tortillas (8 inch)
2   cups packed fresh spinach leaves

1. In medium bowl, beat cream cheese with electric mixer on medium speed 30 seconds. Add goat cheese, milk, garlic and pepper; beat until smooth. Stir in roasted peppers and basil.

2. Spread mixture evenly over tortillas to within ½ inch of edges. Arrange spinach over filling. Carefully roll up tortillas tightly; wrap in plastic wrap. Refrigerate at least 2 hours or up to 24 hours.

3. To serve, use sharp knife to cut each roll-up into 6 pieces.

1 Serving: Calories 60 (Calories from Fat 20); Total Fat 2g (Saturated Fat 1g; Trans Fat 0g); Cholesterol 0mg; Sodium 130mg; Total Carbohydrate 7g (Dietary Fiber 1g); Protein 3g **% Daily Value:** Vitamin A 10%; Vitamin C 10%; Calcium 4%; Iron 2% **Exchanges:** ½ Starch, ½ Fat **Carbohydrate Choices:** ½

a little bit more

Don't feel deprived or guilty! Have 4 roll-ups for 120 calories.

blt tomato cups

Prep Time: 30 Minutes   **Start to Finish:** 30 Minutes   **Makes:** 24 appetizers

6 slices bacon, cut into ½-inch slices	2 tablespoons ranch dressing
12 small plum (Roma) tomatoes	2 tablespoons coarsely crushed garlic- and butter-flavor croutons
3 cups coarsely chopped romaine lettuce	

25 Calories

1. In 10-inch nonstick skillet, cook bacon 5 to 7 minutes over medium heat until crisp; drain on paper towels.

2. Meanwhile, with serrated knife, cut each tomato in half crosswise. Using teaspoon, scoop out seeds and pulp from each tomato half, leaving enough tomato for a firm shell. If necessary, cut small slice from bottom so tomato half stands upright.

3. In medium bowl, toss lettuce and dressing. Using small tongs or fingers, fill tomato shells evenly with lettuce mixture. Sprinkle with bacon and croutons. Serve immediately or refrigerate up to 1 hour before serving.

1 Appetizer: Calories 25 (Calories from Fat 15); Total Fat 1.5g (Saturated Fat 0g; Trans Fat 0g); Cholesterol 0mg; Sodium 65mg; Total Carbohydrate 1g (Dietary Fiber 0g); Protein 1g **% Daily Value:** Vitamin A 15%; Vitamin C 4%; Calcium 0%; Iron 0% **Exchanges:** ½ Vegetable, ½ Fat **Carbohydrate Choices:** 0

a little bit more

Sprinkle about 2 tablespoons of finely shredded Cheddar cheese over tops of appetizers for an added 60 calories per serving.

lemon-dill dip

Prep Time: 10 Minutes   **Start to Finish:** 10 Minutes   **Makes:** 12 servings (2 tablespoons each)

25 Calories

1 cup plain fat-free yogurt	½ teaspoon grated lemon peel
½ cup reduced-fat sour cream	Assorted vegetable dippers (such as carrot sticks, zucchini, yellow summer squash, fresh pea pods or bell pepper strips)
1 tablespoon finely chopped drained capers	
2 teaspoons chopped fresh dill weed or thyme leaves or ½ teaspoon dried dill weed or thyme leaves, crushed	

1. In a small bowl, stir together yogurt, sour cream, capers, dill and lemon peel. Serve immediately, or cover and refrigerate until serving.

2. Stir before serving. Garnish with shredded lemon peel and additional fresh dill weed or thyme, if desired. Serve with vegetable dippers.

1 Serving: Calories 25 (Calories from Fat 10); Total Fat 1.5g (Saturated Fat 1g; Trans Fat 0g); Cholesterol 0mg; Sodium 40mg; Total Carbohydrate 2g (Dietary Fiber 0g); Protein 1g **% Daily Value:** Vitamin A 0%; Vitamin C 0%; Calcium 6%; Iron 0% **Exchanges:** ½ Fat **Carbohydrate Choices:** 0

thai spinach dip

Prep Time: 15 Minutes   **Start to Finish:** 2 Hours 15 Minutes   **Makes:** 20 servings
(2 tablespoons each)

50 Calories

1 cup chopped fresh spinach
¾ cup fat-free sour cream
¾ cup plain fat-free yogurt
¼ cup chopped fresh mint leaves
¼ cup finely chopped unsalted peanuts
¼ cup reduced-fat peanut butter
1 tablespoon honey

1 tablespoon reduced-sodium soy sauce
1 to 2 teaspoons crushed red pepper flakes
Assorted vegetable dippers (such as ready-to-eat baby-cut carrots, zucchini slices, pea pods, yellow summer squash strips or red bell pepper strips)

1. In medium bowl, mix spinach, sour cream and yogurt. Stir in mint, peanuts, peanut butter, honey, soy sauce and pepper flakes. Cover; refrigerate at least 2 hours or up to 24 hours.

2. Stir before serving. Garnish with additional chopped unsalted peanuts and fresh mint leaves, if desired. Serve with vegetable dippers.

1 Serving: Calories 50 (Calories from Fat 20); Total Fat 2g (Saturated Fat 0g; Trans Fat 0g); Cholesterol 0mg; Sodium 65mg; Total Carbohydrate 5g (Dietary Fiber 0g); Protein 2g **% Daily Value:** Vitamin A 4%; Vitamin C 0%; Calcium 4%; Iron 0% **Exchanges:** ½ Starch, ½ Fat **Carbohydrate Choices:** ½

a little bit more

Serve crusty whole wheat bread cubes with the dip instead of the vegetable dippers. A ½ cup portion of bread cubes (about ½ slice) with 2 tablespoons dip is about 65 calories.

seven-layer taco dip

180 Calories

1½ lb ground turkey breast

1 jalapeño chile, seeded, finely chopped, if desired

1 package (1 oz) 40%-less-sodium taco seasoning mix

2 packages (8 oz each) ⅓-less-fat cream cheese (Neufchâtel), softened

2 cans (16 oz each) fat-free refried beans

3 ripe avocados, pitted, peeled

2 tablespoons fresh lemon juice

½ cup fat-free sour cream

½ cup fat-free mayonnaise

2 cups shredded reduced-fat Cheddar cheese (8 oz)

½ cup chopped green onions, if desired

2 cups shredded fresh spinach

3 medium tomatoes, chopped (about 2 cups)

Assorted vegetable dippers and/ or baked tortilla chips

1. Heat oven to 325°F. In large skillet, cook turkey, chile and 2 tablespoons of the taco seasoning mix over medium heat 8 to 10 minutes, stirring occasionally, until turkey is no longer pink; drain. Set aside.

2. Spread cream cheese in bottom of ungreased 13×9-inch (3-quart) glass baking dish. Spread refried beans over cream cheese. In medium bowl, mash avocados with lemon juice; spread over refried bean layer.

3. In small bowl, stir together sour cream, mayonnaise and remaining 2 tablespoons taco seasoning mix. Spread sour cream mixture over avocado layer. Top with turkey mixture and cheese.

4. Bake uncovered about 25 minutes or until thoroughly heated and cheese is melted. Sprinkle with onions, spinach and tomatoes. Serve with vegetable dippers and/or baked tortilla chips.

1 Serving: Calories 180 (Calories from Fat 90); Total Fat 10g (Saturated Fat 4g; Trans Fat 0g); Cholesterol 40mg; Sodium 450mg; Total Carbohydrate 10g (Dietary Fiber 3g); Protein 13g **% Daily Value:** Vitamin A 15%; Vitamin C 4%; Calcium 10%; Iron 6% **Exchanges:** ½ Starch, ½ Vegetable, 1 Very Lean Meat, ½ Lean Meat, 1½ Fat **Carbohydrate Choices:** ½

sweet pea-wasabi hummus with wonton chips

Prep Time: 20 Minutes   **Start to Finish:** 40 Minutes   **Makes:** 24 servings

90 Calories

HUMMUS

1	bag (12 oz) frozen sweet peas
1	can (15 oz) chickpeas (garbanzo beans), drained, rinsed
2	tablespoons canola oil
1	tablespoon sesame oil
2	teaspoons wasabi paste
2	teaspoons chopped gingerroot
½	teaspoon salt
2	cloves garlic, finely chopped
2	tablespoons water

WONTON CHIPS

36	wonton skins (3½-inch square)
	Cooking spray
½	teaspoon coarse sea salt

1. Cook peas as directed on bag for minimum cook time; drain.

2. In food processor, place cooked peas and remaining hummus ingredients except water. Cover; process with on-and-off pulses 10 to 15 times or until partially smooth. With food processor running, add water, processing 10 to 15 seconds or until smooth. (Add additional water for a thinner dip.) Transfer to serving bowl. Cover; refrigerate up to 1 day.

3. Heat oven to 375°F. Cut wonton skins diagonally in half. Place half of the skins on ungreased large cookie sheet. Spray with cooking spray; sprinkle with sea salt.

4. Bake 8 to 10 minutes or until golden brown and crisp. Transfer to serving platter. Repeat with remaining wonton skins. Serve hummus with chips.

1 Serving: Calories 90 (Calories from Fat 25); Total Fat 3g (Saturated Fat 0g; Trans Fat 0g); Cholesterol 0mg; Sodium 210mg; Total Carbohydrate 13g (Dietary Fiber 1g); Protein 3g **% Daily Value:** Vitamin A 6%; Vitamin C 0%; Calcium 0%; Iron 6% **Exchanges:** 1 Starch, ½ Fat **Carbohydrate Choices:** 1

smoky spinach hummus with popcorn chips

Prep Time: 10 Minutes   **Start to Finish:** 10 Minutes   **Makes:** 12 servings

120 Calories

1	can (15 oz) chickpeas (garbanzo beans), drained, liquid reserved
1	cup chopped fresh spinach leaves
2	tablespoons fresh lemon juice
2	tablespoons sesame tahini paste
2	teaspoons smoked Spanish paprika
1	teaspoon ground cumin
½	teaspoon salt
2	tablespoons chopped red bell pepper, if desired
6	oz popcorn snack chips

1. In food processor, place chickpeas, ¼ cup of the reserved liquid, the spinach, lemon juice, tahini paste, paprika, cumin and salt. Cover; process with quick on-and-off motions 30 seconds. Scrape side.

2. With food processor running, add additional reserved bean liquid, 1 tablespoon at a time, processing until smooth and desired dipping consistency. Transfer to serving bowl; garnish with bell pepper. Serve hummus with popcorn chips.

1 Serving: Calories 120 (Calories from Fat 35); Total Fat 4g (Saturated Fat 0g; Trans Fat 0g); Cholesterol 0mg; Sodium 280mg; Total Carbohydrate 18g (Dietary Fiber 2g); Protein 3g **% Daily Value:** Vitamin A 8%; Vitamin C 4%; Calcium 2%; Iron 8% **Exchanges:** 1 Starch, ½ Fat **Carbohydrate Choices:** 1

a little bit less

Serve ½ cup jicama sticks with the hummus instead of popcorn chips, for a savings of 40 calories per serving.

garlic potato chips

Prep Time: 5 Minutes   **Start to Finish:** 25 Minutes   **Makes:** 2 servings

1   medium unpeeled potato (6 to 8 oz), cut into ⅛-inch-thick slices
    Cooking spray

⅛   teaspoon garlic salt
    Chopped fresh chives, if desired

1. Heat oven to 450°F. Line large cookie sheet with foil; spray foil with cooking spray. Arrange potato slices in single layer on cookie sheet. Spray potatoes with cooking spray. Sprinkle with garlic salt.

2. Bake 15 to 20 minutes or until potatoes are browned and crisp. (If any slices brown more quickly than others, remove from cookie sheet and keep warm.) Sprinkle with chives.

1 Serving: Calories 110 (Calories from Fat 25); Total Fat 2.5g (Saturated Fat 0g; Trans Fat 0g); Cholesterol 0mg; Sodium 70mg; Total Carbohydrate 18g (Dietary Fiber 2g); Protein 2g **% Daily Value:** Vitamin A 0%; Vitamin C 6%; Calcium 0%; Iron 6% **Exchanges:** ½ Starch, ½ Other Carbohydrate, ½ Fat **Carbohydrate Choices:** 1

a little bit more

Serve these chips with Barbecue Dipping Sauce (below). Two tablespoons of sauce add 35 calories per serving.

Barbecue Dipping Sauce In small bowl, mix ¼ cup fat-free sour cream and 1 tablespoon barbecue sauce.

indian-spiced roasted chickpeas

Prep Time: 15 Minutes   **Start to Finish:** 1 Hour 20 Minutes   **Makes:** 8 servings

160 Calories

2 cans (15 oz each) chickpeas (garbanzo beans), drained
4 teaspoons olive oil
1 teaspoon coarse (kosher or sea) salt

1 teaspoon curry powder
½ teaspoon garam masala

1. Heat oven to 400°F. Thoroughly rinse chickpeas; drain. Place on paper towel–lined tray. Rub gently with another layer of paper towels until very dry, about 2 minutes. Discard papery skins.

2. In medium bowl, toss chickpeas with 2 teaspoons of the oil. Place in single layer in ungreased 15×10×1-inch pan. Roast uncovered 40 minutes, stirring every 15 minutes, until chickpeas make a rattling sound when pan is gently shaken.

3. Meanwhile, in 8-inch skillet, mix salt, curry powder and garam masala. Cook over medium heat 2 minutes, stirring constantly, until curry powder is fragrant. Remove from heat.

4. Remove chickpeas from oven; immediately pour into same medium bowl. Add spice mixture and remaining 2 teaspoons oil; toss to coat thoroughly. Pour back into pan. Roast 10 minutes longer. Cool completely, about 15 minutes. Store tightly covered.

1 Serving: Calories 160 (Calories from Fat 40); Total Fat 4.5g (Saturated Fat 0.5g; Trans Fat 0g); Cholesterol 0mg; Sodium 410mg; Total Carbohydrate 22g (Dietary Fiber 5g); Protein 7g **% Daily Value:** Vitamin A 0%; Vitamin C 0%; Calcium 4%; Iron 15% **Exchanges:** 1½ Other Carbohydrate, 1 Very Lean Meat, 1 Fat **Carbohydrate Choices:** 1½

a little bit more

Top your green salads with a serving of these crunchy little nuggets instead of croutons. You'll add about 3 grams of additional protein.

crispy vanilla-caramel popcorn

Prep Time: 15 Minutes   **Start to Finish:** 45 Minutes   **Makes:** 11 servings

120 Calories

½   cup packed brown sugar
¼   cup granulated sugar
¼   cup 50% to 70% vegetable oil spread

¼   teaspoon salt
1½ teaspoons vanilla
12 cups popped light popcorn

1. Heat oven to 300°F. In 4-quart Dutch oven, mix brown sugar, granulated sugar, vegetable oil spread and salt. Cook and stir over medium heat until just boiling and sugar is dissolved. Remove from heat; stir in vanilla. Add popcorn and toss to coat.

2. Spread coated popcorn in shallow roasting pan. Bake uncovered 15 minutes, stirring once. Spread popcorn on large sheet of foil to cool at least 15 minutes.

1 Serving: Calories 120 (Calories from Fat 45); Total Fat 5g (Saturated Fat 1g; Trans Fat 0g); Cholesterol 0mg; Sodium 170mg; Total Carbohydrate 19g (Dietary Fiber 1g); Protein 0g **% Daily Value:** Vitamin A 4%; Vitamin C 0%; Calcium 0%; Iron 0% **Exchanges:** 1½ Other Carbohydrate, 1 Fat **Carbohydrate Choices:** 1

sweet almond snack mix

Prep Time: 20 Minutes   **Start to Finish:** 1 Hour   **Makes:** 24 servings

130 Calories

4 cups Corn Chex® cereal	2 tablespoons light corn syrup
3 cups Rice Chex® cereal	⅛ teaspoon baking soda
2 cups sourdough pretzel nuggets	¾ cup orange-flavored dried cranberries
⅔ cup sliced almonds	¾ cup dried cranberries, blueberries or cherries
½ cup packed brown sugar	
¼ cup butter	

1. Heat oven to 300°F. In large roasting pan, toss cereals, pretzels and almonds; set aside.

2. In 2-quart saucepan, mix brown sugar, butter and corn syrup. Cook and stir over medium heat until mixture just begins to bubble. Continue cooking at a moderate, steady rate, without stirring, 5 minutes longer. Remove from heat; stir in baking soda. Pour over cereal mixture; stir gently to coat.

3. Bake 15 minutes; stir. Bake 5 minutes longer. Stir in dried fruit. Lightly spray large sheet of foil with cooking spray. Spread mixture on foil to cool. Store tightly covered at room temperature.

1 Serving: Calories 130 (Calories from Fat 30); Total Fat 3.5g (Saturated Fat 1.5g; Trans Fat 0g); Cholesterol 5mg; Sodium 150mg; Total Carbohydrate 22g (Dietary Fiber 1g); Protein 1g **% Daily Value:** Vitamin A 4%; Vitamin C 0%; Calcium 4%; Iron 15% **Exchanges:** ½ Starch, 1 Other Carbohydrate, ½ Fat **Carbohydrate Choices:** 1½

acai berry lava flows

Prep Time: 15 Minutes   **Start to Finish:** 15 Minutes   **Makes:** 4 servings

240 Calories

1 bag (10 oz) frozen unsweetened strawberries	1 cup vanilla fat-free frozen yogurt
¾ cup acai berry juice	2 tablespoons canned cream of coconut (not coconut milk)
½ cup light rum	⅔ cup cold water
¼ cup sugar	4 fresh strawberries, if desired
8 ice cubes	4 sprigs fresh mint, if desired

1. In blender, place frozen strawberries, juice, rum and sugar. Cover; blend on high speed about 1 minute 30 seconds or until smooth. Pour evenly into 4 (8-oz) wine or other stemmed glasses (about ½ cup each). Rinse blender.

2. Add ice cubes to blender. Cover; blend on high speed until crushed. Add frozen yogurt, cream of coconut and water. Cover; blend on high speed about 1 minute 30 seconds or until smooth. Spoon evenly on top of strawberry mixture in glasses (generous ⅓ cup each). Garnish with fresh strawberries and mint sprigs. Serve immediately.

1 Serving: Calories 240 (Calories from Fat 25); Total Fat 3g (Saturated Fat 2.5g; Trans Fat 0g); Cholesterol 0mg; Sodium 40mg; Total Carbohydrate 33g (Dietary Fiber 2g); Protein 3g **% Daily Value:** Vitamin A 6%; Vitamin C 1260%; Calcium 10%; Iron 6% **Carbohydrate Choices:** 2

a little bit less
Substitute ¼ cup acai berry juice for the ½ cup rum and save 110 calories per serving.

cantaloupe granita

Prep Time: 15 Minutes   **Start to Finish:** 3 Hours 15 Minutes   **Makes:** 10 servings (½ cup each)

60 Calories

2 cups cubed cantaloupe or honeydew melon	3 tablespoons honey
2 cups soymilk	¾ teaspoon ground ginger

1. In blender, place all ingredients. Cover; blend on high speed about 30 seconds or until smooth. Pour into 8- or 9-inch square glass baking dish.

2. Freeze 30 minutes. When ice crystals begin to form at edges of dish, stir mixture with fork. Freeze 2 hours 30 minutes to 3 hours longer, stirring every 30 minutes, until firm.

3. To serve, spoon into individual bowls.

1 Serving: Calories 60 (Calories from Fat 10); Total Fat 1g (Saturated Fat 0g; Trans Fat 0g); Cholesterol 0mg; Sodium 35mg; Total Carbohydrate 11g (Dietary Fiber 1g); Protein 2g **% Daily Value:** Vitamin A 25%; Vitamin C 20%; Calcium 6%; Iron 4% **Exchanges:** ½ Other Carbohydrate, ½ Very Lean Meat **Carbohydrate Choices:** 1

a little bit more

For a frosty, slushy drink, make the recipe as directed, spoon into 10 serving glasses and gently stir ¼ cup ginger ale into each glass for 100 more calories per serving.

mango freezer pops

Prep Time: 15 Minutes   **Start to Finish:** 11 Hours 15 Minutes   **Makes:** 12 to 16 servings

80 Calories

2   ripe medium mangoes, seeds removed, peeled and cut up
½   cup water
¼   cup sugar
¼   cup fresh lemon juice

3   containers (6 oz each) vanilla fat-free yogurt
12   to 16 ice pop molds or paper cups (2 to 4 oz) and craft sticks (flat wooden sticks with round ends)

1. In blender, place mangoes, water, sugar and lemon juice. Cover; blend on high speed until smooth. Add yogurt. Cover; blend until combined. Transfer mixture to 13×9-inch (3-quart) glass baking dish. Cover; freeze about 3 hours, stirring two or three times, until edges are firm but center is still slightly soft.

2. Scrape mango mixture into chilled large bowl. Beat with electric mixer on medium speed until smooth. Divide mixture among ice pop molds. (If using paper cups, pour mixture into cups and cover with foil. With knife, make small slit in center of foil piece and slide craft stick through hole.) Freeze at least 8 hours or overnight until firm.

3. To serve, remove pops from molds or peel off paper cups.

1 Serving: Calories 80 (Calories from Fat 0); Total Fat 0g (Saturated Fat 0g; Trans Fat 0g); Cholesterol 0mg; Sodium 20mg; Total Carbohydrate 18g (Dietary Fiber 1g); Protein 1g **% Daily Value:** Vitamin A 15%; Vitamin C 40%; Calcium 6%; Iron 0% **Exchanges:** ½ Starch, ½ Fruit **Carbohydrate Choices:** 1

a little bit more

Substitute orange juice for the water for a tropical treat. It adds only 5 calories per serving.

lemon dessert shots

Prep Time: 30 Minutes   **Start to Finish:** 1 Hour   **Makes:** 12 servings

110 Calories

2   oz ⅓-less-fat cream cheese (Neufchâtel), softened
½   cup marshmallow creme (from 7-oz jar)
1   container (6 oz) fat-free Greek honey vanilla yogurt

½   cup lemon curd (from 10-oz jar)
36   raspberries
10   gingersnap cookies, crushed
½   cup frozen (thawed) reduced-fat whipped topping

1. In medium bowl, beat cream cheese and marshmallow creme with electric mixer on low speed until smooth. Beat in yogurt until blended. Spoon mixture into 1-quart resealable food-storage plastic bag; seal bag. Spoon lemon curd into 1-pint resealable food-storage plastic bag; seal bag. Cut ⅛-inch opening diagonally across bottom corner of each bag.

2. In bottom of each of 12 (2-oz) shot glasses, place 1 raspberry. In each glass, pipe about 2 teaspoons yogurt mixture over raspberry. Pipe ¼-inch ring of lemon curd around edge of glass; sprinkle with about 1 teaspoon cookies. Repeat.

3. Garnish each dessert shot with dollop of about 2 teaspoons whipped topping and 1 raspberry. Place in 9-inch square pan. Refrigerate 30 minutes until chilled but no longer than 3 hours.

1 Serving: Calories 110 (Calories from Fat 25); Total Fat 3g (Saturated Fat 1.5g; Trans Fat 0g); Cholesterol 15mg; Sodium 70mg; Total Carbohydrate 18g (Dietary Fiber 0g); Protein 2g **% Daily Value:** Vitamin A 2%; Vitamin C 2%; Calcium 4%; Iron 0% **Exchanges:** ½ Starch, ½ Other Carbohydrate, ½ Fat **Carbohydrate Choices:** 1

a little bit more

Serve with a bowl full of extra gingersnaps on the side, for guests to grab. One gingersnap cookie adds 30 calories per serving.

pomegranate-tequila sunrise jelly shots

Prep Time: 30 Minutes **Start to Finish:** 4 Hours **Makes:** 12 servings

50 Calories

¾ cup pulp-free orange juice
2 envelopes unflavored gelatin
6 tablespoons silver or gold tequila
½ cup 100% pomegranate juice

¼ cup sugar
¼ cup water
Orange slices, if desired

1. Lightly spray 12 (2-oz) shot glasses with cooking spray; gently wipe any excess with paper towel. In 1-quart saucepan, pour orange juice; sprinkle 1 envelope gelatin evenly over juice to soften. Heat over low heat, stirring constantly, until gelatin is completely dissolved; remove from heat. Stir in tequila.

2. Divide orange juice mixture evenly among shot glasses (about 2 tablespoons per glass). In 9-inch square pan, place shot glasses. Refrigerate 30 minutes or until almost set. (Setting the first layer helps to give the 2-layer appearance and also ensures the desserts will release from the glasses in 1 piece, rather than 2 separate layers.)

3. Meanwhile, in same saucepan, stir pomegranate juice, sugar and water. Sprinkle remaining 1 envelope gelatin evenly over juice to soften. Heat over low heat, stirring constantly, until gelatin is completely dissolved; remove from heat.

4. Remove shot glasses from refrigerator (orange layer should appear mostly set). Pour pomegranate mixture evenly over top of orange layer in glasses (about 4 teaspoons per glass). Refrigerate at least 3 hours until completely chilled and firm.

5. Just before serving, dip a table knife in hot water; slide knife along inside edge of shot glass to loosen. Shake jelly shot out of glass onto plate (or serve from glass with a spoon); repeat with remaining jelly shots. Serve each jelly shot on orange slice.

1 Serving: Calories 60 (Calories from Fat 0); Total Fat 0g (Saturated Fat 0g; Trans Fat 0g); Cholesterol 0mg; Sodium 0mg; Total Carbohydrate 7g (Dietary Fiber 0g); Protein 1g **% Daily Value:** Vitamin A 0%; Vitamin C 4%; Calcium 0%; Iron 0% **Exchanges:** ½ Fruit **Carbohydrate Choices:** ½

strawberry-orange dessert shots

Prep Time: 30 Minutes   **Start to Finish:** 1 Hour   **Makes:** 12 servings

60 Calories

1 container (6 oz) vanilla fat-free yogurt
2 oz ⅓-less-fat cream cheese (Neufchâtel)
¼ cup frozen (thawed) reduced-fat whipped topping
1 tablespoon orange-flavored liqueur

½ teaspoon grated orange peel
1 cup finely chopped fresh strawberries
48 cubes (¾ inch) angel food cake (2 cups)
6 teaspoons finely grated semisweet baking chocolate

1. In small bowl, mix yogurt, cream cheese, whipped topping, liqueur and orange peel until smooth and well blended. Spoon mixture into 1-quart resealable food-storage plastic bag; seal bag.

2. In each of 12 (2-oz) shot glasses, place 1 rounded teaspoon strawberries. Top each with 2 cake cubes. Squeeze bag to pipe about 1 tablespoon yogurt mixture on cake in each glass. Repeat layers. Sprinkle with grated chocolate.

3. Place shot glasses in 9-inch square pan. Refrigerate uncovered 30 minutes or until chilled but no longer than 3 hours.

1 Serving: Calories 60 (Calories from Fat 15); Total Fat 2g (Saturated Fat 1g; Trans Fat 0g); Cholesterol 0mg; Sodium 80mg; Total Carbohydrate 9g (Dietary Fiber 0g); Protein 1g **% Daily Value:** Vitamin A 2%; Vitamin C 15%; Calcium 2%; Iron 0% **Carbohydrate Choices:** ½

a little bit more

Serve with a Cocoa Square (page 306) for an additional 140 calories.

bittersweet chocolate cake with berries

Prep Time: 25 Minutes   **Start to Finish:** 2 Hours 5 Minutes   **Makes:** 12 servings

170 Calories

¾ cup sugar
½ cup water
1 tablespoon instant espresso coffee powder or 2 tablespoons instant coffee granules
3 oz bittersweet baking chocolate, chopped
2 egg yolks
1 teaspoon vanilla
½ cup unsweetened baking cocoa

⅓ cup all-purpose flour
¼ teaspoon baking powder
5 egg whites
1½ cups frozen (thawed) reduced-fat whipped topping
1½ cups mixed fresh berries (raspberries, blackberries and/or blueberries)
Additional unsweetened baking cocoa, if desired

1. Heat oven to 350°F. Lightly spray 9-inch springform pan with cooking spray.

2. In 2-quart saucepan, mix sugar, water and coffee powder. Cook and stir over medium-low heat until sugar is dissolved and mixture almost boils. Stir in chocolate until melted. Remove from heat. Place egg yolks in small bowl. Gradually stir chocolate mixture into egg yolks; stir in vanilla (mixture may appear slightly grainy). Set aside.

3. In medium bowl, mix ½ cup cocoa, the flour and baking powder. Stir in chocolate–egg yolk mixture until smooth. In large bowl, beat egg whites with electric mixer on medium speed until stiff peaks form. Stir small amount of egg whites into chocolate mixture to lighten. Fold chocolate mixture into remaining egg whites. Spread in pan.

4. Bake about 30 minutes or until top springs back when lightly touched. Cool in pan on cooling rack 10 minutes. Loosen and remove side of pan. Cool completely. (Cake may fall slightly but evenly during cooling.)

5. To serve, cut cake into wedges; place on dessert plates. Top with whipped topping and berries. Sprinkle plates with additional cocoa.

1 Serving: Calories 170 (Calories from Fat 60); Total Fat 6g (Saturated Fat 4g; Trans Fat 0g); Cholesterol 30mg; Sodium 45mg; Total Carbohydrate 24g (Dietary Fiber 3g); Protein 4g **% Daily Value:** Vitamin A 0%; Vitamin C 2%; Calcium 4%; Iron 10% **Exchanges:** 1½ Starch, 1 Fat **Carbohydrate Choices:** 1½

a little bit more

Drizzle 1 tablespoon chocolate fudge topping over each wedge of cake and berries for a decadent 65 extra calories.

dark chocolate cupcakes

Prep Time: 35 Minutes   **Start to Finish:** 1 Hour 10 Minutes   **Makes:** 12 cupcakes

170 Calories

CUPCAKES

1½ oz bittersweet baking chocolate (3 squares from 4-oz bar), finely chopped

6 tablespoons unsweetened dark baking cocoa

½ teaspoon instant espresso coffee powder or granules

½ cup fat-free (skim) milk

¾ cup white whole wheat flour

¾ teaspoon baking soda

¼ teaspoon salt

¼ cup fat-free egg product

½ cup granulated sugar

¼ cup packed brown sugar

3 tablespoons canola oil

2 teaspoons vanilla

GLAZE

2 teaspoons fat-free (skim) milk

1 tablespoon unsweetened dark baking cocoa

1 oz fat-free cream cheese (from 8-oz package)

⅓ cup powdered sugar

⅛ teaspoon vanilla

Dash salt

¼ oz bittersweet baking chocolate (½ square from 4-oz bar), grated

1. Heat oven to 350°F. Place paper baking cup in each of 12 regular-size muffin cups.

2. In small bowl, place 1½ oz chocolate, 6 tablespoons cocoa and the espresso powder. In small microwavable measuring cup, microwave ½ cup milk uncovered on High 30 seconds or until steaming but not boiling. Pour over chocolate mixture; stir. Cover; let stand 5 minutes. Stir until smooth.

3. In medium bowl, mix flour, baking soda and ¼ teaspoon salt; set aside. In large bowl, beat egg product with electric mixer on medium speed 30 seconds. Gradually add granulated sugar and brown sugar, about ¼ cup at a time, beating well after each addition; beat 2 minutes longer. Beat in oil and 2 teaspoons vanilla. Alternately add flour mixture, about one-third at a time, and chocolate mixture, about half at a time, beating on low speed until blended.

4. Divide batter evenly among muffin cups, filling each about two-thirds full. Bake 20 to 25 minutes or until tops spring back when touched lightly in center. Cool 5 minutes; remove from muffin cups to cooling rack. Cool completely.

5. In small microwavable bowl, heat 2 teaspoons milk uncovered on High about 10 seconds or until hot. Stir in 1 tablespoon cocoa until smooth. In another small bowl, stir cream cheese until smooth; stir in cocoa mixture until blended. Stir in powdered sugar, ⅛ teaspoon vanilla and dash salt until glaze is smooth and shiny.

6. Spoon about 1 teaspoon glaze over each cupcake; spread to edge with back of spoon. Sprinkle about ¼ teaspoon grated chocolate over each glazed cupcake.

1 Cupcake: Calories 170 (Calories from Fat 60); Total Fat 6g (Saturated Fat 2g; Trans Fat 0g); Cholesterol 0mg; Sodium 190mg; Total Carbohydrate 26g (Dietary Fiber 2g); Protein 3g **% Daily Value:** Vitamin A 2%; Vitamin C 0%; Calcium 4%; Iron 8% **Exchanges:** 1 Starch, ½ Other Carbohydrate, 1 Fat **Carbohydrate Choices:** 2

frozen hazelnut-mocha pie

Prep Time: 15 Minutes   **Start to Finish:** 3 Hours 25 Minutes   **Makes:** 10 servings

170 Calories

½ cup light mocha-flavored Frappuccino beverage (from 9.5-oz bottle)

½ cup fat-free sweetened condensed milk (not evaporated)

2 tablespoons fat-free hazelnut-flavored liquid nondairy creamer

1 tablespoon instant espresso coffee powder or 2 tablespoons coffee granules

2 cups frozen (thawed) fat-free whipped topping

1 oz bittersweet baking chocolate, shaved

1 creme-filled chocolate sandwich cookie crumb crust (6 oz)

1. In medium bowl, mix mocha beverage, condensed milk, creamer and coffee powder. Stir in 1 cup of the whipped topping until well blended. Reserve 1 teaspoon shaved chocolate for garnish. Stir remaining chocolate into filling. Pour into crust.

2. Freeze 3 to 4 hours or until frozen. Remove from freezer 10 minutes before cutting. Garnish each slice with dollop of remaining 1 cup whipped topping. Sprinkle evenly with reserved 1 teaspoon shaved chocolate.

1 Serving: Calories 170 (Calories from Fat 50); Total Fat 6g (Saturated Fat 2g; Trans Fat 0g); Cholesterol 0mg; Sodium 110mg; Total Carbohydrate 27g (Dietary Fiber 1g); Protein 3g **% Daily Value:** Vitamin A 0%; Vitamin C 0%; Calcium 6%; Iron 6% **Exchanges:** 1 Starch, 1 Other Carbohydrate, 1 Fat **Carbohydrate Choices:** 2

incredible apple tart

Prep Time: 30 Minutes   **Start to Finish:** 2 Hours   **Makes:** 16 servings

130 Calories

⅔ cup quick-cooking oats
½ cup whole wheat flour
¼ cup pecans, toasted*, ground
1 package (8 oz) ⅓-less-fat cream cheese (Neufchâtel), softened
2 tablespoons butter, softened
2 tablespoons packed brown sugar
1 teaspoon grated orange peel
¼ teaspoon baking soda

¼ teaspoon salt
⅓ cup fat-free Greek plain yogurt (from 6-oz container)
¼ cup powdered sugar
1 egg white
¼ cup low-sugar orange marmalade
⅛ teaspoon ground cardamom
2 medium red cooking apples, cut crosswise into ⅛-inch slices

1. In small bowl, mix oats, flour and ground pecans; set aside. In large bowl, beat 4 oz of the cream cheese and the butter with electric mixer on high speed 30 seconds. Add brown sugar, orange peel, baking soda and salt; beat on medium speed until well mixed. Beat in as much of the oat mixture as you can with the mixer. Using wooden spoon, stir in any remaining oat mixture. If necessary, cover and refrigerate dough 30 to 60 minutes or until easy to handle.

2. Heat oven to 375°F. Lightly spray 9-inch tart pan with removable bottom with cooking spray. Pat dough evenly on bottom and up side of pan. Spray double thickness of foil with cooking spray; place foil, sprayed side down, on pastry. Bake 4 minutes. Remove foil. Bake 3 minutes longer. Cool completely on cooling rack.

3. Meanwhile, in medium bowl, beat remaining 4 oz cream cheese, the yogurt, powdered sugar, egg white, 2 tablespoons of the marmalade and the cardamom with electric mixer until smooth. Spread in bottom of partially baked crust. Arrange apple slices in concentric rings on cream cheese mixture, overlapping slices slightly.

4. Cover top of tart with foil. Bake 35 minutes. Uncover; bake 10 to 15 minutes longer or until crust is golden brown and apples are just tender.

5. In small microwavable bowl, place remaining 2 tablespoons marmalade. Cover; microwave on Medium (50%) 10 seconds. Stir; microwave about 10 seconds longer or until melted. Brush over apples. Serve tart slightly warm or cool.

*To toast nuts, heat oven to 350°F. Spread nuts in ungreased shallow pan. Bake uncovered 6 to 10 minutes, stirring occasionally, until light brown.

1 Serving: Calories 130 (Calories from Fat 60); Total Fat 6g (Saturated Fat 3g; Trans Fat 0g); Cholesterol 15mg; Sodium 125mg; Total Carbohydrate 15g (Dietary Fiber 1g); Protein 3g **% Daily Value:** Vitamin A 4%; Vitamin C 0%; Calcium 4%; Iron 2% **Exchanges:** 1 Starch, 1 Fat **Carbohydrate Choices:** 1

mixed berry pie

Prep Time: 20 Minutes   **Start to Finish:** 3 Hours 30 Minutes   **Makes:** 10 servings

1⅓ cups finely crushed zwieback or graham crackers
2 tablespoons packed brown sugar
1 egg white
2 tablespoons butter, melted
¾ cup strawberry fruit spread

6 cups mixed fresh berries (such as raspberries, blackberries, blueberries and halved strawberries)
2 containers (6 oz each) fat-free Greek honey vanilla yogurt

1. Heat oven to 350°F. Spray 9-inch glass pie plate with cooking spray.

2. In medium bowl, mix zwieback and brown sugar. Add egg white and melted butter; stir until well mixed. Press mixture evenly on bottom and up side of pie plate. Bake 10 to 12 minutes or until edge is browned. Cool completely on cooling rack.

3. In small saucepan, melt fruit spread over medium-low heat. Transfer to large bowl; cool slightly. Add berries; toss gently.

4. Spread yogurt into crust. Spoon berries over yogurt. Cover; refrigerate 3 to 6 hours before serving.

1 Serving: Calories 190 (Calories from Fat 35); Total Fat 3.5g (Saturated Fat 1.5g; Trans Fat 0g); Cholesterol 10mg; Sodium 65mg; Total Carbohydrate 35g (Dietary Fiber 3g); Protein 4g **% Daily Value:** Vitamin A 4%; Vitamin C 25%; Calcium 8%; Iron 4% **Exchanges:** 1½ Starch, ½ Fruit, ½ Other Carbohydrate, ½ Fat **Carbohydrate Choices:** 2

creamy tropical banana pie

Prep Time: 45 Minutes   **Start to Finish:** 5 Hours   **Makes:** 10 servings

230 Calories

PASTRY
- 1⅓ cups all-purpose flour
- ¼ teaspoon salt
- ¼ cup canola oil
- 3 tablespoons fat-free (skim) milk

FILLING
- ¼ cup sugar or artificial sweetener equivalent to ¼ cup sugar
- ¼ cup cornstarch
- 1½ cups fat-free (skim) milk
- 1 can (12 oz) evaporated fat-free milk
- ¼ cup fat-free egg product
- 3 tablespoons flaked coconut, toasted*
- ½ teaspoon vanilla
- ¼ teaspoon rum extract or additional vanilla
- 2 medium bananas, sliced
- 1½ cups frozen (thawed) fat-free whipped topping
- Additional toasted coconut, if desired

1. Heat oven to 450°F. In medium bowl, mix flour and salt. Stir in oil and 3 tablespoons milk with fork. If necessary, stir in 1 more tablespoon milk to moisten (dough will appear crumbly). Shape dough into a ball.

2. On lightly floured surface, slightly flatten dough ball. Starting at center, roll dough to 12-inch round. Carefully roll pastry around rolling pin. Carefully transfer pastry to 9-inch glass pie plate (pastry will be very tender). Ease into pie plate, being careful not to stretch pastry. Trim pastry to ½ inch beyond edge of plate. Fold edge under and crimp as desired. Prick pastry all over with a fork. Line with double thickness of foil. Bake 8 minutes. Remove foil. Bake 5 to 6 minutes longer or until golden. Cool on cooling rack.

3. Meanwhile, in 2-quart heavy saucepan, mix sugar and cornstarch. Gradually stir in 1½ cups milk and the evaporated milk. Cook and stir over medium heat until thickened and bubbly. Cook 2 minutes longer, stirring constantly. Remove from heat. In medium bowl, gradually stir about 1 cup of the hot mixture into egg product. Return mixture to saucepan. Cook and stir over medium-low heat 2 minutes. Remove from heat. Stir in 3 tablespoons coconut, the vanilla and rum extract. Cool 30 minutes, stirring occasionally.

4. Arrange bananas in baked shell. Pour filling over bananas. Cover surface with plastic wrap. Refrigerate 4 hours.

5. Just before serving, spoon whipped topping onto pie. Sprinkle with additional toasted coconut.

   *To toast coconut, heat oven to 350°F. Spread coconut in ungreased shallow pan. Bake uncovered 5 to 7 minutes, stirring occasionally, until golden brown.

1 Serving: Calories 230 (Calories from Fat 60); Total Fat 7g (Saturated Fat 1g; Trans Fat 0g); Cholesterol 0mg; Sodium 135mg; Total Carbohydrate 36g (Dietary Fiber 1g); Protein 6g **% Daily Value:** Vitamin A 6%; Vitamin C 2%; Calcium 15%; Iron 6% **Exchanges:** 2 Starch, ½ Other Carbohydrate, 1 Fat **Carbohydrate Choices:** 2½

triple chocolate pie

Prep Time: 20 Minutes   **Start to Finish:** 4 Hours 20 Minutes   **Makes:** 10 servings

190 Calories

1	box (4-serving size) chocolate fat-free sugar-free instant pudding and pie filling mix
1¾	cups fat-free (skim) milk
1	teaspoon vanilla
4	oz (half of 8-oz package) fat-free cream cheese, softened
1½	cups frozen (thawed) reduced-fat whipped topping

1 chocolate-flavor crumb crust (6 oz)
1 tablespoon grated semisweet chocolate
1 cup fresh or frozen (thawed) raspberries

1. Prepare pudding as directed on package, using the 1¾ cups milk. Stir in vanilla; set aside.

2. In large microwavable bowl, microwave unwrapped cream cheese uncovered on High 15 seconds; stir. Microwave 15 seconds longer. Beat with electric mixer on medium speed 15 seconds. Add half of the pudding; beat until smooth. Add remaining pudding; beat until smooth. Fold in ¾ cup of the whipped topping. Spread filling in crust. Refrigerate 4 hours until set or up to 24 hours.

3. Cut pie into slices. Dollop each slice with remaining whipped topping; sprinkle with grated chocolate. Garnish with raspberries.

1 Serving: Calories 190 (Calories from Fat 50); Total Fat 6g (Saturated Fat 2.5g; Trans Fat 0g); Cholesterol 0mg; Sodium 340mg; Total Carbohydrate 28g (Dietary Fiber 1g); Protein 5g **% Daily Value:** Vitamin A 4%; Vitamin C 6%; Calcium 10%; Iron 6% **Exchanges:** 1½ Starch, ½ Other Carbohydrate, 1 Fat **Carbohydrate Choices:** 2

a little bit more

For an unforgettable dessert experience, pair this pie with a cup of Mexican Coffee (below) for 90 calories extra.

Mexican Coffee In Dutch oven, combine 12 cups water, ½ cup packed brown sugar, ¼ cup ground cinnamon and 4 whole cloves. Heat to boiling, stirring to dissolve sugar. Stir in 1 cup ground coffee (regular grind); reduce heat to medium-low. Cover and simmer 5 minutes. Stir in ½ cup chocolate-flavor syrup and 1 teaspoon vanilla; remove from heat. Let stand 5 minutes for coffee grounds to settle. Strain into coffee server or individual cups; discard grounds mixture. Serve with whipped cream topping if desired. Makes 10 servings.

banana brownie skillet

Prep Time: 20 Minutes   **Start to Finish:** 1 Hour 40 Minutes   **Makes:** 12 servings

200 Calories

1 cup semisweet chocolate chips (6 oz)	2 egg whites
⅔ cup whole wheat flour	⅓ cup buttermilk
⅔ cup granulated sugar	1 teaspoon vanilla
⅓ cup instant nonfat dry milk	1 large banana, sliced
⅓ cup unsweetened baking cocoa	Lemon juice
1 teaspoon ground cinnamon	2 tablespoons powdered sugar
½ teaspoon baking soda	1½ cups sliced fresh strawberries
¼ teaspoon salt	1½ cups frozen (thawed) fat-free whipped topping

1. Heat oven to 350°F. Lightly spray 8- or 9-inch springform pan or cast-iron skillet with cooking spray.

2. In large bowl, mix chocolate chips, flour, granulated sugar, dry milk, cocoa, cinnamon, baking soda and salt. In medium bowl, beat egg whites, buttermilk and vanilla with fork or whisk. Make well in center of flour mixture; add egg white mixture all at once and stir until combined.

3. Spread batter in pan. Arrange banana slices on top; lightly brush banana slices with lemon juice.

4. Bake 35 to 40 minutes or until toothpick inserted in center comes out clean and brownie starts to pull away from side of pan. If using springform pan, cool on cooling rack 10 minutes; loosen side of pan and cool 30 minutes before removing side of pan. If using skillet, cool on cooling rack 30 minutes before serving.

5. Cut brownie into wedges. Sprinkle with powdered sugar. Serve each wedge with 2 tablespoons strawberries and 2 tablespoons whipped topping.

1 Serving: Calories 200 (Calories from Fat 45); Total Fat 5g (Saturated Fat 3g; Trans Fat 0g); Cholesterol 0mg; Sodium 125mg; Total Carbohydrate 36g (Dietary Fiber 3g); Protein 3g **% Daily Value:** Vitamin A 0%; Vitamin C 10%; Calcium 4%; Iron 6% **Exchanges:** 1 Starch, 1½ Other Carbohydrate, 1 Fat **Carbohydrate Choices:** 2½

no-bake lime bars

Prep Time: 20 Minutes   **Start to Finish:** 8 Hours 20 Minutes   **Makes:** 9 bars

150 Calories

6 low-fat honey graham cracker squares, finely crushed (½ cup)

2 tablespoons butter, melted

1 teaspoon sugar

1 box (4-serving size) sugar-free lime-flavored gelatin

¾ cup boiling water

1 container (16 oz) fat-free cottage cheese

1 package (8 oz) fat-free cream cheese, softened

1 container (8 oz) frozen fat-free whipped topping, thawed

Lime wedges, if desired

1. In small bowl, mix crushed crackers, butter and sugar. Press mixture in bottom of 8-inch square glass baking dish. Refrigerate.

2. In large bowl, stir gelatin and boiling water until gelatin is dissolved. In blender or food processor, place cottage cheese and cream cheese. Cover; blend on medium speed until smooth, stopping to scrape sides as needed. Stir ½ cup of the cottage cheese mixture into gelatin with whisk. Stir in remaining cottage cheese mixture until smooth. Fold in whipped topping.

3. Spoon filling over chilled crumb crust. Cover; refrigerate 8 hours until filling is firm or up to 24 hours. Cut into 3 rows by 3 rows. Garnish bars with lime wedges.

1 Bar: Calories 150 (Calories from Fat 35); Total Fat 3.5g (Saturated Fat 2.5g; Trans Fat 0g); Cholesterol 15mg; Sodium 460mg; Total Carbohydrate 19g (Dietary Fiber 0g); Protein 10g **% Daily Value:** Vitamin A 6%; Vitamin C 0%; Calcium 15%; Iron 0% **Exchanges:** 1 Starch, ½ Other Carbohydrate, 1 Very Lean Meat, ½ Fat **Carbohydrate Choices:** 1

cocoa squares

Prep Time: 20 Minutes   **Start to Finish:** 1 Hour 45 Minutes   **Makes:** 24 squares

140 Calories

1 cup all-purpose flour	½ cup canola oil
1 cup whole wheat flour	⅓ cup fat-free (skim) milk
¼ cup ground flaxseed or wheat germ	1 cup shredded peeled or unpeeled zucchini
¼ cup unsweetened baking cocoa	1 medium ripe banana, mashed (½ cup)
2 teaspoons baking powder	½ cup miniature semisweet chocolate chips
½ teaspoon salt	
½ cup fat-free egg product	
¾ cup sugar	

1. Heat oven to 350°F. Lightly spray 13×9-inch pan with cooking spray.

2. In large bowl, mix flours, flaxseed, cocoa, baking powder and salt. In medium bowl, beat egg product, sugar, oil and milk with whisk. Stir in zucchini and banana. Make well in center of flour mixture; add zucchini mixture all at once and stir just until moistened. Fold in chocolate chips. Pour batter in pan.

3. Bake about 25 minutes or until top springs back when lightly touched. Cool completely on cooling rack, about 1 hour. Cut into 6 rows by 4 rows.

1 Square: Calories 140 (Calories from Fat 60); Total Fat 6g (Saturated Fat 1g; Trans Fat 0g); Cholesterol 0mg; Sodium 100mg; Total Carbohydrate 19g (Dietary Fiber 1g); Protein 2g **% Daily Value:** Vitamin A 0%; Vitamin C 0%; Calcium 4%; Iron 4% **Exchanges:** ½ Starch, 1 Other Carbohydrate, 1 Fat **Carbohydrate Choices:** 1

a little bit more

Love frosting? Spread 1 container (16 ounces) milk chocolate creamy ready-to-spread frosting on cooled squares for an added 75 calories per serving.

baked berry cups with crispy cinnamon wedges

Prep Time: 15 Minutes   **Start to Finish:** 1 Hour 5 Minutes   **Makes:** 4 servings

130 Calories

2 teaspoons sugar	1 teaspoon grated orange peel, if desired
¾ teaspoon ground cinnamon	1½ cups fresh blueberries
1 balanced-carb whole wheat tortilla (6 inch)	1½ cups fresh raspberries
Butter-flavor cooking spray	1 cup fat-free whipped cream topping (from aerosol can)
¼ cup sugar	
2 tablespoons white whole wheat flour	

1. Heat oven to 375°F. In sandwich-size resealable food-storage plastic bag, place 2 teaspoons sugar and ½ teaspoon of the cinnamon. Spray both sides of tortilla with butter-flavor cooking spray, about 3 seconds per side; cut tortilla into 8 wedges. Place wedges in bag; seal bag and shake to coat evenly with cinnamon-sugar.

2. On ungreased cookie sheet, place wedges. Bake 7 to 9 minutes, turning once, until just beginning to crisp (wedges will continue to crisp while cooling). Cool about 15 minutes.

3. Meanwhile, spray 4 (6-oz) custard cups or ramekins with cooking spray; place cups on cookie sheet. In medium bowl, stir ¼ cup sugar, the flour, orange peel and remaining ¼ teaspoon cinnamon until blended. Add berries; toss gently. Divide berry mixture evenly among custard cups.

4. Bake 15 minutes; stir gently. Bake 5 to 7 minutes longer or until liquid is bubbly around edges. Cool 15 minutes.

5. To serve, top each cup with ¼ cup whipped cream topping; insert 2 tortilla wedges into topping. Serve warm.

1 Serving: Calories 130 (Calories from Fat 15); Total Fat 2g (Saturated Fat 0g; Trans Fat 0g); Cholesterol 0mg; Sodium 60mg; Total Carbohydrate 24g (Dietary Fiber 7g); Protein 3g **% Daily Value:** Vitamin A 0%; Vitamin C 15%; Calcium 4%; Iron 4% **Exchanges:** 1 Starch, ½ Fruit, ½ Fat **Carbohydrate Choices:** 1½

a little bit more

Savor a bit of chocolate with this berry dessert without blowing your entire day! Serve smooth dark chocolate pieces—for 40 calories each.

carrot and zucchini bars

Prep Time: 20 Minutes   **Start to Finish:** 1 Hour 45 Minutes   **Makes:** 24 bars

170 Calories

1½ cups all-purpose flour	½ cup raisins
1 teaspoon baking powder	½ cup chopped walnuts
½ teaspoon ground ginger	⅓ cup canola oil
¼ teaspoon baking soda	¼ cup unsweetened applesauce
¼ teaspoon salt	¼ cup honey
½ cup fat-free egg product	1 teaspoon vanilla
1½ cups shredded carrot	1 package (8 oz) ⅓-less-fat cream cheese (Neufchâtel), softened
1 medium zucchini, shredded (1 cup)	1 cup powdered sugar
¾ cup packed brown sugar	

1. Heat oven to 350°F. In large bowl, mix flour, baking powder, ginger, baking soda and salt. In another large bowl, stir egg product, carrot, zucchini, brown sugar, raisins, walnuts, oil, applesauce, honey and vanilla. Add carrot mixture to flour mixture, stirring just until combined. Spread batter in ungreased 13×9-inch pan.

2. Bake about 25 minutes or until toothpick inserted in center comes out clean. Cool completely on cooling rack, about 1 hour.

3. In medium bowl, beat cream cheese and powdered sugar with electric mixer on medium speed until fluffy. Frost bars. Cut into 6 rows by 4 rows.

1 Bar: Calories 170 (Calories from Fat 60); Total Fat 7g (Saturated Fat 1.5g; Trans Fat 0g); Cholesterol 5mg; Sodium 105mg; Total Carbohydrate 25g (Dietary Fiber 1g); Protein 3g **% Daily Value:** Vitamin A 25%; Vitamin C 0%; Calcium 4%; Iron 4% **Exchanges:** 1 Starch, ½ Other Carbohydrate, 1½ Fat **Carbohydrate Choices:** 1½

a little bit less

Omit the raisins and walnuts and save 25 calories per serving.

pick-me-up bars

Prep Time: 20 Minutes   **Start to Finish:** 1 Hour   **Makes:** 24 bars

100 Calories

3   tablespoons honey
¼   cup orange juice
2   tablespoons fresh lemon juice
1   package (8 oz) pitted whole dates, chopped
2½ cups whole wheat flour

½   teaspoon baking soda
¼   teaspoon baking powder
¼   cup unsweetened applesauce
3   tablespoons real maple syrup
2   egg whites
1   tablespoon canola oil

1. Heat oven to 350°F. Line 13×9-inch pan with foil, leaving foil overhanging at 2 opposite sides of pan; lightly spray foil with cooking spray.

2. In small bowl, mix honey, orange juice and lemon juice. Stir in dates; set aside.

3. In large bowl, mix flour, baking soda and baking powder. In medium bowl, stir applesauce, syrup, egg whites and oil until blended. Add applesauce mixture to flour mixture. Beat with electric mixer just until combined (mixture will be crumbly). Stir in date mixture. Spoon into pan; press evenly with fingers or back of spoon.

4. Bake 12 to 15 minutes or until toothpick inserted in center comes out clean. Cool on cooling rack. Use foil to lift out of pan. Cut into 6 rows by 4 rows.

1 Bar: Calories 100 (Calories from Fat 10); Total Fat 1g (Saturated Fat 0g; Trans Fat 0g); Cholesterol 0mg; Sodium 35mg; Total Carbohydrate 21g (Dietary Fiber 2g); Protein 2g **% Daily Value:** Vitamin A 0%; Vitamin C 0%; Calcium 0%; Iron 4% **Exchanges:** ½ Starch, 1 Other Carbohydrate **Carbohydrate Choices:** 1½

homemade snickerdoodles

Prep Time: 1 Hour   **Start to Finish:** 2 Hours   **Makes:** 4 dozen cookies

⅓ cup butter, softened	⅓ cup fat-free sour cream
1 cup sugar	¼ cup fat-free egg product
1 teaspoon baking powder	1 teaspoon vanilla
½ teaspoon ground nutmeg	2 cups all-purpose flour
¼ teaspoon baking soda	2 tablespoons sugar

1. In large bowl, beat butter with electric mixer on medium speed 30 seconds. Add 1 cup sugar, the baking powder, nutmeg and baking soda; beat until combined. Beat in sour cream, egg product and vanilla. Beat in as much of the flour as you can with the mixer. Using wooden spoon, stir in any remaining flour. Cover; refrigerate dough 1 to 2 hours or until easy to handle.

2. Heat oven to 375°F. Lightly spray 2 cookie sheets with cooking spray. In small bowl, place 2 tablespoons sugar. Shape dough into 1-inch balls. Roll balls in sugar. Place 2 inches apart on cookie sheets.

3. Bake 10 to 11 minutes or until edges are golden brown. Transfer cookies from cookie sheets to cooling racks.

1 Cookie: Calories 50 (Calories from Fat 10); Total Fat 1.5g (Saturated Fat 1g; Trans Fat 0g); Cholesterol 0mg; Sodium 35mg; Total Carbohydrate 9g (Dietary Fiber 0g); Protein 0g **% Daily Value:** Vitamin A 0%; Vitamin C 0%; Calcium 0%; Iron 0% **Exchanges:** ½ Other Carbohydrate, ½ Fat **Carbohydrate Choices:** ½

a little bit more

Add a mug of hot apple juice or cider with your cookie on a cold day for about 80 calories per 6-ounce cup. Many apple juices and ciders don't contain much more than calories; look for a variety that has added vitamin C.

strawberry-nut thumbprints

60 Calories

Prep Time: 30 Minutes **Start to Finish:** 2 Hours 40 Minutes **Makes:** 3 dozen cookies

¼	cup butter, softened	½	teaspoon vanilla
½	cup packed brown sugar	½	cup all-purpose flour
½	teaspoon baking powder	¼	cup whole wheat flour
¼	teaspoon ground cinnamon or cardamom	1	cup quick-cooking oats
⅛	teaspoon baking soda	½	cup finely chopped walnuts or pecans
3	egg whites	¼	cup sugar-free strawberry or apricot preserves

1. In large bowl, beat butter with electric mixer on medium speed 30 seconds. Add brown sugar, baking powder, cinnamon and baking soda; beat until combined, scraping side of bowl occasionally. Beat in 2 of the egg whites and the vanilla. Beat in as much of the flours as you can with the mixer. Using wooden spoon, stir in oats and any remaining flour. Cover; refrigerate dough about 2 hours or until easy to handle.

2. Heat oven to 375°F. Lightly spray 2 large cookie sheets with cooking spray or line with cooking parchment paper. Shape dough into ¾-inch balls. In small bowl, lightly beat remaining 1 egg white. Roll balls in egg white, then coat with nuts. Place on cookie sheets. Using thumb, make indentation in center of each ball.

3. Bake 7 to 8 minutes or until edges are golden brown. If necessary, gently press the back of a measuring teaspoon into indentations after removing cookies from oven. Cool 1 minute. Remove cookies to cooling rack.

4. Just before serving, spoon preserves into indentations in cookies.

1 Cookie: Calories 60 (Calories from Fat 25); Total Fat 2.5g (Saturated Fat 1g; Trans Fat 0g); Cholesterol 0mg; Sodium 30mg; Total Carbohydrate 8g (Dietary Fiber 0g); Protein 1g **% Daily Value:** Vitamin A 0%; Vitamin C 0%; Calcium 0%; Iron 0% **Exchanges:** ½ Starch, ½ Fat **Carbohydrate Choices:** ½

a little bit more

A glass of milk with your cookie is not only delicious but smart. One 8-ounce glass of skim milk adds 90 calories, 300 milligrams of calcium and 8 grams protein.

fudgy almond cookies

Prep Time: 30 Minutes   **Start to Finish:** 1 Hour 55 Minutes   **Makes:** 3 dozen cookies

80 Calories

⅓ cup butter, softened
¾ cup packed brown sugar
1 teaspoon instant espresso coffee powder or granules
¾ teaspoon baking soda
2 egg whites
⅓ cup plain fat-free yogurt

½ teaspoon almond extract
⅔ cup unsweetened baking cocoa
1½ cups white whole wheat flour
2 oz white chocolate baking bars or squares
½ teaspoon shortening
36 whole almonds, toasted*

1. In large bowl, beat butter with electric mixer on medium speed 30 seconds. Add brown sugar, coffee powder and baking soda; beat until combined, scraping side of bowl occasionally. Add egg whites, yogurt and almond extract; beat until combined. Beat in cocoa. Beat in as much of the flour as you can with the mixer. Using wooden spoon, stir in any remaining flour. If necessary, cover and refrigerate dough 1 to 2 hours or until easy to handle.

2. Heat oven to 350°F. Shape dough into 1-inch balls. Place balls 2 inches apart on ungreased cookie sheets.

3. Bake 6 to 8 minutes or just until edges are firm. Transfer cookies from cookie sheets to cooling racks; cool completely.

4. In small saucepan, heat white chocolate and shortening over low heat, stirring until melted and smooth. Spoon small amount of melted chocolate over each cookie. Dip each almond halfway into melted white chocolate; place on each cookie. Let stand until set.

*To toast nuts, cook in an ungreased skillet over medium heat for 5 to 7 minutes, stirring frequently, until nuts begin to brown, then stirring constantly until nuts are light brown.

1 Cookie: Calories 80 (Calories from Fat 30); Total Fat 3g (Saturated Fat 1.5g; Trans Fat 0g); Cholesterol 0mg; Sodium 50mg; Total Carbohydrate 10g (Dietary Fiber 1g); Protein 1g **% Daily Value:** Vitamin A 0%; Vitamin C 0%; Calcium 0%; Iron 2% **Exchanges:** ½ Starch, ½ Fat **Carbohydrate Choices:** ½

dark chocolate-cherry multigrain cookies

Prep Time: 40 Minutes   **Start to Finish:** 40 Minutes   **Makes:** 1½ dozen cookies

150 Calories

½ cup packed brown sugar
3 tablespoons granulated sugar
⅓ cup canola oil
1 egg or ¼ cup fat-free egg product
2 teaspoons vanilla
1 cup white whole wheat flour

¾ cup uncooked 5-grain rolled hot cereal
½ teaspoon baking soda
¼ teaspoon salt
½ cup dried cherries
⅓ cup bittersweet chocolate chips

1. Heat oven to 375°F. In medium bowl, mix brown sugar, granulated sugar, oil, egg and vanilla with whisk. Stir in flour, cereal, baking soda and salt until blended (dough will be slightly soft). Stir in cherries and chocolate chips.

2. Onto ungreased cookie sheet, drop dough by rounded tablespoonfuls 2 inches apart. Bake 7 to 8 minutes or until light golden brown around edges (centers will look slightly underdone). Cool 1 minute; remove cookies from cookie sheet to cooling rack. Store cooled cookies in tightly covered container.

1 Cookie: Calories 150 (Calories from Fat 50); Total Fat 6g (Saturated Fat 1g; Trans Fat 0g); Cholesterol 10mg; Sodium 125mg; Total Carbohydrate 23g (Dietary Fiber 2g); Protein 2g **% Daily Value:** Vitamin A 0%; Vitamin C 0%; Calcium 0%; Iron 4% **Exchanges:** ½ Starch, 1 Other Carbohydrate, 1 Fat **Carbohydrate Choices:** 1½

angel orange trifles

Prep Time: 45 Minutes   **Start to Finish:** 2 Hours 45 Minutes   **Makes:** 10 servings

120 Calories

2   cups fat-free (skim) milk

1   box (4-serving size) vanilla fat-free sugar-free instant pudding and pie filling mix

2   teaspoons grated orange peel

¼   cup orange juice

4   oz (half of 8-oz package) ⅓-less-fat cream cheese (Neufchâtel), softened

3   cups assorted citrus fruit sections (such as blood oranges, tangelos, grapefruit or navel oranges)

4   cups cubes (1 inch) angel food cake (4 oz)

Finely shredded orange peel, if desired

1. In medium bowl, beat milk and pudding mix with electric mixer on low speed 2 minutes. Beat in grated orange peel and 2 tablespoons of the orange juice. In large bowl, beat cream cheese with electric mixer on medium speed 30 seconds. Gradually add pudding mixture, beating until combined.

2. Divide half of the fruit among 10 (6-oz) dessert glasses or dishes. Top with half of the cake cubes. Drizzle with 1 tablespoon of the remaining orange juice. Spoon half of the pudding mixture over cake. Repeat layers. Cover; refrigerate at least 2 hours or up to 6 hours before serving. Garnish with shredded orange peel.

1 Serving: Calories 120 (Calories from Fat 25); Total Fat 3g (Saturated Fat 1.5g; Trans Fat 0g); Cholesterol 10mg; Sodium 190mg; Total Carbohydrate 19g (Dietary Fiber 1g); Protein 4g **% Daily Value:** Vitamin A 15%; Vitamin C 45%; Calcium 10%; Iron 0% **Exchanges:** 1 Other Carbohydrate, ½ Skim Milk, ½ Fat **Carbohydrate Choices:** 1

a little bit more

Add a crunchy twist to the trifle by topping each serving with 2 teaspoons slivered almonds for an additional 25 calories per serving.

ricotta cheesecake with apple topper

Prep Time: 30 Minutes   **Start to Finish:** 8 Hours 30 Minutes   **Makes:** 12 servings

230
Calories

CHEESECAKE
- 1 container (15 oz) part-skim ricotta cheese
- 12 oz ⅓-less-fat cream cheese (Neufchâtel), softened
- ⅓ cup sugar
- ¼ cup honey
- ¼ cup unsweetened applesauce
- 2 tablespoons all-purpose flour
- 2 egg yolks
- 4 egg whites

APPLE TOPPER
- 6 cups thinly sliced cooking apples (3 Jonathan or 4 McIntosh)
- 1 teaspoon apple pie spice or ground cinnamon
- ¼ cup water
- 2 tablespoons honey

1. Heat oven to 325°F. Wrap outside bottom and side of 9-inch springform pan with heavy-duty foil; spray inside bottom and side of pan with cooking spray.

2. In large bowl, beat ricotta cheese, cream cheese, sugar, ¼ cup honey, the applesauce and flour with electric mixer on medium speed until smooth. Add egg yolks; beat on low speed just until combined. In medium bowl with clean beaters, beat egg whites on high speed until stiff peaks form. Fold about one-fourth of the egg whites into ricotta mixture. Fold in remaining egg whites.

3. Spoon filling into pan and spread evenly. Bake 1 hour or until edge of cheesecake is set at least 2 inches from edge of pan but center of cheesecake still jiggles slightly when moved. Turn oven off; open oven door at least 4 inches. Let cheesecake remain in oven 30 minutes. Run small metal spatula around edge of pan to loosen cheesecake. Cool in pan on cooling rack 30 minutes (cheesecake may crack). Refrigerate 6 hours or up to 24 hours.

4. In large skillet, toss apple slices with apple pie spice. Add water; heat to boiling. Cover; cook over medium-high heat about 5 minutes or until apples are just tender, stirring occasionally. Drizzle with 2 tablespoons honey; toss gently to coat. Cool to room temperature.

5. To serve, run small metal spatula around edge of pan; carefully remove side of pan. Just before serving, spoon apple topper over cheesecake (or spoon over individual slices if not serving whole cheesecake at one time).

1 Serving: Calories 230 (Calories from Fat 90); Total Fat 10g (Saturated Fat 6g; Trans Fat 0g); Cholesterol 60mg; Sodium 160mg; Total Carbohydrate 27g (Dietary Fiber 1g); Protein 8g **% Daily Value:** Vitamin A 8%; Vitamin C 2%; Calcium 15%; Iron 2% **Exchanges:** 1½ Starch, ½ Other Carbohydrate, ½ Lean Meat, 1½ Fat **Carbohydrate Choices:** 2

apple-mango crisp

Prep Time: 25 Minutes **Start to Finish:** 1 Hour 25 Minutes **Makes:** 16 servings

220 Calories

¾ cup all-purpose flour
¾ cup old-fashioned oats
½ cup wheat germ, toasted
½ cup packed brown sugar
1½ teaspoons ground cinnamon
¼ cup canola oil
4 tart green apples (such as Granny Smith), chopped

2 sweet red apples (such as Gala, Fuji or Rome Beauty), chopped
3 tablespoons fresh lime juice
2 medium mangoes, seeds removed, peeled and chopped
⅓ cup finely chopped pecans
4 cups frozen (thawed) fat-free whipped topping or low-fat vanilla frozen yogurt

1. Heat oven to 375°F. Spray 13×9-inch (3-quart) glass baking dish with cooking spray.

2. In medium bowl, mix ½ cup of the flour, the oats, wheat germ, brown sugar and cinnamon. Stir in oil; set aside. In large bowl, toss apples with lime juice. Stir in remaining ¼ cup flour. Fold in mangoes. Spoon fruit mixture into baking dish. Evenly sprinkle flour-oat mixture over fruit.

3. Bake 30 minutes. Sprinkle with pecans. Bake 10 to 15 minutes longer or until apples are tender. Cool slightly, about 15 minutes.

4. To serve, spoon ¼ cup crisp into individual dessert bowls. Top each with ¼ cup whipped topping.

1 Serving: Calories 220 (Calories from Fat 60); Total Fat 6g (Saturated Fat 1g; Trans Fat 0g); Cholesterol 0mg; Sodium 10mg; Total Carbohydrate 38g (Dietary Fiber 3g); Protein 2g **% Daily Value:** Vitamin A 10%; Vitamin C 15%; Calcium 2%; Iron 6% **Exchanges:** ½ Starch, ½ Fruit, 1½ Other Carbohydrate, 1 Fat **Carbohydrate Choices:** 2½

peach-berry cobbler

Prep Time: 25 Minutes   **Start to Finish:** 55 Minutes   **Makes:** 9 servings (⅔ cup each)

150 Calories

BISCUIT TOPPING

1	cup all-purpose flour
2	tablespoons sugar
¾	teaspoon baking powder
¼	teaspoon baking soda
¼	teaspoon ground allspice, cardamom or cinnamon
⅛	teaspoon salt
⅓	cup plain fat-free yogurt
¼	cup fat-free egg product
2	tablespoons butter, melted

FILLING

4	cups sliced peeled fresh peaches or frozen (thawed) sliced peaches
¼	cup cold water
2	tablespoons sugar
4	teaspoons cornstarch
1	tablespoon lemon juice
¼	teaspoon ground allspice, cardamom or cinnamon
2	cups fresh or frozen (thawed) raspberries

1. Heat oven to 400°F. In medium bowl, mix flour, 2 tablespoons sugar, the baking powder, baking soda, ¼ teaspoon allspice and the salt. In small bowl, stir together yogurt, egg and butter; add to flour mixture, stirring just until moistened. Set aside.

2. In 3-quart saucepan, stir all filling ingredients except raspberries. Let stand 10 minutes. Cook and stir over medium heat until thickened and bubbly. Stir in raspberries; heat through, stirring gently.

3. Spoon hot filling into 2-quart round or square baking dish. Immediately drop biscuit topping into small mounds on hot filling.

4. Bake about 20 minutes or until browned and toothpick inserted into biscuit topping comes out clean. Serve warm.

1 Serving: Calories 150 (Calories from Fat 30); Total Fat 3g (Saturated Fat 1.5g; Trans Fat 0g); Cholesterol 5mg; Sodium 150mg; Total Carbohydrate 28g (Dietary Fiber 3g); Protein 3g **% Daily Value:** Vitamin A 8%; Vitamin C 10%; Calcium 6%; Iron 6% **Exchanges:** 1 Starch, ½ Fruit, ½ Other Carbohydrate, ½ Fat **Carbohydrate Choices:** 2

creamy custards

Prep Time: 30 Minutes   **Start to Finish:** 5 Hours 30 Minutes   **Makes:** 4 servings

240 Calories

⅔ cup sugar
3 eggs, slightly beaten

2 containers (6 oz each) fat-free Greek plain yogurt
1 teaspoon vanilla

1. Heat oven to 325°F. In 8-inch heavy skillet, cook ⅓ cup of the sugar over medium-high heat until sugar starts to melt, shaking skillet occasionally to heat sugar evenly. Do not stir. Once sugar starts to melt, reduce heat to low. Cook about 5 minutes or until all of the sugar is melted and golden brown, stirring as needed with wooden spoon.

2. Immediately divide caramelized sugar among 4 (6-oz) custard cups; tilt cups to coat bottoms evenly. Cool slightly. Meanwhile, in medium bowl, stir eggs, yogurt, vanilla and remaining ⅓ cup sugar with whisk.

3. Place custard cups in 13×9-inch pan. Divide egg mixture among custard cups. Place pan on oven rack. Pour hottest tap water available into pan around cups to a depth of about ½ inch.

4. Bake 30 to 35 minutes or until knife inserted near center comes out clean. Remove cups from water. Cool on cooling rack. Cover; refrigerate in cups 4 hours until chilled or up to 24 hours.

5. To unmold, slip point of knife between custard and side of cup. Place dessert plate upside down over cup; turn plate and cup over. Remove cup. Spoon any caramelized sugar that remains in cups on top of custards.

1 Serving: Calories 240 (Calories from Fat 35); Total Fat 4g (Saturated Fat 1g; Trans Fat 0g); Cholesterol 145mg; Sodium 90mg; Total Carbohydrate 39g (Dietary Fiber 0g); Protein 11g **% Daily Value:** Vitamin A 10%; Vitamin C 0%; Calcium 20%; Iron 2% **Exchanges:** 1 Starch, 1 Other Carbohydrate, ½ Skim Milk, ½ Medium-Fat Meat **Carbohydrate Choices:** 2½

a little bit more
Serve each custard with ¼ cup fresh blueberries for an additional 20 calories per serving.

banana pudding

Prep Time: 20 Minutes   **Start to Finish:** 3 Hours 20 Minutes   **Makes:** 16 servings (about ¾ cup each)

200 Calories

3 cups fat-free (skim) milk	1 container (8 oz) frozen fat-free whipped topping, thawed
2 boxes (4-serving size each) French vanilla instant pudding and pie filling mix	48 reduced-fat vanilla wafer cookies
4 containers (6 oz each) banana crème or French vanilla fat-free yogurt	6 small bananas, sliced
	Additional banana slices, if desired

1. In large bowl, beat milk and pudding mix with electric mixer on low speed until well blended; beat in yogurt. Fold in whipped topping.

2. In ungreased 13×9-inch (3-quart) glass baking dish, place 24 of the vanilla wafers in single layer. Spoon half of the pudding mixture over wafers. Top with 6 sliced bananas. Spoon remaining pudding mixture over bananas. Arrange remaining 24 vanilla wafers over pudding.

3. Cover; refrigerate at least 3 hours but no longer than 8 hours. Just before serving, garnish with additional banana slices.

1 Serving: Calories 200 (Calories from Fat 15); Total Fat 1.5g (Saturated Fat 0.5g; Trans Fat 0g); Cholesterol 0mg; Sodium 260mg; Total Carbohydrate 42g (Dietary Fiber 1g); Protein 3g **% Daily Value:** Vitamin A 6%; Vitamin C 8%; Calcium 10%; Iron 2% **Exchanges:** 1 Starch, 2 Other Carbohydrate **Carbohydrate Choices:** 3

a little bit more

Sprinkle each serving with 1 tablespoon dark chocolate chips for an added 50 calories per serving.

freezy chocolate-banana shakes

Prep Time: 5 Minutes   **Start to Finish:** 5 Minutes   **Makes:** 2 servings (1 cup each)

1¼ cups fat-free (skim) milk
1 container (6 oz) vanilla fat-free yogurt
1 medium banana, sliced, frozen*

3 tablespoons unsweetened baking cocoa
2 tablespoons honey
1 teaspoon vanilla

1. In blender, place all ingredients. Cover; blend on high speed until smooth and frothy.

2. Pour into 2 glasses. Serve immediately.

*To freeze banana, peel and slice. Place slices in single layer on cookie sheet lined with plastic wrap. Freeze about 1 hour or until firm.

1 Serving: Calories 230 (Calories from Fat 15); Total Fat 1½g (Saturated Fat 1g; Trans Fat 0g); Cholesterol 5mg; Sodium 110mg; Total Carbohydrate 48g (Dietary Fiber 4g); Protein 11g **% Daily Value:** Vitamin A 8%; Vitamin C 10%; Calcium 30%; Iron 8% **Exchanges:** 0 Starch, ½ 1 Fruit, Other Carbohydrate, 1½ Skim Milk **Carbohydrate Choices:** 3

a little bit more

For a festive finish, top off these shakes with 2 tablespoons fat-free whipped topping (from an aerosol can) and 1 teaspoon mini semisweet chocolate chips for an additional 30 calories per serving.

cherry-raspberry ice cream

Prep Time: 45 Minutes   **Start to Finish:** 4 Hours 45 Minutes   **Makes:** 18 servings (½ cup each)

120 Calories

¾   cup sugar
1   envelope unflavored gelatin
4   cups whole milk
4   eggs, beaten
1   pound fresh dark sweet cherries, pitted and halved, or 1½ bags (10 oz each) frozen sweet cherries

1   bag (10 oz) frozen unsweetened raspberries or 2½ cups fresh raspberries
¼   cup frozen (thawed) orange juice concentrate

1. In large saucepan, mix sugar and gelatin. Stir in milk. Cook and stir over medium heat just until mixture starts to boil. Remove from heat. Stir about 1 cup of the hot mixture into beaten eggs; return all to saucepan. Cook and stir 2 to 3 minutes or until mixture coats the back of a metal spoon. Do not boil. Remove from heat.

2. Stir in cherries, raspberries and orange juice concentrate. Cover; refrigerate 4 to 24 hours or until set.

3. Transfer mixture to 4- or 5-quart ice cream freezer; freeze according to manufacturer's directions. Serve immediately or, if desired, ripen for 4 hours.

1 Serving: Calories 120 (Calories from Fat 30); Total Fat 3g (Saturated Fat 1.5g; Trans Fat 0g); Cholesterol 45mg; Sodium 40mg; Total Carbohydrate 19g (Dietary Fiber 1g); Protein 4g **% Daily Value:** Vitamin A 4%; Vitamin C 10%; Calcium 10%; Iron 2% **Exchanges:** 1 Starch, ½ Other Carbohydrate, ½ Fat **Carbohydrate Choices:** 1

a little bit more

Serve a scoop of ice cream with a Cocoa Square (page 306) for an extra 140 calories.

metric conversion guide

Volume

U.S. Units	Canadian Metric	Australian Metric
¼ teaspoon	1 mL	1 ml
½ teaspoon	2 mL	2 ml
1 teaspoon	5 mL	5 ml
1 tablespoon	15 mL	20 ml
¼ cup	50 mL	60 ml
⅓ cup	75 mL	80 ml
½ cup	125 mL	125 ml
⅔ cup	150 mL	170 ml
¾ cup	175 mL	190 ml
1 cup	250 mL	250 ml
1 quart	1 liter	1 liter
1½ quarts	1.5 liters	1.5 liters
2 quarts	2 liters	2 liters
2½ quarts	2.5 liters	2.5 liters
3 quarts	3 liters	3 liters
4 quarts	4 liters	4 liters

Weight

U.S. Units	Canadian Metric	Australian Metric
1 ounce	30 grams	30 grams
2 ounces	55 grams	60 grams
3 ounces	85 grams	90 grams
4 ounces (¼ pound)	115 grams	125 grams
8 ounces (½ pound)	225 grams	225 grams
16 ounces (1 pound)	455 grams	500 grams
1 pound	455 grams	0.5 kilogram

Measurements

Inches	Centimeters
1	2.5
2	5.0
3	7.5
4	10.0
5	12.5
6	15.0
7	17.5
8	20.5
9	23.0
10	25.5
11	28.0
12	30.5
13	33.0

Temperatures

Fahrenheit	Celsius
32°	0°
212°	100°
250°	120°
275°	140°
300°	150°
325°	160°
350°	180°
375°	190°
400°	200°
425°	220°
450°	230°
475°	240°
500°	260°

Note: The recipes in this cookbook have not been developed or tested using metric measures. When converting recipes to metric, some variations in quality may be noted.

Index

Recipe Testing and Calculating Nutrition Information

Recipe Testing:

- Large eggs and 2% milk were used unless otherwise indicated.

- Fat-free, low-fat, low-sodium or lite products were not used unless indicated.

- No nonstick cookware and bakeware were used unless otherwise indicated. No dark-colored, black or insulated bakeware was used.

- When a pan is specified, a metal pan was used; a baking dish or pie plate means ovenproof glass was used.

- An electric hand mixer was used for mixing only when mixer speeds are specified.

Calculating Nutrition:

- The first ingredient was used wherever a choice is given, such as ⅓ cup sour cream or plain yogurt.

- The first amount was used wherever a range is given, such as 3- to 3½-pound whole chicken.

- The first serving number was used wherever a range is given, such as 4 to 6 servings.

- "If desired" ingredients were not included.

- Only the amount of a marinade or frying oil that is absorbed was included.